In Defence of Identity

In Defense of Plants

In DEFENCE OF IDENTITY

The Ethnic Nationalities' Struggle for
Democracy, Human Rights, and Federalism in Burma

A Collection of Writings and Speeches, 2001-2010

Second Print

Lian H. Sakhong

Orchid Press

Layout & Design
Paul Keenan

Type Setting
Sai Mawn

Cover Design
Myo Myint

Orchid Press
PO Box 1046, Silom Post Office,
Bangkok 10504, Thailand

www.orchidbooks.com

ISBN: 978-974-524-133-6

Made in Thailand
Printed by Wanida Press, Chiang Mai, 2010
Second Print 2014

To My Beloved Aapen, David and Laura Sakhong

Contents

PART FOUR: PERSONAL REFLECTIONS

PREFACE

On 28 August 2010, I was arrested, together with 26 Chin political activists who had been living in exile for more than two decades in Mizoram State of India, and sent to Aizawl's police detention facility.

I was giving training for this group regarding the principles of democracy, human rights and federalism, and telling them how we were going to rebuild our country peacefully. But, my lecture was disrupted and within a few hours I found myself in a room behind iron bars.

I entered to the room first, and my friends followed. The room was simply too small for more than ten persons and an awful smell welcomed us. Damp, dirty, and dark: all my senses as a simple living being and all my soul as a human being were not prepared to tolerate such a terrible condition!

It was not a place for a human being; no human being should be placed in such a condition even if they have committed a crime. We had committed no crime! But we were there, forced to dwell in hell on earth? I was reminded, almost like a mantra in my mind, of Allen Ginsberg's verse: "I dwell in Hell on earth to write this rhyme/ I witness Heaven in unholy time". I like this verse because it seemed to me that he was writing about the human condition in Burma today, and, at that moment, it also applied to our current circumstance! But why should we be dwelling in this Hell on earth for so long? And for what reason are we standing as witnesses of Heaven in this unholy time?

Before I fled from my country – Burma, I was arrested and interrogated three times, but never had I been sent to jail. All three times I was interrogated at the Military Interrogation Centre (MIC), also known as MI-6, in the same room. The difference between MI-6 and Aizawl's police cell is that when

I entered into the MI-6, the first thing I realized was that they tried to destroy my integrity as a political activist and my dignity as a human being; they even tried to kill my soul and my identity as a Chin.

The interrogation room at MI-6 was not that dirty but when they closed the door the darkness quickly descended on me no matter whether it was day or night. But, there was a kind of a very small window, more of an opening, almost at the top of the wall. So, when they closed the door from the outside, a very dim light came through that small window, which made me feel like I had been thrown into a very deep... deep hole.

Everyday and night, throughout my detention, they usually interrogated me as many as four to five times a night - one session of interrogation would last for several hours. They simply tried to deprive me of sleep! Whenever they wanted to conduct an interrogation session: they always brought with them a portable table and chairs and they pointed a very bright light directly into my eyes. Within a few minutes, the bright light blinded me and I could no longer see the interrogators sitting just in front of me, all I was aware of was their loud and abusive voices. Unless one is prepared mentally such simple methods of interrogation could tear apart and even destroy one's integrity.

But in Aizawl, India, there was no such mental torture. In Rangoon, as soon as I was arrested: they always blind-folded me but no such thing happened to us in Aizawl. They just deprived us of our liberty and placed us in animal-like conditions.

On the same evening, my Uncle Pu Hi Phei, a former MP of Rajya Sabha (Upper House of the Indian Parliament), came to my rescue. The police officers also realized that I held a Swedish passport with a valid entry visa to India. So, I was released but all my friends were pushed back to the border town of Champhai the next day. They were accused and punished under the so called "foreign case", meaning living illegally in India. I rented a car with two other friends and followed them to the border. Luckily we were able to rescue most of our friends by paying the fines thrust upon them as illegal migrant workers at the border town.

During this short unholy event, I realized that the people of Mizoram—our blood brothers and sisters from *Khua-thlang*: from ordinary people to state government levels are so sympathetic to us. They sympathize not only in regards to what so often happens to us in Mizoram but what has also been happening in our country under the military regime; political suppression, economic hardship and all kinds of social problems that the peoples of Burma have been enduring for more than half a century. Even the police officers who were assigned to push-back my friends to Champhai were friendly to us all the way long.

When we returned from Champhai, I expressed my feelings of gratitude for our blood brothers and sisters in *Khua-thlang* of Mizoram to my friend Dr. Robin from Mizoram University at the dinner table. Robin quickly suggested to me to write a book about what is happening in Burma: politically, economically and socially and describe why so many Chin from *Khua-chak* are in Mizoram. This is a good question: why are so many Chin in Mizoram State of India, despite knowing that they could be arrested, pushed-back, or even jailed. Why are they all fleeing from their homeland? We need to tell the reason for our being in Mizoram to the Mizo people: who tolerate us, sympathize with us, and sometime are angry with us when we have made too much trouble for them!

It is estimated that there are at least sixty to seventy thousands Chin refugees and illegal migrant workers in Mizoram. There are around ten thousands Chin refugees in New Delhi. Another seventy to eighty thousands Chin refugees are in Malaysia seeking the protection of United Nations High Commission for Refugees (UNHCR). Around thirty to forty thousands are lucky enough to get resettlement in third countries around the world. For the Chin population of less than a million in Burma, it is too much for us to bear. How are we going to prevent the collapse of our society?

There are many other ethnic groups who are also fleeing from the country because of the political crisis and sixty years of civil war. Along the Thai-Burma borders, there are tens of

3

thousands of Karen refugees living in the jungle camps many have been there for several decades. Also, there are Karenni, Mon and Shan refugees living along Thailand's borders. In addition to those who are described legally as refugees, there are at least three million illegal migrant workers from Burma are in Thailand.

We also have several thousand Rohingya refugees in Bangladesh. It is hard to estimate how many migrant workers are in Malaysia, Singapore, China and other neighbouring countries. We don't know the number but the question remains – Why are all these people fleeing from their homeland? In other countries, we just become "illegal peoples". There is no such thing as an "illegal human being" but we are described as "illegal peoples" so that we can be arrested, jailed, and pushed-back. And the government in our own country will not take any action. Instead, the regime will arrest us, punish us, and we will face far worst conditions than we faced in other countries. These "illegal peoples" are facing everyday the condition that I encountered over a few hours in Aizawl, Mizoram State of India. Luckily for me, it was just for a few hours but for them, if some of them are unlucky, it could be for a life time.

The problems that we are facing in Burma are real and immense. And I want to tell our story to the world: what are we facing in our homeland? What are we fighting for, for our country and our future? Ethnic nationalities in Burma have already been engaged in over sixty years of civil war, but what we are fighting for is unknown to the world. The military regime in Burma described us as separatists, terrorists, and the one who would cause disintegration of the Union. The other way round is true: we are the founders of the Union at Panglong Conference in 1947, and what we are fighting for is to rebuild the Union according to the Panglong Agreement.

We are engaged in civil war because the regime in Rangoon and now in Naypyidaw refused to solve our problems through political means. We call for political dialogue and negotiated-settlement but the responses are always violent confrontations: bullets on the streets of our capital, and battle fields in the jungle of ethnic homelands. We, the ethnic nationalities in Burma, are holding arms in order to defend ourselves, to defend our peoples, to defend our homelands, to defend our ways of life: our heritage, our culture, our language, and our religion. This is the struggle to defend who we are and what we are as a people, as an ethnic group, and as a religious group: *to defend our identity!* Those sixty years of civil war in Burma can, therefore, be summarized as "fighting for identity".

These are the stories that I want to tell: my individual journey as well as our collective memories and experiences as a people and a nation. But, I do not have time to sit down and write: hoping only that I will be able to do so in the future. As a substitute to my dream of writing a new book, we have published this collection of my writings over the past ten years: 2001-2010.

Since this volume is a collection of my writings and speeches originally intended to address different audiences in different time and places, repetitions are unavoidable. We have to repeat again and again the root cause of political crisis in Burma, until the root cause is properly addressed and solved. The root cause of the crisis remains the same, and we must realize that there are so many social and economic problems stemming from these political problems.

In order to address the problems properly, I include in this book two papers (chapter six and chapter nine) for which I am not the sole author: these are the product of our collective efforts through a long process in which I was deeply involved, and it was I who wrote the first draft of chapter nine. The rest of the papers and speeches are my own writings, though some papers were published previously in the name of the organizations that I have been working for. Acknowledgement will be clearly mentioned in all papers and speeches.

I thank my colleagues Paul Keenan and Sai Mawn for putting all these papers together, especially Paul for editing the text and doing the layout. I also thank my friends at the Chin National Council (CNC), especially those who shared that unholy event with me in Aizawl on 28 August 2010: Pu Thang Yen

(Acting Chairman), Pu Ral Hnin (General Secretary), Pi Tei (Pi Lalhmangeihzuali), Pu Thang Len Piang, Pu Thet Ni and Pu Khua Uk Lian (Coordinator of PAC). I also would like thank my colleagues at the Ethnic Nationalities Council (Union of Burma) and at the Euro-Burma Office in Brussels.

My heartfelt thanks also go to my friends and relatives in Aizawl: though we are divided by international boundaries we are still blood relatives and friends. Pu He Phei and Kapi Khen Hrang nu (Mrs. Hi Phei), who always support me when I am in trouble in Mizoram. Their kindness and love cannot be repaid but I pray for them that the Lord our God will bless them abundantly! I also thank Pu Hia To (Minister of Industries & Tourism, Government of Mizoram), Pu P. P. Thawle (Member of Legislative Assembly of Mizoram State), and Dr. Robin who made all kinds of effort to free us when we were arrested. I also thank countless other friends from *Khua-thlang* who prayed for us and made many efforts to restore our liberty during our ordeals.

Last but not least, I would like to express my deepest love and gratitude to my beloved wife: Aapen, who has stood by me for all these years. Without her love, support, and understanding, I certainly would not be able to do what I have been doing during the past ten years as a political activist. When I started working full time for the *movement* in 2001, our daughter Laura was just one year old, and our son David was four. She raises our most beloved David and Laura almost like a single mother in Sweden as I was travelling most of the time and working in Thailand, India and other part of the world.

With my deepest love and gratitude, I humbly dedicate this book to my beloved Aapen, David and Laura: hoping that one day in the future when you read this book, David and Laura will understand and forgive me, as Mamma has been doing all her life, why Papa is travelling away from home so many times and for so long! You will understand one day that this is for the freedom of our homeland and our people.

Lian Hmung Sakhong, Chiang Mai, 2010

PART ONE

THE STRUGGLE

ONE

Imagine

The following talk was given at the 6th International Conference on Human Rights, "Human Rights, Ethnic Minorities and Religions: An Asia-Europe Dialogue on the Impact of Multinational Institutions", 10-11 November 2003, at the Mandarin Oriental Makati, Manila, Philippines.

Thank you so much for giving me this opportunity to speak about human rights violations and the denial of religious and minority rights in Burma.

But before I speak about Burma, I would like to ask you to think for a moment about your own country. Imagine where you were born, where you were raised, and the country you call "my motherland".

Now! Please close your eyes, and try to see nothing but complete darkness. And behind the darkest screen of your mind:

Imagine your country as a very big prison, that holds 50 millions prisoners;

Imagine your country as a concentration camp, in which there might not be gas chambers like in Auschwitz, but you can see Insein and many other notorious jails which contains hundreds of thousands of political prisoners;

Imagine your country as somewhere where your elected leader is frequently put under house arrest for years at a time simply because of her courageous leadership, her sacrifices for the people and the country, and her love for freedom and democracy;

Imagine your country as a place where the governing party uses rape, torture, arbitrary detention, extra-judicial killings, religious persecution, and various other abuses as a means of remaining in power instead of upholding the result of the election held some thirteen years ago;

Imagine your country as a place where your children, your sons and daughters, as students, are slaughtered in their campuses' simply because of the fact that they are demanding freedom of expression;

Imagine your country as a place where all the schools, all the universities and all of the colleges have been closed for 9 out of the past 14 years simply because of a fear that students might demand their rights, that they might demand the release of their fellow students who are in jail without trial, and that they might demand the return of their fellow students who are forced into exile;

Imagine your country as somewhere where the government instils fear among the people so that nobody can trust each other; where workers fear their fellow workers, where students fear fellow students. Imagine the fear that strikes them when they believe that among them there are government informers spying on them. A fear where friends cannot trust each other, where family members, father and mother, husband and wife, parents and children, brothers and sisters cannot openly discuss anything between them because of such a fear;

Imagine your country as a place where your mother, your sisters and your daughters are raped with impunity by government soldiers in order to terrorise you, in order to subjugate you; simply because you belong to different ethnic and religious groups in the country and simply because you are not a Buddhist but a Christian or a Muslim;

Imagine your country as a place where your government is waging war against your own people, continuing a civil war against ethnic minorities in the country that has already lasted five long decades. A government that relies on a "scorched earth strategy" and clings to the "law of the jungle" where might is right and urban killing is a legitimate means of maintaining law and order;

Imagine your country as somewhere where your government spends 64% of the national budget on the Armed Forces in order to wage war against ethnic groups, and only 7% on health and 3% on education and continue to ignore the fact that the sick are neglected and the schools are almost closed all the time;

Imagine your country in a modern world, where your government has announced that 70% of the currency no longer has any value and almost all of your life savings, almost all of the money you possess are valueless pieces of paper;

Imagine your country as a place where a Mafia runs financial institutions and more than 40% of the banks in the entire country are owned by drug war lords. A country where drug money can be easily deposited in government banks and where money laundering is an intrinsic part of the country's financial system;

Imagine your own country as a place where your government traffics drugs and people, sells your daughters and sisters into the sex industries of neighbouring countries, sends hundreds of thousands of refugees and migrant workers all over the world. A country that sends students and political activists either into jail or into exile in foreign countries, a country which uses forced labour in order to maintain their wealth and power;

Imagine your country as somewhere where your government not only spends so little money on public health but gives AIDS patients treatment not to aid recovery but to finish their lives; imagine a situation where those patients could be your own father, your own mother, your wife, your husband, your son, your daughter, your own brother or sister, your boy friend, your girl friend, your beloved one, your friends, all of whom are prematurely taken away from this world;

If you can imagine all of these images on the screen of complete darkness in your mind, then you will find yourself in Burma.

This is all I was asked to tell you; and I think I have told you enough!

I am also preparing a paper for you where I investigate the root cause of human rights violations and the denial of minority rights, religious, cultural, and ethnic, in fact all kinds of minority rights denied in a country run by a gangster army. I have argued that total denial of human rights in Burma began with the rejection of the right of self-determination for non-Burman ethnic nationalities who joined the Union of Burma voluntarily as an equal partner in 1947.

In so doing, I have explored how the successive governments of the Union of Burma have abused the rights of religious and cultural minority groups, including the collective rights of self-determination, in the name of "nation-building", in the name of "national integration" and in the name of maintaining "national sovereignty". I have argued that during the parliamentary democracy period, U Nu's government adopted the state religion of Buddhism, with the promulgation of Buddhism as State Religion in 1961, as a means of "national integration" by imposing cultural and religious assimilation into the predominant group of Burman/Myanmar Buddhists.

While U Nu opted for cultural and religious assimilation into Buddhism as a means of integration, Ne Win removed the rights of minority groups including religious, cultural, ethnic, civil and basic human rights as a means of creating a homogeneous unitary state. U Nu and Ne Win therefore complemented each other in their strategy, although their approaches in depriving cultural and religious minorities of their rights were different in nature. Despite the fact that their approaches to "National Integration" were different, both U Nu and Ne Win had the same goal of creating a homogeneous nation of the people of Myanmar.

The current military regime also shares the same goal but with a slightly different approach. They apply the method of religious persecution as a means of destroying ethnic identity, especially against the Chin Christians. They use rape as weapon of war against ethnic insurgency, especially among the Shan. In a nutshell, ever since the military coup in 1988, the distinction between the army and state ceased to exist, and gross violations of human rights has become part of everyday life in Burma.

I maintain, in my paper, that the root cause of human rights violations in Burma is related to a constitutional crisis and it must therefore be solved through constitutional means of establishing a democratic federal system of government. A democratic federal system, which is based on the principle of equality for all member states of the Union, which guarantees the right of self-determination for all ethnic nationalities in the Union, and which promotes the democratic rights for all citizens in the country; and this I think is the best means to restore the Union of Burma. So, I can tell you that the ultimate goal of the democracy movement in Burma is to establish a genuine democratic federal union, where various ethnic nationalities from different religious groups, different ethnic groups, and those who come from different cultural and historical backgrounds can live peacefully together.

(Note: The paper that I presented at the conference is included in the chapter three of this volume.)

TWO

A Struggle for Democracy, Equality and Federalism in Burma: An Ethnic Perspective

This paper was first published as chapter fifteen in the 'Between Isolation and Internationalization: The State of Burma' *edited by Johan Lagerkvist, the Swedish Institute of International Affairs, 2008.*

Introduction

On 12 February 1947, the Union of Burma was founded at Panglong by four former British colonies, namely Chinram, Kachin Hills, Federated Shan States and Burma Proper, all of which already had their own constitutions. The British had occupied these four colonies separately as independent countries in different periods of time and had applied different administrative systems in accordance with the different constitutions that the colonial power had promulgated for them. The British officially promulgated the Chinram Constitution, called the "Chin Hills Regulation," in 1896, the "Kachin Hill Tribes Regulation" in 1895, the "1919 Act of Federated Shan States" in 1920, and the "1935 Burma Act" in 1937. The Chin Hills Regulation of 1896 covered present Chin State in Burma, present Mizoram State, Nagaland State, and part of Manipur and Meghalaya States in India. The 1935 Burma Act was applied to the area of the pre-colonial Myanmar/Burman Kingdom, which included the former Arakan and Mon Kingdoms as well as delta areas of Karen country.

Since independence, the twelfth of February has been celebrated as the Union Day of Burma. The observation of

Union Day as an official holiday in Burma implies the recognition of the distinctive national identities of those who signed the Panglong Agreement and ratified the treaty through the constitutional arrangement of 1947. It also implicitly recognizes their political rights—the right to gain their own independence and to establish their own nation-state. The essence of the Panglong Agreement was, and is, mutual recognition and respect, based on the principles of political equality, self-determination and voluntary association.

However, Aung San, who had persuaded the Chin, Kachin, Shan and other ethnic nationalities to join the Union, was assassinated before Burma gained her independence. After his assassination, the 1947 Union Constitution was rushed through to completion without reflecting the spirit of Panglong. As a result, the country was plunged into fifty years of civil war. Burma's political crisis today is therefore not merely an ideological confrontation between military dictatorship and democracy, but also a constitutional problem. The ethnic nationalities joined the Union as equal partners, preserving their rights of self-determination, on the basis of the Panglong Agreement, but Burma's subsequent constitutions have failed to adhere to the spirit of that agreement.

In this paper, I shall argue that federalism is the only viable solution to Burma's current political crisis, including five long decades of civil war. Federalism, therefore, is essential to the ultimate success of the democracy movement, to guarantee political equality for all nationalities, the right of self-determination for all member states of the Union, and democratic rights for all citizens of the Union.

Federalism: Theoretical Analysis

The term Federal is derived from the Latin words *foedus* and *fides*. According to S. R. Davis, the Latin word foedus is translated as "covenant", while its cognate fides means "faith" and "trust." When we find in these terms the idea of a "covenant, and synonymous ideas of promise, commitment, undertaking, or obligation, vowing, plighting one's word to a course of conduct in relations to others, we come upon a vital bonding device of civilization." The idea of covenant involves "the idea of co-operation, reciprocity, mutuality, and it implies the recognition of entities—whether it be persons, a people, or a divine being."[1]

According to Daniel J. Elazar, the first example of a federal state with the essential characteristic of the "idea of a contract, treaty, or alliance" was the ancient Hebrew state, whose principles are mentioned in the Bible.[2] In modern times, the rise of federal political thought went hand in hand with the emergence of a political-theological philosophy of federalism in 16th and early 17th century Renaissance Europe, when the sovereignty of the modern nation-state appeared as a conceptual instrument for the organization of power within the state.

Since the emergence of the modern nation-state, federalism has generally been defined as an approach to government that divides public powers not only horizontally, i.e. division of powers between legislative, administrative and judiciary; but vertically, i.e. separation of powers between two or more levels of government. In other words, federalism is "a constitutional device which provides for a secure, i.e. constitutional, division of powers between central and 'segmental' authorities in such a way that each is acknowledged to be the supreme authority in specific areas of responsibility."[3] The basic essence of federalism, therefore, is "the notion of two or more orders of government combining elements of 'shared rule' for some purposes and regional 'self-rule' for the other."[4] As such, federalism is seen as a constitutionally established balance between shared rule and self-rule: shared rule through common institutions, and regional self-rule through the governments of the constituent units or states. The federal principles of self-rule and shared rule, in turn, are based on "the objective of combining unity and diversity: i.e. of accommodating, preserving and promoting distinct identities within a larger political union."[5]

In a genuine federal system, neither the federal nor state governments (or, the constituent units) are constitutionally subordinate to the other, i.e. each has sovereign powers derived from the constitution rather than from one or other level of government, each is empowered to deal with the citizens in the exercise of its legislative, executive and taxing powers, and each is directly elected by its citizens. The structural characteristics of a genuine federal system, at its full development, can thus be generally defined as follows:

1. Two or more orders of government each acting directly on its citizens, rather than indirectly through the other order;

2. A formal constitutional distribution of legislative and executive authority, and allocation of revenue resources between the orders of government ensuring some areas of genuine autonomy for each other;

3. Provision for the designated representation of distinct regional or ethnic views within the federal policy-making institutions, provided not only by a federal second chamber (i.e., what used to be known in Burma as the Chamber of Nationalities or the Upper House) composed of representatives of the state and regional electorates, but also by state legislatures or governments;

4. A supreme written *federal* constitution, not unilaterally amendable by one order of government, and therefore requiring the consent not only of the federal legislature but also of a significant portion of the constituent units or states, through assent by their legislatures or by referendum of majorities;

5. Written constitutions for all member states of the union, or constituent units, which are to be promulgated, exercised and amended independently and unilaterally by each constituent state for its own state, so long as such procedures are conducted in accordance with the federal constitution;

6. An umpire (in the form of a supreme court, or as in Switzerland provision for referendums) to rule on the interpretation and valid application of the federal constitution;

7. Process and institutions to facilitate inter-governmental collaboration in those areas where governmental responsibilities are shared or inevitably overlap.[6]

What basically distinguishes federations from decentralized unitary systems, on the one hand, and from confederations, on the other, according to Blindenbacher and Watts, is that "in unitary systems the governments of the constituent units ultimately derive their authority from the central government, and in confederations the central institutions ultimately derive their authority from the constituent units and consist of delegates of constituent units."[7] In a federation, however, "each order of government derives its authority, not from each order of government, but from the constitution."[8]

Federalism in the Burmese Context: Lessons Learned from the 1947 Union Constitution

At the Panglong Conference in 1947, the Chin, Kachin, Shan and other non-Burman nationalities were promised, as Silverstein observes, the right to exercise political authority (in the form of administrative, judicial and legislative powers in their own autonomous national states) and to preserve and protect their language, culture and religion, in exchange for voluntarily joining the Burmans in forming a political union and giving their loyalty to a new state.[9]

On the basis of the Panglong Agreement, the Union Constitution was framed. Aung San himself drafted the Union Constitution and submitted it to the AFPFL convention held in May 1947, at the Jubilee Hall in Rangoon. Aung San delivered a long speech at the convention and explained the essence of the Panglong Agreement, which had the aim of establishing a Federal Union. He also argued:

> When we build our new Burma, shall we build it as a Union or as a Unitary State? In my opinion it will not be feasible to set up a Unitary State. We must set up a Union with properly regulated provisions to safeguard the rights of the national minorities.[10]

Aung San also insisted on the right of self-determination for ethnic nationalities who signed the Panglong Agreement to found a new Federal Union with so-called Burma Proper. He referred to his co-signatories, the Chin, Kachin and Shan, as nations, or pyidaung in Burmese. He said:

> The right of self-determination means that a nation can arrange its life according to its will. It has the right to arrange its life on the basis of autonomy. It has the right to enter into federal relation with other nations. It has the right to complete secession.[11]

Moreover, Aung San clarified the nature of ethnic and cultural minority rights and their implications, an issue which many of his contemporaries regarded as problematic:

> What is it that particularly agitates a national minority? A minority is discontented because it does not enjoy the right to use its native language. Permit it to use its native language and this discontentment will pass of itself. A minority is discontented because it does not enjoy liberty of conscience etc. Give it these liberties and it will cease to be discontented. Thus, national equality in all forms (language, schools, etc.) is an essential element in the solution of the national problem [or, ethnic conflict?].

> state law based on complete democracy in the country is required, prohibiting all national privileges without exception and all kinds of disabilities and restrictions on the rights of national minorities.[12]

On the basis of the principles of equality, the right of self-determination, and constitutional protection of ethnic and cultural minority groups, Aung San drafted a new constitution for a new Union of Burma, which was duly approved by the AFPFL convention. According to Aung San's version of the constitution, the Union would be composed of National States, or what he called "Union States," such as the Chin, Kachin, Karen, Karenni (Kayah), Mon, Myanmar (Burman), Rakhine (Arakan) and Shan States. The "original idea," as Dr Maung Maung points out, "was that the Union States should have their own separate constitutions, their own organs of state, viz. Parliament, Government and Judiciary."[13]

However, U Chan Htun reversed all these principles of the Federal Union after Aung San was assassinated. According to U Chan Htun's version of the Union Constitution, Burma Proper or the ethnic Burman/Myanmar did not form their own separate National State; instead they combined the power of the Burman/Myanmar National State with the whole sovereign authority of the Union of Burma. Thus, while one ethnic group, the Burman/Myanmar, controlled the sovereign power of the Union, that is, the legislative, judicial and administrative powers of the Union of Burma, the other ethnic nationalities who formed their own respective National States became akin to "vassal states" of the ethnic Burman/Myanmar bloc. This constitutional arrangement was totally unacceptable to the Chin, Kachin and Shan who signed the Panglong Agreement on the basis of the principle of national equality, a viewed also shared by other nationalities.

Another serious flaw in the 1947 Constitution was the absence of state constitutions for all the member states of the Union. In contrast to the original agreement, according to which Aung San and Chin, Kachin and Shan leaders intended to establish a separate state constitution for each and every state, U Chan Htun's version of the Union Constitution incorporated clauses covering all the affairs of the states. In this way, state affairs became part and parcel of the Union Constitution, with no separate constitutions for the Chin, Kachin, Shan and other ethnic nationalities. Such a constitutional arrangement stated that whatever powers the state governments enjoyed and exercised under the 1947 Constitution were in fact granted to them by the central government and was therefore characteristic of a unitary state system. In a unitary system, power lies in the hands of the central government, and the powers of local governing or administrative units derive from or are devolved to them by the central government.

What the Chin, Kachin, Shan and other ethnic nationalities envisioned in Panglong was a federal system, in which the member, or constituent, states were the basis and founding units of the federation, and whatever powers they exercised or possessed were not given to them by the centre. The powers of the constituent states of a federation are, in principle, derived from the peoples of the respective states, as is stated in most state constitutions in countries that are federal in form. In theory, as Dr. Chao Tzang Yawnghwe observes,

> A federation is formed when a number of states agree for some reason to live and work together under one flag. And because there is an agreement among founding states to band together as equal partners, there arises a need for another level of government to handle matters of common interest. Accordingly, this government—the federal or central government—is given or vested with certain powers by the member states. In a federation, therefore, it is the power of the federal or central government that is derived from, or given to it, by the member states. Thus, in federalism, the federal government is not a superior government that holds all powers. Various and significant powers are held by the member states, and these are clearly spelt out in the state constitutions. In addition, some powers which are shared by all are given to the federal government, and these too are spelt out, this time in the federal constitution. In a federation, therefore, there are two levels of powers as well as two levels of governments, which are intertwined, yet separate. Hence, in a federal system there are two constitutions: one is the federal constitution, and concurrently with it there exists another set of constitutions, those of member states of the Union.[14]

U Chan Htun's version of the 1947 Union Constitution of Burma did not allow for the existence of separate constitutions for the founding member states of the Union, namely, the Chin, Kachin, Shan and other nationalities—including the Burman.

The third point which betrayed the Panglong Agreement and Aung San's policy of federalism was the structure of the Chamber of Nationalities at the Union Assembly. The original idea of the creation of the Chamber of Nationalities was to safeguard not only the rights of non-Burman ethnic nationalities, but also the symbolic and real equality envisaged at the Panglong Conference. Thus, the intention was that each ethnic national state should have the right to send equal numbers of representatives to the Chamber of Nationalities, no matter how big or small their national state might be. But what happened under U Chan Htun's version of the Union Constitution was that, while all the non-Burman nationalities had to send their tribal or local chiefs and princes to the Chamber of Nationalities, it allowed Burma Proper to elect representatives to the Chamber on the basis of its population. Thus, the Burman or Myanmar from Burma Proper, who composed the majority in terms of population, was given dominance in the Union Assembly.

In this way, the Union Assembly, according to U Chan Htun's version of the Union Constitution, was completely under the control of the Burman or Myanmar ethnic nationality. Not only did the powerful Chamber of Deputies (the lower house of the legislature) have the power to thwart the aspirations and interests of the non-Burman nationalities, the Burmans even dominated the Chamber of Nationalities itself. For that reason, the combined votes of the non-Burman nationalities (even in the Chamber of Nationalities) were unable to halt the passage of the "state religion bill" in which U Nu promulgated Buddhism as a state religion in 1961. Thus, all the non-Burman nationalities viewed the Union Constitution itself as an instrument for imposing a tyranny of the majority and not as their protector, and it was this perception that led Burma into fifty years of civil war.

The Panglong Agreement was the most solemn agreement that the Chin, Kachin and Shan had ever signed in their history, and therefore it had to be protected as the covenant on which they built the Union together with the Burman and other ethnic nationalities. However, since the agreement was betrayed or even broken by Burmese politicians after Aung San was assassinated, the Chin and other non-Burman ethnic nationalities in the Union of Burma have had to redefine the covenant, or Union

Constitution, through which they have sought to build a peaceful Union of Burma.

Nation-building and the Problem of Forced Assimilation

When the Chin, Kachin and Shan signed the Panglong Agreement in 1947, what they aimed to achieve was the acceleration of their own search for freedom, together with the Burman and other nationalities, based on the principles of equality, mutual trust and recognition; but not to integrate their societies and their lands into Myanmar Buddhist society and the Burman Kingdom. Thus, for them, the basic concept of independence was independence without integration, that is, what political scientists used to term "coming together", or "together in difference." These phrases refer to a process by which nations come together in order to form a modern nation-state in the form of a Federal Union, or Pyi-daung-suh in Burmese, while maintaining the right of national self-determination and the autonomous status of their nations.

Within this concept of "coming together," it is important to differentiate between "nation" and "state," or what Hannah Arendt refers to as a "secret conflict between state and nation." According to Arendt,

> [The nation] presents the "milieu" into which man is born, a closed society to which one belongs by the right of birth; and a people becomes a nation when it arrives at a historical consciousness of itself; as such it is attached to the soil which is the product of past labour and where history has left its traces. The state on the other hand is an open society, ruling over territory where its power protects and makes law. As a legal institution, the state knows only citizens no matter of what nationality; its legal order is open to all who happen to live on its territory.[15]

The state, far from being identical with the nation, is "the supreme protector of a law which guarantees man his rights as man, his rights as citizen and his rights as a national."[16] By signing the Panglong Agreement, the Chin, Kachin and Shan had co-founded a Federal Union of a multi-national state, which is an administrative and legal unit, but they still wanted to keep their own respective nations, a concept which according to Weber belongs to the sphere of values: culture, language, religion, ethnicity, homeland, shared memories and history, a specific sentiment of solidarity in the face of other groups or people. Thus, what Aung San and the Chin, Kachin, and Shan leaders wanted to achieve at Panglong was to build a Union through a state-building process, not to create a nation through nation-building.

As mentioned above, the Burmese word for "Union" is "*Pyi-daung-shu,*" which means "the coming together of different 'nations' and 'national states.'"[17] As the term indicates, the *Pyi-daung-shu* allows the peaceful co-existing of different ethnic groups with different cultural and religious backgrounds, i.e. different nations, within an administrative and legal unit of political union. It is, therefore, clear that state-building is very different from nation-building, because in the building of a multi-national state, there can be many nation-building processes taking place at the same time for the different member nations.

In contrast to state-building, nation-building excludes from its process other ethnic groups, cultures, religions and everything related to multiculturalism and diversity. Thus, by accepting only one homogeneous set of cultural and religious values as its political values, the very notion of nation-building can produce only a nation-state made by a homogeneous people or nation that claims "pre-state unity based on culture, history or religion."[18] As a result, a nation-state made by a nation through the nation-building process cannot accommodate other cultures, religions and ethnic groups. At best, as Saunders argues, "it can tolerate non-integrated minorities as guests, but not as equal citizens. The status of fully recognized citizen can be attained only by integration. Those who want to become citizens must change their cultural identity." Moreover, as Saunders explains:

> If a cultural minority demands political recognition and identity, the state must reject the claim. Because it is unable to accommodate a fragmented political identity, it will ultimately come into conflict with its minorities.

Either the minorities must be integrated within the majority culture, destroying their original cultural roots, or they must be denied the opportunity to enhance their cultural identity through political means. A fragmented political identity is rejected as a solution, because of is threat to the unity, homogeneity, and the roots of state's existence.[19]

Aung San seemed to have a clear policy of state-building based on the principles of equality and unity in diversity. He maintained that nation-building in the form of "one race, one religion, and one language ha[s] gone obsolete."[20] By inviting the Chin, Kachin, Shan and other ethnic nationalities to form a new Union, Aung San's policy of unity in diversity transcended all different cultures and religions, rejecting them as structural and functional factors to unite the country. By rejecting culture and religion as uniting factors of the country, he opted for a secular state whose political values would be based not on cultural and religious roots but on the equality of individual citizens and the right of self-determination for member states of the Union. Aung San particularly rejected religiously oriented ethno-nationalism, which mixed religion with politics. He thus declared:

> Religion is a matter of individual conscience, while politics is social science. We must see to it that the individual enjoys his rights, including the right to freedom of religious belief and worship. We must draw clear lines between politics and religion because the two are not the same thing. If we mix religion with politics, then we offend the spirit of religion itself.[21]

However, after Aung San was assassinated, U Nu reintroduced cultural and religious values into political debate and abandoned Aung San's policy of unity in diversity together with the state/union-building process. For U Nu, the only means to build a new nation was to revive the pre-colonial cultural unity of Buda-bata Myanmar Lu-myo, which had nothing to do with the Chin, Kachin, Shan and other ethnic nationalities who joined the Union in order to speed up their own freedom.

Although Buddhism had been a powerful integrative force in traditional Myanmar society, a modern multi-national state of the Union of Burma with its multi-religious, multi-cultural, multi-ethnic plural society was a very different country from that of the pre-colonial Myanmar Kingdom. However, leaders like U Nu still believed that Buddhism could make a significant contribution to some aspects of national integration. When he became the Prime Minister of the newly independent Burma, U Nu contradicted Aung San's version of the Union Constitution, particularly the clause that separated religion from politics, by declaring: "In the marrow of my bones there is a belief that government should enter into the sphere of religion."[22] In this way, U Nu's government officially adopted Buddhism as its state religion, as a means of national integration. By this means, an attempt was made to achieve homogeneity by imposing religious and cultural assimilation into the predominant group of Myanmar Buddhists. In 1953, the Ministry of Religious and Cultural Affairs was created to promote the process of assimilation, and eventually it promulgated Buddhism as the state religion of the Union of Burma in 1961.[23]

While U Nu opted for cultural and religious assimilation into Buddhism, or *Buda-bata Myanmar-lumyo*, as a means of integration, General Ne Win, who came to power through military coup in 1962, removed the rights of the country's religious and cultural minorities, including all civil and basic human rights, as a means of creating a homogeneous unitary state. Moreover, General Ne Win imposed his national language policy by declaring *Myanmar-sa* as the only official language in the entire Union of Burma, which therefore was required to be used at all levels of government and public functions, and also to be the only medium of instruction at all levels of schools in the country—from primary to university levels. He not only imposed the *Myanmar-sa* as the official language, but also suppressed the right to learn the other ethnic national languages of the Union.

Nation-building, for both U Nu and Ne Win, was simply based on the notion of "one race, one language and one religion"—that is to say, the ethnicity of *Myanmar-lumyo*, the language of *Myanmar-sa* and the state religion of Buddhism. Thus, what they wanted to achieve through nation-building was to create a homogeneous nation of *Myanmar Naing-ngan*, by drawing its political values from the cultural and religious values of *Maynmar-sa* and Buddhism. Although their approaches to national integration were different, U Nu and Ne Win shared the goal of creating a homogeneous people in the country. While U Nu opted for cultural and religious assimilation into Buddhism as a means of integration, Ne Win used the national language policy of *Myanmar-sa* and denied the rights of the country's religious and cultural minorities as a means of creating a homogeneous unitary state. U Nu and Ne Win thus complemented each other, although their approaches in oppressing the cultural and religious minorities were different in nature.

Supplementing U Nu's policy of state religion and Ne Win's national language policy, the current military regime is opting for ethnicity as a means of national integration, by imposing ethnic assimilation into *Myanmar-lumyo*. The changing of the country name from Burma to *Myanmar*, the name only of the ethnic *Myanmar*, in 1989 is a case in point. When it implemented its policy of ethnic assimilation by force, the present military junta applied various methods: killing people and destroying the livelihoods of ethnic minorities over fifty years of civil war, using rape as a weapon of war against ethnic minorities, and religious persecution as a means of destroying ethnic identity, especially of the Chin, Kachin and Karen Christians. In this way, the successive governments of the Union of Burma—from U Nu to Ne Win to Saw Maung and Than Shwe—have carried out the nation-building process in terms of "one race, one language, one religion," that is—*Myanmar-lunyo, Myanmar-sa, Buddhism.*

In the name of nation-building, the successive governments of the Union of Burma have violated not only basic human rights and civil rights but also all kinds of collective rights. In the name of national sovereignty the rights of self-determination for ethnic nationalities are rejected; in the name of national integration the rights to follow different religions, to practice different cultures, and to speak different languages are deprived; and in the name of national assimilation the rights to up-hold different identities and traditions are denied. In short, the successive governments of the Union of Burma have been practicing ethnic cleansing and cultural genocide for forty years.

State-making and Unity in Diversity: An Option for the Future

As mentioned above, nation-building belongs to what social scientists call "subjective values," that is, culture, language, religion, ethnicity, homeland, shared memories and history, etc., which differentiate one group of people from another—values that cannot be shared objectively. Thus, the nation-building process is impossible to implement in a multi-ethnic, multi-cultural, multi-religious plural society like the Union of Burma. The only way to implement the nation-building process in a plural society is to use coercive force for assimilation, but that approach will definitely result in confrontation and conflict because the very notion of nation-building is "hostile to multiculturalism and diversity."[24] Unfortunately, such conflict is exactly what has occurred in Burma during the past fifty years.

> In a plural society like the Union of Burma, the only good option is federalism with a strong emphasis on decentralization and local autonomy, in which the parallel processes of nation-building for all the national states, i.e. member states of the union, and state-building for the union as a multi-national state, can go hand in hand. Federalism by definition is the division of power between the federal government and state governments, which have their own separate constitutions. When member states of the federal union are composed in terms of ethnicity and historical homeland, each national state can implement its own nation-building process within the territory of its homeland based on its own culture, language, religion, ethnicity, shared memories, etc., by making its own state constitution. Thus, while the purpose of writing a state

constitution is self-rule through a nation-building process allowing for the preservation and promotion of distinct identities, the purpose of making a federal constitution is shared-rule through a state-building process aimed at the establishment of common institutions for multiculturalism and diversity. In summary, while the state constitutions drafting process aims to implement a nation-building process for national states within the Union, the federal constitution aims to complete the state-building process for the Union of Burma. In this way, federalism can combine nation-building and state-building with the objective of unity in diversity, which is "...accommodating, preserving and promoting distinct identities within a larger political union."[25]

Although the state constitution making process through nation-building can be a value-based subjective approach, the federal constitution making process through state-building is purely a matter of objective value; for the federal constitution is "a legal institution, [which] knows only citizens no matter of what nationality, and [whose] legal order is open to all who happen to live on its territory."[26] As a legal institution, federal constitution rules "over territory where its power protects and makes law", which guarantees "man his rights as man, his rights as citizen and his rights as a national."[27] Thus, in a genuine federal system, the federal constitution will never adopt cultural values as political values, and it shall never promulgate a law that aims at the creation of a homogeneous culture, which excludes other cultures.

Conclusion: Finding Equilibrium between Nation-building and State-making

The question of constitution making is usually focused on the structure and function of the state and government; how the state should be formed, how government should be organized, and how people should be governed. In a multicultural plural society like Burma, such simple questions concerned only with good governance are simply not enough. We need to raise more controversial issues such as: Who should govern whom? What majority or majorities should rule over what minorities? Who should control the political power of the state, and with regards to whom? Who should decide the procedure by which it is settled and who should govern whom?

As mentioned above, federalism is an approach to government that divides public powers not only horizontally, but also vertically. Federalism, therefore, has been viewed as a useful way of limiting governmental power in order to secure good governance. In addition to balancing self-rule and shared rule through constitutionally established mechanisms, the recognition and participation of cultural and ethnic minorities can also be achieved through:

1. Emphasis on the political rather than the cultural base of the nation-state;
2. Separation of the state and religious or other socio-cultural powers;
3. Emphasis on human rights as protection of minority rights;
4. Emphasis on separation of powers, formally and informally;
5. Executive power sharing;
6. Multiparty system and proportional rule in elections of the parliament;
7. Decentralization and local autonomy, including bi-cameralism, as a means of vertical power sharing.

In today's Burmese political context, the processes of federal constitution and state constitutions drafting can be defined as finding a political compromise between state-building and nation-building, which will hopefully result in an institutional equilibrium. A political compromise has to be found between a cultural majority having enough power to define a majority regime on the one hand, and cultural minorities seeking recognition within the constitutional framework and participation in political decision making on the other. The institutional equilibrium is always a compromise between a majority regime and institutional forms of minority protection and power sharing.

In the context of the legal system, an institutional equilibrium between state-making and nation-building implies the concept of equality. Thus, a multi-national state or a union that implements this fundamental principle must translate the concept of equality into effective collective rights. Although democracy is based on the principle of majority rule, the majority should not abuse its democratic power by tyrannising its minorities. Federalism can effectively control the tyranny of the majority through not only constitutionally mandated decentralization, but also the equalisation of the majority and the minority before the law and thus recognizes the rights of a minority to be treated equally both as individuals and as communities.

The concept of equality implies both collective rights and individual rights. The protection of the human rights of individuals prevents the authorities of the state from discriminating against individuals who belong to minorities, on the grounds of their language, religion, ethnicity or race. The guarantee of human rights as individual rights according to the law is different from that of tolerance. Tolerance also allows everyone to live within his or her community as a respected individual, free from discrimination on the ground of ethnicity, religion or language. However, those who are tolerated are not part of the governing people, the "We" who form the state; for members of tolerated minorities, the state is "their" state and "their" union, not "our" state or union. Diversity might be respected, but not as a political value. Minorities are respected because that is required by the universal values enshrined in the constitution, as in the 1947 Constitution of the Union of Burma. But in such a situation, diversity is neither a policy nor a goal of the state.

Fifty years of negative experiences of constitution making and practice teaches that federalism is the only good option for the future of Burma. In order that unity in diversity becomes a political value of the Union, state constitutions drafting for "self-rule" must engage in nation-building; federal constitution drafting for "shared-rule" must engage in state-building; and the constitutional structure as a whole must seek equality between these two processes. Thus, the ultimate goal of the democracy movement in Burma is to establish a genuine Federal Union of Burma, which will guarantee democratic rights for all citizens, political equality for all ethnic nationalities, and the rights of self-determination for all member state of the Union within the framework of federal arrangement.

Notes

[1] S. R. Davis, *The Federal Principles: A Journey Through Time in Quest of a Meaning* (London: University of California Press, 1978), p. 3.

[2] Daniel J. Elalzar, "Federalism," in International Encyclopaedia of the Social Sciences, Vol. V (New York, 1968), pp. 361–2.

[3] Alan Smith, "Ethnic Conflict and Federalism: The Case of Burma," in Gunther Bächler (ed.), *Federalism against Ethnicity? Institutional, Legal and Democratic Instruments to Prevent Violent Minority Conflicts* (Zurich: Verlag Ruegger, 1997), pp. 231-267.

[4] Raoul Blindenbacher and Arnold Koller (eds.), *Federalism in a Changing World* (London and Ithaca: McGill-Queen's University Press, 2003), p. 9

[5] Ibid.

[6] Cf. Blindenbacher and Watts (2003), p. 10

[7] Ibid.

[8] Ibid.

[9] Josef Silverstein, "Minority Problems in Burma Since 1962," in Lehman (ed.), *Military Rule in Burma Since 1962* (Singapore, 1981), p. 51.

[10] Aung San, *Burma's Challenge* (Rangoon, 1947), reprinted in Josef Silverstein, The *Political Legacy of Aung San* (New York: Cornell University Press, 1993), cited in Maung Maung, *Burma's Constitution* (The Hague, 1959), p. 169.

[11] *Bogyoke Aung San's Speeches,* pp. 306–307. Also cited in *The 1947 Constitution and the Nationalities, Volume 11* (Rangoon University: University Historical Research Centre, 1999), p. 60.

[12] *Bogyoke Aung San's Speeches,* pp. 306–307.

[13] U Maung Maung, *Burmese Nationalist Movements, 1940–1948* (1989), p. 170.

[14] Chao Tzang Yawnghwe, "Burma: State Constitutions and the Challenges Facing the Ethnic Nationalities," in Yawnghwe and Sakhong (eds.), *Federalism, State Constitutions and Self-determination in Burma* (Chiang Mai, UNLD Press, 2003), pp.99-110

[15] Hannah Arendt, "The Nation," cited by Ronald Beiner, "Arendt and Nationalism," in Dana Villa (ed.), *The Cambridge Companion to Hannah Arendt* (Cambridge University Press: 2000), pp. 44–56.

[16] Ronald Beiner, "Arendt and Nationalism," in Dana Villa (ed.), *The Cambridge Companion to Hannah Arendt* (2000), p. 53.

[17] Chao Tzang Yawnghwe "State Constitutions, Federalism and Ethnic Self-determination," in Yawnghwe and Sakhong (eds.) *Federalism, State Constitutions and Self-determination in Burma* (Chiang Mai: UNLD Press, 2003), pp. 99-110

[18] Cf. Saunders in Blindenbacher and Koller (2003), p. 199

[19] Ibid., p. 201

[20] Aung San's speech entitled "Problems for Burma's Freedom," delivered on January 20, 1946, in Josef Silverstein (ed.), *Political Legacy of Aung San* (Ithaca, New York: Cornell University Press, 1993), p. 96.

[21] Aung San's speech entitled "Problems for Burma's Freedom," delivered on January 20, 1946, in Josef Silverstein (ed.), *Political Legacy of Aung San* (Ithaca, New York: Cornell University Press, 1993), p. 96.

[22] Jerold Schector, *The New Face of Buddha* (1967), p. 106.

[23] Cf. John F. Cady, *A History of Modern Burma* (Ithaca, New York: Cornell University Press, 1960), p. 638.

[24] Saunder (2003), ibid., p. 198

[25] Ibid.

[26] Ronald Beiner in Dana Villa (2000), op.cit., p. 53.

[27] Ibid.

THREE

Human Rights Vioaltions and the Denial of Minority Rights in Burma

This paper was presented at the 6th International Conference on Human Rights, "Human Rights, Ethnic Minorities and Religions: An Asia-Europe Dialogue on the Impact of Multinational Institutions", 10-11 November 2003, at the Mandarin Oriental Makati, Manila, Philippines. It was published as chapter twenty of 'Religious Persecution: A Campaign of Ethnocide against Chin Christians in Burma' *by the Chin Human Rights Organisation, 2004.*

'Burma's thuggish ruling elite traffics in drugs and in people---in forced labor, child labor, slave labor. It throws people into medieval torture chambers at the slightest pretext: for owning a fax machine, for making jokes about the regime, for listening to foreign broadcasts. There are some 1,800 political prisoners. Universities have been shuttered for much of the past decade, and poverty has deepened.'

The Washington Post, July 16, 2001

Introduction

When the Universal Declaration of Human Rights was adopted in 1948, Burma was one of the first newly independent countries that enthusiastically endorsed the Declaration.[1] In fact, the smaller countries in the third world like Burma were very passionate about the Declaration because this was the first international agreement that recognised the equality and dignity of all peoples, regardless of the size of their country and regardless of their geographic or ethnic origin. U Thant, the Burmese Ambassador to the UN and who later became its Secretary General from 1962-1971, said that "the Universal Declaration is the Magna Carta of humankind," for its provisions constitute "a common standard of achievement for all peoples and all nations."[2]

Today, however, we have a military regime in Burma, claiming that the provisions in the Universal Declaration of Human Rights are based on Western concepts of government and human nature, that it is a tool of Western cultural imperialism imposed on us, and that it ignores the distinctive cultural values of the Burmese people. General Saw Maung, Chairman of the SLORC, for example, said, "I tell you if anyone wants to enjoy the human rights they have in the US, England and India, provided the country accepts; I will permit them to leave. But in Myanmar [Burma], I can only grant human rights suitable for Myanmar [Burmese] people."[3] As the regime ruled the country under Martial Law, he also said, "Martial Law is no law at all, but the use of force."[4]

The present military junta in Burma can best be described as one of the most repressive regimes in the world. After the bloody coup in 1988, gross violations of human rights, including the draconian suppression of political freedoms, arbitrary detention, torture, rape, disappearances, extra-judicial killings, oppression of ethnic and religious minorities, and use of forced labour have continuously increased. The Index on Human Misery in 1992, therefore, ranked Burma as one of the world's most miserable countries, estimating that over 16 million of its 46 million inhabitants were living under the poverty line and under insufferable conditions. The year 2003 represented no improvements in human rights in Burma; in fact, the situation of the common people is continuing to worsen. Systematic abuses of economic, social and cultural rights by the regime and army has been continuing to grow as the ruling military junta called the State Peace and Development Council (SPDC) consolidates its power at all costs.[5]

Since 1991, the United Nations General Assembly and the United Nations Commission on Human Rights have for 12 consecutive years adopted consensus resolutions condemning the military's systematic gross abuse of human rights and its refusal to accept the will of the Burmese people as expressed in the 1990 general elections. The International Labour Organisation (ILO) has in effect, expelled Burma from the ILO for the regime's widespread use of forced labour.

Political crisis, civil war and human rights violations in Burma are always related with the notorious golden triangle drug trade. Since the 1950's, unable to repel the Chinese Kuomintang troops and unable to pay local defence forces, the Burma Army authorised militias to trade in opium to finance their operations. In the 1960's more militia to fight Shan nationalists were raised and again they were paid by allowing them to trade in opium. Worse yet, in 1989, fearing that some ethnic armies would join the democracy movement; the military signed cease-fires with them. In exchange for not joining the democracy movement, some of the ethnic armies, among them is the United Wa State Army (UWSA), were given the right to 'trade' without any restrictions. So, until recently, Burma was the biggest producer of opium and heroin. The current level of annual production is about 2,000 tons. However, the drug lords in Burma are now switching from heroin to the production of amphetamines which is more lucrative. The fact that cash can be deposited in Burmese banks with no questions asked, and the fact that Burma's drug lords are now known as successful 'entrepreneurs' in Burma's new economy and live in Rangoon, all point to the fact that the regime benefits from the drug trade.

In addition to drugs, Burma is a major source of HIV/AIDS infection, which will in the long run affect regional stability. Burma after India and Thailand has the highest incidence of HIV/AIDS in Asia. It is understandable that India with a population of 1 billion has the highest number. Thailand's HIV/AIDS problem is caused by its rampant sex trade. But through public education and good policies, the situation is slowly being brought under control. Burma's HIV/AIDS epidemic is mainly caused by drug addiction. It is illegal in Burma to own a needle. Addicts, therefore, share needles. In testing drug addicts in northern Burma over 90% tested positive. The problem is compounded by contaminated blood. When the military requires blood transfusions, the blood is taken from prisoners. There is no screening. The next factor is the fact that more and more Burmese women and girls are being sold into the sex trade in Thailand. When they test positive, they are shipped home without any explanation and the military sends them back to their home villages. There is no information, education or treatment program. The military in Burma is still denying that HIV/AIDs is a problem. The World Health Organisation and other independent sources estimated at least 500,000 HIV/AIDs positive cases in Burma.

Another major problem, which has a bearing on the matter, is the fact that education in Burma has virtually become non-existent. In the past 14 years, universities have been closed for about 9 nine years. This means that Burma does not now have educated people who can help develop the country. Unable to win the allegiance of students, the military has opted for keeping the universities closed and students scattered rather than provide them with an education for fear that they will organise anti-regime demonstrations which could spark nation-wide unrest. In addition to university closures, an even more disturbing trend was reported by the World Bank recently. According to statistics provided by the regime, in 1989 the education budget was Kyat 1,200 per child per year.

In 1999, this figure had decreased to Kyat 100 per child per year! The World Bank also reported that half of the primary school-aged children are malnourished and on average it takes a Burmese child 9.5 years to complete 5 years of primary school. This means that Burma is facing an enormous crisis. Without an educated population, how can anyone build a nation? The statistics take on an even more disturbing aspect when it is realised that this neglect of education is a deliberate policy and not an oversight. During the period that the education budget has been declining, the regime has more than doubled the size of its army from 180,000 men to 450,000 men and purchased US$ 1.8 billion worth of arms from China. The question is why?

Burma has no external enemies. The only possible answer is that the regime intends to remain in power at all cost even to the extent of sacrificing the future of Burma's children.[6]

In this paper, I will investigate the political roots of human rights violations and the denial of minority rights in Burma. Instead of compiling detail accounts of human rights violations, I will argue from an historical point of view that human rights violations in Burma began with the denial of minority rights by the successive governments of the Union of Burma, even during the so called parliamentary democracy period, in the name of maintaining national sovereignty. Though a certain level of individual rights were guaranteed constitutionally during the parliamentary democracy period, minority rights on the other hand were violated, this in turn became the main source of political crisis as well as the basis of gross violations of human rights in present Burma.

While human rights are mainly concerned with individual rights, minority rights are particularly concerned, as Swedish scholar Alf Tergel points out, with collective rights and "with a view to preserving and developing their specific character and the people's right to self-determination."[7] The central argument of this paper, therefore, will be the issue of "self-determination"; and I try to point out that when the rights of self-determination for minority groups in the country are abused by the power holders of the state, the state itself became a mechanism by which the people's rights are abused instead of maintaining the state's fundamental ideal of being an instrument for ensuring civil, political, social and cultural rights.

The main objective of this paper, therefore, is to investigate how the successive governments of the Union of Burma have violated minority rights, including collective rights of self-determination, in the name of "nation-building", how they abused the rights of minority religious groups in the name of "national integration", and how the basic human rights are denied in the name of maintaining "national sovereignty".

Human Rights vs. Traditional Burmese Political Values

In his article "Traditional Values and Universal Rights", Jack Donnelly argues that every society possesses a perception of human dignity, a particular view of the inner natural worth of the human person and his or her personal relations to society, perceptions that are reflected in its institutions and practices. He nevertheless maintains that the idea that a person is entitled to equal respect and a wide range of inalienable personal rights is alien to most non-Western societies, where social structures and the underlying social visions of human dignity rest mainly on social status, hierarchies and duties, not on rights. He concludes his argument, saying that "persons are not seen as bearers of rights but rather as bearers of duties."[8]

The concept of human persons as the bearers of duties, not as the bearer of rights, was well developed under the absolute monarchy of traditional Burmese authoritarianism and it was still practiced by General Ne Win and his successors, including the current military junta, the State Peace Development Council. Maung Maung Gyi, therefore, argues in his *Burmese Political Values: the Socio-Political Roots of Authoritarianism,* that the military coup of 1962 and its consequences of authoritarianism under General Ne Win were "the culmination of a political process"; stemming from a pre-colonial "authoritarian system of native Burmese monarchical rules."[9]

As Maung Maung Gyi observes, "from 1044 to 1885, for over 800 years, the Burmese lived under an absolute monarchy. Its authority was never challenged by any liberal forces during these years until it was overthrown by alien power in 1885."[10] The Burman pattern of thought on the government was therefore moulded during these 800 years, and "the nature of kingship largely determined the pattern of thought."[11] Though the "British conquest of Burma in 1885 laid the foundations for a significant change in the infrastructure of Burmese political culture", he argues, "the impact of British administration was not such as to bring about a revolutionary change in the medieval Burmese mind."[12] Another way of putting it is to say that the British administration destroyed "the old Burmese officialdom", but its "ethos was never broken." And Maung Maung Gyi concludes his argument by saying:

> Suffice it to say that the medieval mind underwent no essential change after being ruled by the British over 60 years (in upper Burma) to over 100 years (in lower Burma). One should not, therefore, have serious doubts as to whether the reversion to a one-man-dominated authoritarian rule pattern in 1962 was not an atavistic trends, a return to the age-old Burmese political system with modern trappings of communist genre, which itself is an offshoot of authoritarianism.[13]

In a society where "one-man-dominated rule" is practiced, "duty" becomes a mechanism of power relations between the ruler and their subjects; for the ruler it is his tools of power through which his wills are imposed upon the society, and for the people or the subjects on the other hand, "duty" is the mechanism through which they respond to the ruler by obeying his orders. Thus, a society based on "duties" does not recognize "rights"; for "rights are legal recognition of individual will [not the will of the ruler]."[14] Another way of putting the same idea, as Costas Douzinas argues, is that "a society based on rights does not recognize duties; it acknowledges only responsibilities arising from the reciprocal nature of rights in the form of limits on rights for the protection of the rights of others."[15]

"Human Rights" is a combined term. They refer to "the human, to the humanity or human nature" and the reference to "rights" refer to the concept that "all human being are entitled to the same basic rights", which are indissolubly linked with the movement of humanism and its legal reform. In this sense, human rights are "both creations and creators of modernity"; originating from classical Greek philosophy, continuing via the Magna Carta of 1215, the 1689 Bills of Rights and the French Declaration of the Rights of Man and Citizen of 1789, and ending with the Universal Declaration of Human Rights in 1948. Thus, the Universal Declaration of Human Rights, as Douzinas claims, is "the greatest political and legal invention of modern political philosophy and jurisprudence; First, they mark a profound turn in political thought from "duty" to "rights", from *civitas* and *communitas* to civilization and humanity; Secondly, they reverse the traditional priority between the individual and society." [16]

There is, therefore, no need to build a foundation for human rights on any particular traditional values; not even on "natural human dignity". It may be tempting to relate, as Michael Ignatieff observes, "the idea of human rights to propositions like the following: that human being have an innate or natural dignity, that they have a natural and intrinsic self-worth, that they are sacred."[17] However, "these ideas about dignity, worth, and human sacredness appear to confuse what is, with what ought to be, they are controversial, and because they are controversial, they are likely to fragment commitment to the practical responsibilities entailed by human rights instead of strengthening them." Michael Ignatieff, therefore, suggests:

> We must work out a belief in human rights on the basis of human beings as they are, working on assumptions about the worst we can do, instead of hopeful expectations of the best. In other words, we do not build foundations on human nature but on human history, on what we know is likely to happen when human being do not have the protection of rights. We build on the testimony of fear, rather than on the expectations of hope. This...is how human rights consciousness has been built since the Holocaust.[18]

The struggle for human rights in Burma, therefore, needs no reference to Burmese traditional political culture or religious value. Human rights—in terms of both idea and practice—is not a subjective value but objective truth, and the creation of human history; it is not an account of what is good but what is right, and which can be applied universally.

Human Rights and Self-determination

The concept of self-determination has been advanced since the time of the French Revolution, with the idea of the "nation" as the whole people, as the object of ultimate political loyalty, and as endowed with an inalienable right to self-determination and separate statehood. When the League of Nations was founded after the First World War, the right to self-determination had become an international phenomenon. The "minority protection" scheme under the League of Nations was in particular a formulation of "the principles of national self-determination"; as Woodrow Wilson put it, "Every people have a right to choose the sovereignty under which they shall live."[19]

However, the League of Nations' scheme for "minority protection" was seriously abused by the Nazis, who encouraged German minorities in Czechoslovakia and Poland to escalate their demands for minority rights. When the Czechoslovak and Polish governments were unable to meet these demands, the Nazis used this as a pretext for invasion. Consequently, when the United Nations adopted its Universal Declaration of Human Rights, all references to the rights of ethnic minorities were deleted. The hope was that the new emphasis on "human rights" and the principle of non-discrimination would resolve minority conflicts. Rather than protecting vulnerable groups directly, through special rights for the members of particular groups, cultural minorities would be protected indirectly, by guaranteeing basic civil and political rights to all individuals, regardless of group membership.[20]

During the cold war, from 1948 to 1989, both camps of Liberal West and Socialist East put greater emphasis on territorial integrity than on national self-determination. The consensus among the major powers, as Wallensteen explains, was "to describe anti-colonial conflicts as a particular category of conflict", mainly due to the fact that "the anti-colonial movements provided a potential dilemma and challenge as they argued in terms of self-determination". And he argues:

> The goal in the decolonization process was the creation of new states from the territories legally and militarily held by colonial powers. Thus, the issue was control over territory within what was, formally speaking, one state. Some colonial territories were highly integrated into the colonial "motherland", even with representation in the National Assembly.[21]

The neglect of minority cultures, as Vernon Van Dyke argues, is not a new phenomenon arising during the cold war, but has deep roots in the Western political tradition.[22] In liberal tradition, as Van Dyke explains, the fundamental issue for political theory is the proper relationship between the individual and the state. He argues that the relentless individualism of the traditional liberal approach makes it incapable of explaining some inherently collective features of political life, including the formation of the state itself, "which suggest in principle that liberalism cannot be trusted to deal adequately with the question of status and rights for ethnic communities, most of which are minorities within the state".[23] Liberalism, in Van Dyke's view, cannot and does not offer a clear basis for the right of nations or peoples to self-determination, as a right accruing to groups. The liberal tradition, with its individual conception, is he says "unduly limited", and "it is not enough to think in terms of two-level relations, with the individual at one level and the state at another".[24]

The problem with the liberal tradition, according to Van Dyke, is that "its theorists have often taken for granted that citizens feel themselves to constitute a distinct group, sharing a common language and a common desire to live together", and that this community has organized itself into a state through some form of social "contract". Contrary to this assumption, only in very few countries in the world do all citizens share the same language, or belong to the same ethno-national group. In many countries, he argues, there are two or more ethno-cultural communities living together in a single state. Since liberalism ignores the group basis for political life, "it is blind to the injustices suffered by minority cultures, which can only be rectified by supplementing liberalism with a theory of collective rights". The flaw of liberalism, in a nutshell, is "its individualism, which cannot accord any status to groups between the individual and the state".[25]

In the name of "internationalism", Marxist tradition, on the other hand, ignored the right of self-determination for ethnic minorities during the cold war. In *The Communist Manifesto*, Marx mentioned that the proletariat have no nationality—they are workers of the world. Marxist tradition therefore views cultural and national divisions as temporary stopping points, whether it is a question of language rights or national autonomy.[26] Thus, in their understanding of national questions, Marxists define their theory in terms of "historical vs. non-historical nations". For Marx and Engels, "historical nations" or "modern nations" came into existence "through the embryonic capitalist economy in transition from feudalism to capitalism. As a direct result of this process, the feudal society was slowly united under the structure of the embryonic modern state."[27]

The concept of "non-historical nations", on the other hand, implied "the people (*Völker*) who had proved to be unable to build a state over a period of time".[28] Marx and Engels repeatedly argued that "national communities incapable of constituting 'proper national states' should vanish by being assimilated into more 'progressive' and 'vital' nations."[29] They therefore accepted the right of "the great national subdivisions of Europe" to independence, and hence supported the unification of France, Italy, Poland and Germany, and the independence of England, Hungary, Spain and Russia. But they rejected the idea that the smaller "nationalities" had any such rights, such as the Czechs, Basques, Welsh, Bulgarians, Romanians and Slovenes. These smaller nationalities were expected to assimilate to one of the "greater nations", without the benefits of any minority rights, whether it be language rights or national autonomy.

During the cold war, the socialist bloc, led by the Soviet Union, strongly supported non-interference and territorial integrity rather than the rights to self-determination. One of the reasons, as Wallensteen observes, is that "the Soviet Union was the country that had made the largest territorial gains as a result of the Second World War. This included the annexation of the Baltic States, the incorporation of territory which formerly was part of Eastern Poland and Germany, and taking over Bessarabia from Romania."[30] Thus, the Soviet Union and the eastern bloc became a strong defender of the territorial *status quo*. However, during the cold war, the Soviet Union applied double standards in their international relations: on the one hand, its concern for secure borders and political influence in Europe made it a strong defender of territorial integrity; on the other, anti-colonial movements in the Third World, which were very much anti-Western and anti-capitalist, made it a supporter of self-determination. However, as Wallensteen points out, "Soviet support for [self-determination] applied only to colonial situations".[31]

As we have seen, both liberal individualism and socialist internationalism clearly led to a denial of the rights of minority cultures, especially the right to self-determination, during the cold war. International communities and bodies, including the United Nations, followed the lead given by the two superpowers. Moreover, there is relatively little recognition in international law for substantive minority rights, such as the right to self-determination, although it has been based primarily on the non-discrimination model.[32] Rather than protecting collective rights directly, the UN's Universal Declaration of Human Rights focuses only on basic civil and political rights for individuals, regardless of group membership.

However, it has become increasingly clear, as Kymlicka argues, that existing human rights standards are simple unable to resolve some of the most important and controversial questions relating to cultural minorities.

> The right to free speech does not tell us what an appropriate language policy is; the right to vote doesn't tell us how political boundaries should be drawn, or how powers should be distributed between levels of government; the right to mobility doesn't tell us what an appropriate immigration and naturalization policy is. These questions have been left to the usual process of majoritarian decision-making within each state. The result has been to render cultural minorities vulnerable to significant injustice at the hands of the majority, and to exacerbate ethno-cultural conflict.[33]

Since the end of the cold war, there has been increasing interest at the international level in supplementing traditional human rights principles with a theory of minority rights.

For example, the Conference on Security and Cooperation in Europe adopted a declaration on the Rights of National Minorities in 1991, and established a High Commissioner on National Minorities in 1993. The United Nations has debated both a Declaration on Rights of Persons Belonging to National or Ethnic, Religious and Linguistic Minorities (1993) and a Draft Universal Declaration on Indigenous Rights (1988). In 1992, the Council of Europe adopted a declaration on minority language rights (the European Charter for Regional or Minority Languages).[34] This new development, after the collapsed of Soviet, is the most encouraging sign for our struggle for democracy and human rights in Burma.

During the cold war, however, ethnic nationalities in Burma did not receive enough support, internally or internationally, in their struggle for the right of self-determination, including greater autonomous status for their national states within the Union. Instead, most of the international community, especially the UN and neighbouring countries such as India, supported the territorial integrity of the newly independent Burma. Thus, in the 1950s and 1960s, the newly independent Burmese government's efforts towards "nation building", "national integration" etc. were directly and consciously influenced by historical developments in the West, and also by the anti-colonial movements in their fellow developing countries.

Thus, human rights violation and denial of minority rights in Burma should be analysed within the historical context of "state formation conflict" which began soon after Burma's independence. State formation conflict in Burma is a vertical conflict between a Burman military-monopolized "state" and ethnic nationalities whose rights have for so long been suppressed by the "state"; not a horizontal ethnic conflict between different segments of the country's population. The political crisis in Burma is therefore a constitutional problem stemming from the reversal of Aung San's policy of federalism and the principle of "unity in diversity" on which the historic Panglong Agreement was based. We therefore need to take a closer look at how Aung San's policy, particularly his policy relating to the Panglong Agreement, was constitutionally reversed by his successor, U Nu.

Human Rights, Religion and Nation Building

Aung San, who persuaded the Chin, Kachin, Shan and other ethnic nationalities to join the Union, had a clear policy of "nation building" based on the principles of "equality" and "unity in diversity". He criticized the notion of religious-oriented traditional Burmese nationalism of "our race, our religion, our language", which he said "have gone obsolete now". And he clearly states "religion is a matter of individual conscience, while politics is social science. We must see to it that the individual enjoys his rights, including the right to freedom of religious belief and worship. We must draw clear lines between politics and religion because the two are not the same thing. If we mix religion with politics, then we offend the spirit of religion itself."[35]

However, after Aung San was assassinated, U Nu adopted the state religion of Buddhism as a means of "national integration". Buddhism, indeed, had been inseparably intertwined with the Myanmar national identity, as an old saying so clearly put it: *Buddha bata, Myanmar Lumyo* ("To be a Myanmar is to be a Buddhist"). Thus, it was quite reasonable for leaders like U Nu to believe that Buddhism could make a significant contribution to some aspects of national integration. Historically, Buddhism had played a most important role in binding together diverse ethnic groups such as the Burman, Mon, Shan and Rakhine (Arakanese).[36]

Although Buddhism had been a powerful integrative force in traditional Burman/Myanmar society, the modern, multi-ethnic, multi-religious and multi-cultural nation-state of the Union of Burma was a very different country from the pre-colonial Myanmar Kingdom. Thus, the fundamental question for the Union of Burma is: Can Buddhism, a vital source of political legitimacy for traditional Burmese kingship, provides equally effective support for the present democratic regime? The question of legitimacy is closely related to the psychological problem of identity. The concomitant questions are therefore: Can Buddhism provides the values needed to create a modern Burmese national identity? In an attempt to solve the problems of political legitimacy and national identity through religion, what happens to religious minorities and the delicate fabric of national unity?

It seemed that that answer for U Nu was "Yes"; and when he became the leader of the Burmese independence movement and Prime Minister of the newly independent Burma, he reversed Aung San's version of Union Constitution, particularly the clause of separation between religion and politics, declaring: "In the marrow of my bones there is a belief that government should enter into the sphere of religion."[37] U Nu's government, therefore, adopted state religion of Buddhism as a means of "national integration"; that is, an attempt was made to achieve homogeneity by imposing religious and cultural assimilation into the predominant group of Myanmar Buddhists. In so doing, Ministry of Religious and Cultural Affairs was created to promote the process of assimilation, even before Buddhism was promulgated as a state religion.[38] The official view, as John Cady observes, was that:

> A unity of culture existed among the people of the Union and those existing differences are only expressions of the same culture at different stages of development. The Burman and Pyu peoples had long since been amalgamated; the Mon had almost been absorbed, the Shan assimilation was in progress. The Karens, Kachins, and Chins were also mainly Tibeto-Burman, and all were allegedly suitable for becoming parts of a closely knit cultural organism.[39]

U Nu's official government policy of "unity in culture" was oversimplified. The Chin, for instance, never accepted Buddhism either as a culture or as a religion. In contrast to the government's view, the amalgamation of the Burman and Pyu, or the extinction of the Pyu, was a historical reminder which served to awaken the Chin people's self-awareness of a separate national identity, without which they might one day cease to exist as the Pyu people had once done. The Chin therefore, far from accepting assimilation, took the view that U Nu's confessional policy of religion, or what the government called

47

"unity in culture", must be resisted at all costs; and they took arms to defend themselves from assimilation in 1964.

The revision of Aung San's version of the Union Constitution thus proved to be the end of his policy for a secular state and pluralism in Burma, which eventually led to the promulgation of Buddhism as the state religion of the Union of Burma in 1961.

Denial of Religious and Cultural Rights under Ne Win's Dictatorship

As mentioned above, U Nu adopted state religion of Buddhism as a means of national integration. In this section, I will analyse the nature of General Ne Win's dictatorship, and how the de facto government of the military regime legitimized itself through traditional Burmese political concepts. As David Steinberg observes, "there have been five foci for the legitimization of Burmese governments or pretenders to power in the twentieth century: nationalism, Buddhism, socialism, military leadership and election".[40] Since the independence movement, nationalism had been an enduring element of the Burmese concept of political legitimacy, the "sine qua non of political life", as Steinberg so aptly puts it. As we have seen earlier, U Nu apparently mixed nationalism with Buddhism in his attempt to legitimize his government. General Ne Win, on the other hand, mixed nationalism with socialism, and he also used military leadership as a means to introduce national integration to achieve homogeneity in the country.

Nationalism, for both U Nu and Ne Win, was simply based on the notion of "one race, one language and one religion"— that is to say, the Burman or Myanmar race, *Myanmar-sa* and Buddhism. Although their approaches to "national integration" were different, U Nu and Ne Win both had the same goal of creating a homogeneous people in the country. While U Nu opted for cultural and religious assimilation into Buddhism as a means of integration, Ne Win removed the rights of the country's religious and cultural minorities, including all civil and basic human rights, as a means of creating a homogeneous unitary state. U Nu and Ne Win thus complemented each other, although their approaches in depriving cultural and religious minorities of their rights were different in nature.

In his campaign against the rights of minority cultures and religions in the country, General Ne Win targeted Christianity as an unwanted foreign religion, while viewing Christian missionaries as people who kept "imperialism alive". Consequently, he expelled all foreign missionaries from Burma in 1966. Until 1966 when the missionaries were expelled, non-Christian Burman nationalists like General Ne Win viewed and understood the existence of Christians in Burma merely in terms of the church's social missions, such as schools and hospitals, and the presence of foreign missionaries in the country. Without these two factors, they thought that "the church will soon weaken and die".[41]

Thus, in order to suppress both Christian movements and different ethnic nationalist movements, General Ne Win's government not only expelled foreign missionaries, but also nationalized all the missionary schools and hospitals in the country. At the same time, the government intensified its military campaign against the Chin, Kachin, Karen and other ethnic nationalist movements. Ironically, when the government suppressed the military aspects of the Chin nationalist movements, the *indigenous form of Christianity,* that is, the church without foreign missionaries became a more valid expression of the Chin national identity in Burma.

Restrictions on Religious Freedom

The nationalisation of private Christian schools and hospitals had made it clear that so called "religious freedom" under General Ne Win's regime did not include permission to maintain such Christian institutions.[42] Likewise, the expulsion of foreign missionaries from the country in 1966 indicated that, under the military regime of the Revolutionary Council, religious freedom did not include the right of Christians in Burma (mainly Chin, Kachin and Karen) to invite missionaries from abroad to assist the churches within the country. In addition, the continuing inability of Christians to secure Burmese passports to enable them to attend international Christian conferences was an indication of a further limitation in their freedom of religion.

It was in the area of Christian publications that the increased governmental control was felt very keenly. In 1965, the Revolutionary Council issued the "Censor Law", requiring four copies of any manuscript of a religious nature to be submitted for approval before it could be published. This order included magazines, tracts, and Sunday school materials, as well as books. No arrangements had been made to read or pass on such manuscripts unless they were written in either the Burmese or the English language. Along with manuscripts written in any language other than these two, four copies of a translation into Burmese or English had to be submitted along with the originals. Although a considerable amount of Christian publishing was done in Burmese, nevertheless there was a very great demand for Sunday school materials, hymnals, etc. in the languages of the Chin, Kachin, Karen, and others who constituted the overwhelming majority of the Christians in the country. As can well be imagined, having to translate manuscripts from these languages into Burmese or English entailed a great deal of work, increased time for preparation, and extra expense.

Once the application to the government had been made, after a period of three weeks as minimum and perhaps several months as a maximum, one could expect information as to whether or not the government had approved the manuscript. Upon receipt of approval, an order could then be given to a printer to do the work. The printer, on the basis of the order, then applied for permission to purchase from the government the paper needed for the job. When that permission finally came through, the printer very often found that he had been granted less paper than requested, and often of a different size and of poorer quality! Average and better qualities of paper were reserved for government printing; only the cheaper qualities were available for the general public, including religious organisations.

Thus, in the printing of any piece of religious material it was always necessary to anticipate a delay of a number of months, even years. It was obvious how difficult and trying this could be, especially in publishing materials which have a time limit such as Sunday School lessons.[43]

The 1962 Printers and Publishers Registration Law and the 1965 Censor Law immediately hit not only the publication of Christian literature, but also all the literature of non-Burman nationalities. Following the nationalisation of schools, which used to be the centre of learning for the literatures of non-Burman Christian nationalities, such as the Chin, Kachin and Karen, "successive BSPP administrations embarked on what ethnic minority leaders allege was a straightforward policy of Burmanization" or Myanmarnization. Since then, as Martin Smith correctly observes:

> Minority language are rarely taught or used beyond the fourth grade in school; ethnic minority publications are restricted to little more than folksy, housewife magazines, such as the Karen *Our Home* and *Go Forward*. The distribution of religious literature, including the Bible, has been restricted and BSPP officials and censors have complained to Christian pastors about the militant language of the Old Testament, which they claim, is incitement to rebellion.[44]

Since the military government came to power in 1962, as Martin Smith point out, the Christians in Burma, especially non-Burman nationalities have mostly been unable to print the Holy Bible in their own language inside Burma. Chin Christians, for instance, printed the Bile in the Chin language in India, and smuggled it into Burma in the 1970s and 1980s. Even the Holy Bible in Burmese, which was translated by Rev. Judson in the 1820s, never received permission to be reprinted from the Censor Board of the BSPP, or at least the Old Testament never did. Only the New Testament, together with Psalms and Proverbs, once received permission to be printed during the entire period of BSPP administrations, that is, from 1962 to 1988.

Restrictions on Freedom of Expression

As far as social change under the military regime was concerned, the most drastic change took place in the realm of the press and other publications. The RC imposed the strongest ever restrictions and pressures, not only on the press but also on libraries and publishing companies. Newspapers were operated either by the government, which had founded The Working People's Daily, or else completely under government control. All news from abroad was channelled to the papers through the News Agency, Burma (NAB), a government news office. In this way, "Burma's previously lively press was effectively brought under state control within a few years of the coup."[45]

Prior to the military take-over, Burma had had more than thirty newspapers. Apart from the leading ones in Burmese and English, there were also five in Chinese, two in Hindi and one each in Urdu, Tamil, Telegu and Gujarati. Moreover, there were many locally run newspapers in non-Burmese languages, such as in Karen, Kachin and Chin. A well-known weekly newsmagazine in Chin, Hruaituthar (literally: New Leaders), run by Rev. James Sang Awi, was also banned by the military government.

The same restrictions were placed, as indicated above, on libraries and publishing companies. The RC promulgated the "Printers and Publishers Regulation Law" in 1962, which scrutinised not only "the text, language and subject of new books and journals but even the number of copies printed." This resulted, as Martin Smith observes, "in a plethora of privately-owned magazines containing only short stories, for these were easier to replace if rejected. All were for entertainment; no news periodicals were permitted. Over the years the same laws were extended to film, music and video companies."[46]

In short, the 1962 Press Act and the 1965 Censor Act nullified the rights to freedom of opinion and expression, which have been guaranteed to all the people by Article 19 of the Universal Declaration of Human Rights and International Covenant on Civil and Political Rights, for the people of Burma.

Religious Persecution under the Current Military Junta (A Case of the Chin Christians)

Since the military coup in 1988, the distinction between the army and state ceased to exist, and gross violations of human rights become part of everyday life in Burma. In addition to gross violation of human rights, the State Peace and Development Council (SPDC) has been launching relentlessly the campaign of "Myanmarnization" or "Burmanizing" the country by systematically destroying significant and symbolic identities of non-Burman ethnic groups.

Since the early 1990, the regime has turned its attention to the north-western part of the country, particularly the Chin State, to expand its military establishment there in an effort to gain effective control over the Chin population, who had hitherto remained relatively free from direct Burman control. Although only one army battalion was stationed in Chin State prior to 1988, more than 10 infantry battalions, about five thousand soldiers, are now active in the area. The junta's justification was to meet Chin insurgent threat, a movement which began in 1988 with the formation of the Chin National Front by a few exiled politicians and students and youths who fled to India in the aftermath of the 1988 nation-wide democracy uprising. The Chin National Front is fighting for the restoration of democracy in Burma and self-determination for the Chin people. Neither the SLORC nor SPDC have acknowledged the CNF in the state-run media; nor do they mention the CNF when speaking of the "armed groups" that have yet to "return to the legal fold."[2] In stead, some officials refer to them as "misguided youths" who would sooner or later see the light and would return to the "legal fold".

Because Chin State has the largest concentration of Christians in the whole of Burma in terms of percentage, it was not only a large army of soldiers that was brought into by the Burmese regime. In the name of "Hill Regions Buddhist Mission" the junta brought in an army of Buddhist monks who were then dispatched to various towns and villages across Chin State. Protected by the soldiers, these Buddhist monks have considerable powers over the Chin population. In many cases, local people have pointed out that the monks are military intelligence operatives who are more powerful than local army commanders. The Chin Human Rights Organization reported about the monks stationed around Matupi Township as follow:

The monks who live at Zakam, Rezua, Leisen, Vangvai and Tinsi villages rule the communities. Anyone who doesn't abide by the monks orders is reported to the SLORC/SPDC army and he/she is punished by the army. The monks give judgment on all cases. For those who become Buddhist, they are free from any persecution such as forced labour, portering, extortion of money, etc. Whenever and wherever a monk visits, he is accompanied by the army and they arrange a porter to carry the monk's particulars. The villagers were forced to build a Buddhist monastery and temple. But they refused, insisting "we are Christians". Even though the army threatened action against them, they didn't build it yet. Now the monks and army are holding a meeting to discuss this. Nobody knows what will happen.[48]

According to the Chin Human Rights Organization report, the method that the "Hills Regions Buddhists Mission" is applying is as follows:

1. To attack Christian families and the progress of Christians.
2. To criticize against the sermons which are broadcast from Manila, Philippines.
3. To criticize God as narrow-minded and egotistical who himself claimed that "There is no god except eternal God".
4. To criticize Christian ways of life as corrupted and inappropriate culture in Burma.
5. To criticize the preaching of Christians wherever it has penetrated.
6. To criticize Christianity by means of pointing out its delicacy and weakness.
7. To stop the spread of the Christian movement in rural areas.
8. To criticize by means of pointing out "there is no salvation without purchased by the blood of Christ".
9. To counterattack by means of pointing out Christianity's weakness and overcome this with Buddhism.

10. To counter the Bible after thorough study.
11. To criticize that "God loves only Israel but not all the races".
12. To point out ambiguity between the two testaments.
13. To criticize on the point that Christianity is partisan religion.
14. To criticize Christianity's concept of the Creator and compare it with the scientific concept.
15. To study and access the amount given in offerings.
16. To criticize the Holy Bible after thorough study.
17. To attack Christians by means of both non-violence and violence.[49]

A 40-year-old Chin Christian from Matupi Township recounted how he was converted to Buddhism, recruited and trained to be part of a campaign against Christians, as follows:

> I was invited to attend social welfare training by the [SLORC (now SPDC)] authority from Matupi on 27/2/95. When I arrived at the place, the authority told us that it is to attend Buddhist hill tract missionary training run by a Buddhist monk named U Razinn at Mindat. As we are Christian, we said we didn't want to go. But the monk persuaded us saying, 'it is no problem if you are Christian, it is just religious training'. So 5 other persons and I took part in the 10 day training. In the training, we were taught the 17 facts of how to attack and disfigure Christians.[50]

Since they came into power, the military junta has ordered the removal of several crosses erected by local Chin Christians on tops of mountains beside a number of villages and towns throughout Chin State. Since early 1980s, Chin communities in various villages and towns have erected wooden crosses on mounds and hill tops beside their villages and towns to symbolize their faith in Christianity, and to remind themselves of the fact that Christianity has played an important role in shaping their modern society and culture. In some cases, however, the erection of these crosses were in response to what the Chin regarded was the State-sponsored importation of Buddhism into Chin State with the construction of pagodas and temples in certain urban areas in Chin State which began in the 1970s.

Destruction of crosses and churches started around early 1990's with the rapid increase in army battalions being established across Chin State. Since then, almost every cross in all the nine townships in Chin State had been destroyed by the regime. Destruction is usually ordered by the township authorities or by army battalion commanders in whose jurisdiction the cross is erected. After an order is issued, the church or community responsible for erecting the cross is given a timeframe during which they must dismantle the cross. Failure to do so within the given period often meant the cross being destroyed by the authorities and Church leaders being arrested for defiance of order.

While crosses have been removed in several townships, perhaps the most publicized case so far was the removal of a cross in Thantlang Township in January of 1999. The year 1999 marked one hundredth year of Christianity among the Chins. The Centennial Celebration was originally planned for March 15 in Haka, the capital of Chin State where the first American missionaries established their mission centre in 1899. However, before the official celebration in Haka, advance celebrations were also held locally in various townships under the leadership of local churches. In Thantlang, the celebration was organized jointly by all the different denominations in town from January 1 to 3, 1999. The CHRO reported the accident as follows:

> On January 5, when the celebration was over, the organizers erected a Centennial Memorial Cross on a hilltop on Vuichip ridge, located west of the town. Though it was erected primarily in remembrance of the early American missionaries, the selection of the location for the cross had other significance. In addition to its good view from town, the spot has a spiritual and religious dimension to it. Before the advent of Christianity, Thantlang residents had traditionally believed that Vuichip ridge was the dwelling place of evil spirits and there had been legends of the spirits roaming the ridge. The erection of the cross on that particular location was to signify that evil spirits

have been defeated by the crucifixion of Jesus Christ on the cross. The cross was decorated with looking glasses so that it would be more recognizable when it glows with the reflection from the sun.

On the very night the cross was erected, the Township Peace and Development Council ordered the destruction of the cross, compelling the very people who had erected the cross to destroy it. When the people refused, a section of local police were sent to destroy the cross. Six Christian pastors responsible for organizing the Centennial Celebration and the erection of the Memorial cross, Rev. Thawng Kam, Rev. Biak Kam, Rev. Thantu, Rev. Tha Ceu, Rev. Cung Bik and Pastor Beauty Lily were arrested and interrogated by the army. In response, on January 6, the whole town stage a silent protest by closing down their businesses and refusing to go to work, and by observing a 24-hour fast and prayer vigil in their local churches and homes. Fearing the news of protest might spread to other towns; the authorities shut down telephone connections of Thantlang and arrested 20 more Church leaders. Nevertheless, on January 9, Churches in the Chin State capital, Haka, joined the protest, prompting Chairman of the Chin State Peace and Development Council in Haka to go to Thantlang to end the strike by threatening and intimidating them.[51]

The leaders of the Church, Rev. Thawng Kam and Rev. Biak Kam were arrested, and put into jail without trail. In addition to destruction of the Chin Christian symbol of the cross, the soldiers also disrupted worship services and religious ceremonies, and rounded up people going to Church for forced porters. Moreover, the military has tried to coerce people into converting into Buddhism by targeting Christians for forced labour and other abuses. In many instances, Christian pastors have been physically abused and mocked by Burmese soldiers. The junta has refused to grant permission to construct new Church buildings and other Christian religious buildings while it has allocated State funds to construct new Buddhist pagodas in various parts of Chin State.

In many major towns in Chin State, partially completed church buildings are still standing unfinished because the State Peace and Development Council does not grant permission to resume construction. The Carson Memorial Hall was being built in Haka, the capital of Chin State in 1999 by the Haka Baptist Church to be inaugurated on the occasion of one-hundredth anniversary of Christianity among the Chins since the first arrival of American missionaries, Arthur and Laura Carson in the late 1890s. The construction was set to be completed before the start of the Centennial Celebration which was scheduled for March 15, 1999. But the junta halted the construction half-way saying that the Church did not obtain authorization from the Ministry of Home and Religious Affairs in Rangoon, although the Hall was constructed within the parameters of Church properties.

As much evidence has pointed out, the Burmese military regime has actively sought symbolic targets in its campaign of Burmanization and ethnocide against various ethnic groups in the country, and has used religious persecution as a means of destroying religious and ethnic identity in the country.

Conclusion

In this paper, I have investigated the root cause of human rights violations and the denial of the rights of religious and cultural minorities, instead of compiling detail account of human rights violations and the denial of democracy in Burma. I have argued that total denial of human rights in Burma began with the rejection of the right of self-determination for non-Burman ethnic nationalities, who joined the Union of Burma voluntarily as equal partner in 1947.

In so doing, I have explored how successive governments of the Union of Burma have abused the rights of religious and cultural minority groups, including the collective rights of self-determination, in the names of "national-building", "national integration" and maintaining "national sovereignty". I argued that during the parliamentary democracy era, U Nu's government had adopted the state religion of Buddhism as a means of "national integration" by imposing cultural and religious assimilation into the predominant group of Burman/Myanmar Buddhists, as occurred with the promulgation of Buddhism as State Religion act in 1961.

While U Nu opted for cultural and religious assimilation into Buddhism as a means of integration, Ne Win removed the rights of the country's religious and cultural minorities, including all civil and basic human rights, as a means of creating a homogeneous unitary state. U Nu and Ne Win thus complemented each other, although their approaches in depriving cultural and religious minorities of their rights were different in nature. The current military regime also shares the same goal but with a slightly different approach; they apply the method religious persecution as a means of destroying ethnic identity, especially against Chin Christians. In short, ever since General Ne Win took over state power in 1962, the distinction between the army and state has ceased to exist, and gross violations of human rights became part of everyday life in Burma.

I maintain, in this paper, that the root of human rights violations in Burma is related to the constitutional crisis and it must therefore be solved through the constitutional means of establishing a democratic federal system of government. A democratic federal system—based on the principle of equality for all member states of the Union, the right of self-determination for all ethnic nationalities, and the democratic rights for all citizens of the Union—is the best means to restore the Union of Burma. Thus, for all the democratic forces and ethnic nationalities in Burma, the ultimate goal of the democracy movement should be to establish a genuine democratic federal union, where various ethnic nationalities from different religious, racial, cultural and historical backgrounds can live peacefully together.

Notes

[1] In 1948, the UN had fifty-six member countries; forty-eight countries voted for the Universal Declaration of Human Rights, and eight countries abstained. Among the eight countries that abstained, six were from the Soviet Bloc, and the other two were Saudi Arabia and South Africa.

[2] Harn Yawnghwe, "The UN Declaration of Human Rights and Its Impact on Asian Values and Democratic Principles" in Jeffrey Hopkins (ed.), *The Art of Peace: Nobel Peace Laureates Discuss Human Rights, Conflict and Reconciliation*, (Ithaca, New York: Snow Lion Publication, 2000), pp.145-146. On that occasion, Harn Yawnghwe spoke on behalf of Aung San Suu Kyi.

[3] Human Rights Year Book 1994: Burma, pp.

[4] Ibid.

[5] Military regime has changed its name from "State Law and Order Restoration Council" (SLORC) to "State Peace and Development Council" (SPDC) in 1996.

[6] Cf. Harn Yawnghwe, "Current political situation in Burma", a paper presented at the South-East Asia Seminar of the Committee of 100, Rauhanasema, Helsinki, Finland, on 13-14 May 2000

[7] Alf Tergel, *Human Rights in Cultural and Religious Traditions*, (Uppsala University, 1998), pp. 22-23

[8] Jack Donnelly, "Traditional Values and Universal Rights: Caste in India" in Claude E. Welch Jr. and Virginia A. Leary (eds.): *Asian Perspectives on Human Rights* (Oxford University Press, 1990), pp.55-90

[9] Maung Maung Gyi, *Burmese Political Values: The Socio-Political Roots of Authoritarianism* (New York: Preager Publishers, 1983), p. 3.

[10] Ibid., pp. 13-14

[11] Ibid.

[12] Ibid., p. 10

[13] Ibid., p. 13

[14] Costas Douzinas, *The End of Human Rights* (Oxford, 2000), p. 12

[15] Ibid., p. 10

[16] Ibid., p. 18

[17] Michael Ignatieff, *Human Rights as Politics and Idolatry* (Princeton and Oxford: Princeton University Press, 2001), p.54

[18] Ibid., p. 80

[19] Cited in Vernon Van Dyke, "The Individual, the State, and Ethnic Communities in Political Theory", in Will Kymlicka (ed.), *The Rights of Minority Cultures* (Oxford University Press: 1995), pp. 31–56.

[20] Cf. Will Kymlicka (ed.), *The Rights of Minority Cultures* (Oxford University Press: 1995), see especially the introduction.

[21] Peter Wallensteen, *Understanding Conflict Resolution* (2002), op. cit., p. 165.

[22] Vernon Van Dyke, "The Individual, the State, and Ethnic Communities in Political Theory", in Will Kymlicka (ed.), *The Rights of Minority Cultures* (Oxford University Press: 1995), pp. 31–56.

[23] Ibid., p. 32.

[24] Ibid., p. 31.

[25] Ibid., p. 32; see also Kymlicka's introduction.

[26] Will Kymlicka (ed.), *The Rights of Minority Cultures* (1995), p. 5.

[27] Ephraim Nimni, "Marx, Engels, and the National Question", in Will Kymlicka (ed.), *The Rights of Minority Cultures* (1995), pp. 57–75.

[28] Ibid., p. 67.

[29] Ibid., p. 63.

[30] Peter Wallensteen, *Understanding Conflict Resolution* (2002), p. 168.

[31] Ibid., p. 169.

[32] Cf. Will Kymlicka (ed.), *The Rights of Minority Cultures* (Oxford University Press: 1995), see especially the introduction.

[33] Ibid., p. 18.

[34] Ibid., p. 18.

[35] Aung San's speech entitled "Problems for Burma's Freedom", delivered on January 20, 1946, in Josef Silverstein (ed.), *Political Legacy of Aung San* (Ithaca, New York: Cornell University Press, 1993), p. 96.

[36] Burmese political history from the Pagan Dynasty (1044–1287) to the British conquest (1824–86) was characterized by endless struggles between the Burman, Mon, Rakhine (Arakan) and Shan. However, by adopting Buddhism from each other during their long struggles for power and domination, these four ethnic groups shared common values with regard to political systems, customary law and culture, stemming from their common religion of Buddhism.

[37] Jerold Schector, *The New Face of Buddha* (1967), p. 106.

[38] Cf. John F. Cady, *A History of Modern Burma* (Ithaca, New York: Cornell University Press, 1960), p. 638.

[39] Ibid., p. 639, footnote 31.

[40] David Steinberg, "The State, Power, and Civil Society in Burma-Myanmar: The Status and Prospects for Pluralism", in Morten Pedersen, Emily Rudland and R. J. May (eds.), *Burma-Myanmar: Strong Regime, Weak State* (London: Crawford House Publishing, 2000), pp. 91–122.

[41] See Herman Tegenfeldt, *Through the Deep Water: The Final Hours of Christian Mission in Burma* (Valley Forge: Judson Press, 1968), pp. 13–14.

[42] General Ne Win's regime under Revolutionary Council (1962-74) and the Burma Socialist Program Party (1974-1988), officially claimed that "Religious Freedom" is protected by law but it was merely "Freedom of Worship".

[43] Ibid., pp.18-19

[44] Martin Smith (1996), op.cit., p. 205

[45] Bertil Lintner (1994), op. cit., 179.

[46] Ibid, p.205.

[47] Chin Human Rights Organization's report : "*All Quiet on the Western Front?*"

[48] Chin Human Rights Organization's Report: "*Religious Persecution: A Campaign of Ethnocide against Chin Christians in Burma*" (2003), p.5

[49] Ibid.

[50] Ibid., p. 6

[51] Ibid., p. 11

PART TWO

SEARCHING FOR A POLITICAL SOLUTION

FOUR

The Democracy Movement towards a Federal Union: The Role of the UNLD in the Struggle for Democracy and Federalism in Burma

This paper was first presented at the UNLD-LA Conference in 2001, and published as chapter seven in the 'The New Panglong Initative: Rebuilding the Union of Burma' *edited by Chao Tzang Yawnghwe and Lian H. Sakhong, UNLD Press, 2004*

Introduction

The United Nationalities League for Democracy (UNLD), an umbrella political organization of non-Burman or non-Myanmar nationalities in Burma,[1] was formed in 1988 following the nationwide democracy movement against three decades of General Ne Win's dictatorship. From the very beginning, the UNLD adopted a policy aimed at the establishment of a genuine federal union based on democratic rights for all citizens, political equality for all nationalities and the rights of self-determination for all member states of the Union. It openly declared that democracy without federalism would not solve the political crisis in Burma including the civil war which had already been fought for four decades. Thus for the UNLD, the ultimate goal of the democratic movement in present-day Burma is not only to restore democratic government but to establish a genuine federal union. In other words, the UNLD views the root of political crisis in Burma today as a constitutional problem rather than a purely ideological confrontation between democracy and dictatorship.

In this paper, I shall explore the role of the UNLD in the on-going struggle for democracy and federalism in Burma. In doing this, attention will be given to the basic principles of federalism and democratic decentralization, which of course is the goal of the movement and the aim of the UNLD. However, instead of presenting a theoretical paper on the basic principles of federalism, I shall focus my attention to the quest for federalism within the historical framework of so-called, "religious and ethnic conflicts" in modern Burma. In this way, I shall argue that the democracy movement in Burma since the military *coup d'état* in 1962 is the continuation of the "federal movement" during the parliamentary democratic period in the 1950s and early 1960s. The central argument in this paper therefore will run through the military coup in 1962 as "the culmination of political process" stemming from the political crisis during the parliamentary democratic period.[2]

I shall then try to point out how and why we can view the role of the UNLD in present struggle as the continuation of the Supreme Council of the United Hills Peoples (SCOUHP), which played a leading role in the federal movement during the late 1950s and early 1960s. Another way of putting it is to say that what the UNLD is trying to achieve at present is what the SCOUHP attempted to do even before the military coup in 1962. But because the federal movement led by the SCOUHP was abruptly interrupted by the military coup in 1962, the struggle for democracy and federalism needs to be continued today.

Background History

The Union of Burma is a multi-nation-state of diverse ethnic nations (ethnic nationalities), founded in 1947 at the Panglong Conference by pre-colonial independent ethnic nationalities such as the Chin, Kachin, Karen, Karenni, Mon, Rakhine (Arakan), Myanmar (Burman), and Shan, based on the principle of equality. As it was founded by formerly independent peoples in 1947 through an agreement, the boundaries of the Union of Burma today are not historical. Rather, the Union of Burma, or

Burma in its current form, was born of the historic Panglong Agreement signed in 1947.

In order to understand the complex background of religious and ethnic diversity in Burma, one might firstly note that there is an age-old identification of Burman/Myanmar ethnicity and Buddhism, which has been the dominant ideological and political force in what is today called the Union of Burma or Myanmar. Secondly, there are other ethnic nations or nationalities such as the Mon, Rakhine (Arakan), and Shan, who are Buddhists, but feel dominated by the Burman/Myanmar majority. Thirdly, there are ethnic nationalities who are predominantly Christians within a Baptist tradition. The most prominent Christian groups are the Chin, Kachin and Karen. They — like the Mon and the Shan — form ethnic communities which transcend the boundaries of the modern nation-states of Burma, Bangladesh, India, China, and Thailand. The present state of relations between majority Burman/ Myanmar Buddhists and minority Christian ethnic groups must be understood against the background of colonial history.

The British annexed "Burma Proper", i.e., the Burman or Myanmar Kingdom, in three Anglo-Burmese wars fought in 1824-26, 1852 and 1885. As a result, the British took over Burma Proper in three stages: the Rakhine (Arakan) and Tenasserim coastal provinces in 1826, Lower Burma (previously Mon Kingdom) including Rangoon — the present capital of Burma — in 1852, and Upper Burma including Mandalay, the last capital of the Burman Kingdom in 1885. When the last King of Burma, Thibaw, was deposed and exiled to India, the possessions of the Burman Kingdom — including semi-independent tributaries of the Burman king, such as the Arakan and the Mon — were transferred to the British. However, this arrangement did not include the Chin, Kachin, Shan and Karenni, who were completely independent peoples, and had never been conquered by the Burman King. Thus, the British separately conquered or "pacified" them during a different period of time. The Chin people, for instance, were "pacified" only ten years after the fall of Mandalay, and their land Chinram, or Chinland,[3] was not declared a part of British India until 1896.

During the colonial period, the British applied two different administrative systems: "direct rule" and "indirect rule". The first was applied to the peoples and areas they conquered together with the Burman Kingdom, i.e., "Burma Proper". "Indirect rule", on the other hand, was applied to the peoples who were "pacified" or added by treaty (the Shan principalities, for example) to the British Empire after the annexation of the Burman kingdom. Under the British policy of "indirect rule", the traditional princes and local chiefs of the Chin, Kachin and the Shan were allowed to retain a certain level of administrative and judiciary powers within their respective territories.

In 1937, when the Burma Act of 1935 was officially implemented, Burma Proper was separated from British India and given a Governor of its own. The 1935 Act also created a government structure for Burma Proper, with a Prime Minister and cabinet. The Legislative Council for Burma Proper was also created, although essential power remained firmly in the hands of the British Governor and Westminster. From that time on, Burma Proper was commonly known as "Ministerial Burma". In contrast to this, the term "Excluded Areas" was used to denote the Chin, Kachin and Shan States (Federated Shan States), which were not only subject to "indirect rule", but also excluded from the Legislative Council of Ministerial Burma. The term "Excluded Areas", however, was superseded by the term "Frontier Areas" when the British government created a "Frontier Area Administration" soon after the Second World War.

The Second World War and the Japanese invasion of Burma brought British rule to an abrupt end. Accompanied and helped by the Burma Independence Army (BIA) led by General Aung San (later, U Aung San, upon leaving the armed services), the Japanese easily eliminated the British and captured Rangoon. In May 1942, the Governor of Burma fled to Simla, India, and established the British Burma government in exile there. Having successfully driven the British into India, the Japanese occupied Burma Proper and set up a military administration along their lines of advance.

When the BIA was allowed by the Japanese to be stationed in the Irrawady delta where the majority of the population were Karen, who were loyal to the British, communal violence erupted between the two sides. The Japanese ended the bloodbath but only after more than 1,000 Karen civilians had lost their lives. Because of that event, a full-scale war broke out between the Karen and the newly independent Burmese government in 1949. This ethnic conflict was the beginning of civil war in modern Burma, in which hundreds of thousands of lives have been lost over more than five decades and which is still in progress. As will be explained, only in the case of the Karen, can the term "ethnic conflict" be applied, but not, for example, the Chin, Kachin, Shan, etc...

After expelling the Japanese, the British returned to Burma in the spring of 1945. They outlined their long-term plan for the future of Burma in the form of a White Paper. This plan provided for a three-year period of direct rule under the British Governor, during which economic rehabilitation from the ravages of war was to be undertaken. Next, the Legislative Council of Ministerial Burma would be restored in accordance with the 1935 Burma Act. Only after the elections had been held under this Act would the legislature be invited to frame a new constitution "which would eventually provide the basis on which Burma would be granted dominion status."[4]

For the Frontier Areas, the White Paper provided a means of maintaining the pre-war status quo. The Karenni (Kayah) State was still bound by the pre-colonial treaty as an independent nation. Since the Chinram, the Kachin State and the Federated Shan States were excluded from the administration of Burma Proper, they would, according to the White Paper, have "a special regime under the Governor."[5] When Stevenson became the Director of the Frontier Areas Administration, he even promoted plans to create a "United Frontier Union" for the Chin, Kachin, Karen, Shan and other non-Burman nationalities. However, the plans did not come to fruition as the British Conservative Party of Prime Minister Winston Churchill, lost the general election in 1945.

In the early stage of the post-war period, the British strongly highlighted the rights and interests of the Chin, Kachin, Karen and other non-Burman nationalities from the Frontier Areas who had loyally defended the British Empire during the war. But when the Labour Government came to power, Britain reversed its policy, and Burma's political agenda became largely a matter of bilateral negotiation between the British Labor government and Aung San's AFPFL (Anti-Fascist People's Freedom League).[6] Thus, in December 1946, the Labor government invited only Aung San, the undisputed leader of the Burmese nationalist movement. The delegation, which did not include a single representative from the Frontier Areas, went to London to discuss "the steps that would be necessary to constitute Burma a sovereign independent nation."[7] Since Attlee's Labour Government had already prepared to grant Burma's independence either within or without the Commonwealth, the London talks were largely a formality, at most putting into more concrete form the principles to which they had already agreed.[8] It might be said -- as Churchill stated in parliament -- the people of the Frontier Area were abandoned by the British and left to salvage what they could of their former independent status with Aung San and the AFPFL.

The Question of Non-Burman Nationalities

At the London Talks in December 1946, the Burman delegates demanded that "the amalgamation of the Frontier Areas and Ministerial Burma should take place at once, and that the Governor's responsibility for the Frontier Areas should end."[9] As noted already, the London Talks was bilateral negotiation between the British Labor government and Aung San's AFPFL without a single representative from non-Burman nationalities. Although there were at least three Karen members in the Constituent Assembly of the Interim Burmese government, none of them were included in the London Talks. Instead, Aung San included several councilors, civil servants and politicians in the delegation. He even included his main rival politicians such as U Saw and Ba Sein.

On the demand of the amalgamation of the Frontier Areas with Ministerial Burma, the British countered the AFPFL's demand with the following position:

> HMG for their part are bound by solemn undertakings to the people of those Areas to regard their wishes in this matter, and they have deep obligations to those peoples for the help that they gave during the war. According to the information available to HMG the Frontier Areas are not yet ready or willing to amalgamate with Burma Proper.[10]

During the talk, Attlee received a cable from the Shan Sawbwas (princes), through the Frontier Areas Administration and the Governor, stating that Aung San and his delegation did not represent the Shan and the Frontier Areas.[11] Stevenson, Director of Frontier Areas Administration, also cabled to London, saying that,

> We understand that the Hon'ble U Aung San and the Burman Mission visiting London will seek the control of FA. If this is the case we wish to state emphatically that neither the Hon'ble Aung San nor his colleagues has any mandate to speak on behalf of FA.[12]

In short, Aung San and his delegation had no right to discuss the future of the Frontier Areas.

Indeed, it might rightly be said that Aung San and his delegation neither represented nor had the right to discuss the future of the peoples of the Frontier Areas, especially the Chin, Kachin, and Shan because they were independent peoples before the colonial period and were conquered separately by the British, and they were not part of Ministerial Burma (Burma Proper). Aung San could therefore legitimately represent only Burma Proper, or Ministerial Burma, which belonged to an old Burman or Myanmar kingdom before the colonial period. In the pre-colonial period, no Burman or Myanmar King had ever conquered, for instance, the Chin people and their land, Chinram. That was the reason the British had applied two different administrative systems. Thus, when Burma and India were to be given independence by the British, Chinram was not to be handed over to either India or Burma since it was not annexed by the British as a part of either country. They had the full right to be a sovereign independent state by themselves when the British withdrew its imperial administration from British India and Burma. In a nutshell, Aung San did not and could not represent the Chin and/or other nationalities from the Frontier Areas without any mandate from the peoples themselves.

During this critical period, Aung San showed not only his honesty but also his ability for great leadership, which eventually won the trust of the non-Burman nationalities. He acknowledged the fact that the non-Burman nationalities from the Frontier Areas had the right to regain their freedom, independence, and sovereign status because they were not the subjects of the pre-colonial Burman or Myanmar Kingdom. Thus, they had the very right of self-determination: to decide on their own whether they would like to gain independence directly from Great Britain, and to found their own sovereign nation-states, or to jointly obtain independence with Burma, or even to remain as Provinces of the Commonwealth of Great Britain. Aung San reassessed his position and bravely and wisely put his signature to the historic agreement, the Aung San-Attlee Agreement, signed on January 27, 1947. This historic agreement spelled out the position of the Frontier Areas vis-à-vis independence that was to be granted Ministerial Burma, as below:

8. Frontier Areas:

(b) The leaders and the representatives of the peoples of the Frontier Areas shall be asked, either at the Panglong Conference to be held at the beginning of next month or at a special conference to be convened for the purpose of expressing their views upon the form of association with the government of Burma which they consider acceptable during the transition period . . .

(c) After the Panglong Conference, or the special conference, His Majesty's government and the government of Burma will agree upon the best

method of advancing their common aims in
accordance with the expressed views of the peoples
of the Frontier Areas.[13]

However, on that particular issue of non-Burman nationalities,
two members of the Burman delegation refused to sign the
Aung San-Attlee Agreement. One was U Saw, the former Prime
Minister, and the other was Thakin Ba Sein, who had shared
with Thakin Tun Ok the leadership of the minority faction of
Dobama Asi-Azone after it split earlier (in 1938).[14] In their view,
the clause concerning the Frontier Area in the Agreement carried
an implicit threat of "dividing Burma into two parts."[15] Thus,
they not only ignored the history of non-Burman nationalities
such as the Chin, Kachin and Shan, but also the will of the people
from the Frontier Areas.[16] Upon their return to Rangoon, U Saw
and Thakin Ba Sein joined Ba Maw and Paw Tun, another former
Prime Minister, and formed the National Opposition Front, and
accused Aung San of having sold out for the sake of holding
office.[17]

Aung San, however, was not unduly troubled by the
accusations of his political opponents and plunged
straight into negotiation with pre-colonial independent
nationalities such as the Chin, Kachin and Shan. As
mentioned above, the Aung San-Attlee Agreement had
left the future of the Frontier Areas to the decision of
its people.[18]

Jointly gaining Independence with Burma

After having successfully negotiated with the British, Aung
San turned his attention to the non-Burman nationalities and
persuaded them to jointly obtain independence with Burma.
He promised the frontier peoples separate status with full
autonomy within the Burma Union, active participation at the
centre within a Senate-like body, protection of minority rights,
and the right of secession.19 He also promised to make the
agreed terms into law as a guarantee of their right for the future,
and told them they need have no fear of the Burman.20 The
negotiations between Aung San, as the sole representative of

the interim Burmese government, and the Chin, Kachin and Shan, were held at the Panglong Conference in February 1947.

Aung San successfully persuaded the Chin, Kachin, and Shan to join Independent Burma as equal, co-independent partners, and the historic Panglong Agreement was thus signed on February 12, 1947. The essence of the Panglong Agreement — the Panglong Spirit — was that the Chin, Kachin, and Shan did not surrender their rights of self-determination and sovereignty to the Burman. They signed the Panglong Agreement as a means to speed up their own search for freedom together with the Burman and other nationalities in what became the Union of Burma. Thus, the preamble of the Panglong Agreement declares:

> Believing that freedom will be more speedily achieved by the Shans, the Kachins, and the Chins by their immediate co-operation with the interim Burmese government.[21]

The Panglong Agreement therefore represented a joint vision of the future of the pre-colonial independent peoples: namely the Chin, Kachin, Shan and the interim Burmese government led by Chief Minister Aung San, who came into power in August 1946 according to the Burma Act of 1935. The interim Burmese government was a government for the region formerly known as Burma Proper or Ministerial Burma, which included such non-Burman nationalities as the Mon, Rakhine (Arakan), and Karen. The Arakan and Mon were included because they were occupied by the British not as independent peoples but as the subjects of the kingdom of Burman or Myanmar.[22] The Karens were included in the Legislative Council of Ministerial Burma according to the 1935 Burma Act because the majority of the Karens (more than two-thirds of the population) were living in delta areas side by side with the Burmans.[23] Since these peoples were included in the Legislative Council of Ministerial Burma, Aung San could represent them in Panglong as the head of their government. Thus, the Panglong Agreement should be viewed as an agreement to found a new sovereign, independent nation-state between peoples from pre-colonial independent nations of what they then called Frontier Areas and Burma Proper, who in principle had the right to regain their independence directly from Great Britain, and to form their own respective nation-states. In other words, the Panglong Agreement was an agreement signed between the peoples of a post-colonial nation-state-to-be.[24]

Ever since the Union of Burma gained independence in 1948, the date the Panglong Agreement was signed has been celebrated as Union Day. The observance of February12th as Union Day means the mutual recognition of the Chin, Kachin, Shan and other nationalities, including the Burmans, as "different people historically and traditionally due to their differences in their languages as well as their cultural life."[25] It is also the recognition of the distinct national identity of the Chin, Kachin, Shan, and other nationalities that had the right to gain their own independence separately and to found their own nation-state separately. In other words, it is the recognition of pre-colonial independent status of the Chin, Kachin, and Shan, and other nationalities as well as their post-colonial status of nation-state-to-be.

Conditions Underpinning the Creation of the Union of Burma

According to the Aung San-Attlee Agreement, the Frontier Areas Committee of Enquiry (FACE) was formed to inquire through an additional and specific consultation about the wishes of the frontier peoples. The British government appointed Col. D. R. Rees-William as Chairman. Since the committee conducted its inquiry after the signing of the Panglong Agreement during March and April 1947, the evidence they heard was generally in favour of cooperation with Burma but under the condition of:

    i.   Equal rights with Burman,
    ii. Full internal autonomy for Hill Areas [that is, ethnic national states], and
    iii. The right of secession from Burma at any time.26

The commission finally concluded its report to the Government that the majority of witnesses who supported cooperation with Burma demanded the "right of secession by the States at any time."[27]

The FACE report, particularly the right of secession, was strongly criticized by such Burman nationalists as U Saw and Thakhin Ba Sein who had earlier refused to sign the Aung San-Attlee Agreement. They accused Aung San of having given up Burman territory and argued that the Frontier Areas were just the creation of the colonial policy of "divide and rule". Aung San dismissed this criticism as historically unfounded and politically unwise. And he said, "The right of secession must be given, but it is our duty to work and show (our sincerity) so that they don't wish to leave."[28] And in keeping with his promise to the Chin, Kachin and Shan leaders at the Panglong Conference to make agreed term into law, the right of secession was provided for in the 1947 Union Constitution of Burma, Chapter X, Article 201, and 202:

Chapter (X): The Right of Secession

201. Save as otherwise expressly provided in this Constitution or in any Act of Parliament made under section 199, every state shall have the right to secede from the Union in accordance with the condition hereinafter prescribed.

202. The right of secession shall not be exercised within ten years from the date on which this Constitution comes into operation.

Although the "right of secession" was put into law in the Union Constitution, Burma did not become a genuine federal union.

The End of Aung San's Policies of Pluralism and Federalism

At the Panglong Conference in 1947, the Chin, Kachin, Shan and other non-Burman nationalities were promised, as Silverstein observes, the right to exercise political authority of [administrative, judiciary, and legislative powers in their own autonomous national states] and to preserve and protect their language, culture, and religion in exchange for voluntarily joining the Burman in forming a political union and giving their loyalty to a new state.[29]

Unfortunately, Aung San, who persuaded the Chin, Kachin, Shan and other non-Burman nationalities to join Independent Burma as equal partners, was assassinated by U Saw on July 19, 1947. He was succeeded by U Nu as leader of the AFPFL. When U Nu became the leader of the AFPFL, Burman politics shifted in a retro-historical direction, backward toward the Old Kingdom of Myanmar or Burman. The new backward-looking policies did nothing to accommodate non-Myanmar/Burman nationalities who had agreed to join Independent Burma only for the sake of "speeding up freedom".

As a leader of the AFPFL, the first thing U Nu did was to give an order to U Chan Htun to re-draft Aung San's version of the Union Constitution, which had already been approved by the AFPFL Convention in May 1947. U Chan Htun's version of the Union Constitution was promulgated by the Constituent Assembly of the interim government of Burma in September 1947. Thus, the fate of the country and the people, especially the fate of the non-Burman/Myanmar nationalities, changed dramatically between July and September 1947. As a consequence, Burma did not become a genuine federal union, as U Chan Htun himself admitted to historian Hugh Tinker. He told Tinker, "Our country, though in theory federal, is in practice unitary."[30]

On the policy of religion, U Nu also reversed Aung San's policy after the latter was assassinated. Although Aung San, the hero of independence and the founder of the Union of Burma, had opted for a "secular state" with a strong emphasis on "pluralism" and the "policy of unity in diversity" in which all different religious and racial groups in the Union could live together peacefully and harmoniously, U Nu opted for a more confessional and exclusive policy on religion.[31] The revision of Aung San's version of the Union Constitution thus proved to be the end of his policy for a secular state and pluralism in Burma, which eventually led to the promulgation of Buddhism as the state religion of the Union of Burma in 1961.

For the Chin and other non-Burman nationalities, the promulgation of Buddhism as the "state religion of the Union of Burma" in 1961 was the greatest violation of the Panglong Agreement in which Aung San and the leaders of the non-Burman nationalities agreed to form a Union based on the principle of equality. They therefore viewed the passage of the state religion bill not only as religious issue, but also as a constitutional problem, in that this had been allowed to happen. In other words, they now viewed the Union Constitution as an instrument for imposing "a tyranny of majority", not as their protector. Thus, the promulgation of Buddhism as the state religion of Burma became not a pious deed, but a symbol of the tyranny of the majority under the semi-unitary system of the Union Constitution.

There were two different kinds of reaction to the state religion reforms from different non-Burman nationalities. The first reaction came from more radical groups who opted for an armed rebellion against the central government in order to gain their political autonomy and self-determination. The most serious armed rebellion as a direct result of the adoption of Buddhism as the state religion was that of the Kachin Independence Army, which emerged soon after the state religion of Buddhism bill was promulgated in 1961. The "Christian Kachin", as Graver observes, "saw the proposal for Buddhism to be the state religion as further evidence of the Burmanization [*Myanmarization*] of the country,"[32] which they had to prevent by any means, including an armed rebellion. The Chin rebellion, led by Hrang Nawl, was also related to the promulgation of Buddhism as the state religion, but the uprising was delayed until 1964 owing to tactical problems. Thus, the Chin rebellion was mostly seen as the result of the 1962 military coup, rather than the result of the promulgation of Buddhism as the state religion in 1961.

The second reaction came from more moderate groups, who opted for constitutional means of solving their problems, rather than an armed rebellion. The most outstanding leader among these moderate groups was Sao Shwe Thaike of Yawnghwe, a prominent Shan Sawbwa, who was elected as the first President of the Union of Burma. Although a devout Buddhist, he strongly opposed the state religion bill because he saw it as a violation of the Panglong Agreement. As a president of the Supreme Council of United Hills People (SCOUHP), formed during the Panglong Conference, he invited leaders of not only the Chin, Kachin and Shan, the original members of the SCOUHP, but also other non-Burman nationalities — the Karen, Kayah, Mon, and Rakhine (Arakan) — to Taunggyi, the capital of Shan State, to discuss constitutional problems. Unfortunately, these problems still remain unsolved. The conference was attended by 226 delegates and came to be known as the 1961 Taunggyi Conference, and the movement itself was known later as the Federal Movement.

The Federal Movement in 1961-62

At the Taunggyi Conference, all delegates, except three who belonged to U Nu's party,[33] agreed to amend the Union Constitution based on Aung San's draft, which the AFPFL convention had approved in May 1947. At the AFPFL convention, Aung San had asked, "Now when we build our new Burma shall we build it as a Union or as Unitary State?.... "In my opinion", he answered, "it will not be feasible to set up a Unitary State. We must set up a Union with properly regulated provisions to safeguard the right of the national minorities."[34] According to Aung San's version of the constitution, the Union would be composed of National States, or what he called "Union States" such as the Chin, Kachin, Shan and Burman States and other National States such as Karen, Karenni (Kayah), Mon and Rakhine (Arakan) States. "The original idea", as Dr. Maung Maung observes, "was that the Union States should have their own separate constitutions, their own organs of state, viz. Parliament, Government and Judiciary."[35]

U Chan Htun had reversed all these principles of a Federal Union after Aung San was assassinated. According to U Chan Htun's version of the Union Constitution, Burma Proper or the ethnic Burman/Myanmar did not form their own separate

National State; instead they combined the power of the Burman/ Myanmar National State with sovereign authority of the whole Union of Burma. Thus, while one ethnic group, the Burman/ Myanmar, controlled the sovereign power of the Union, that is, legislative, judiciary, and administrative powers of the Union of Burma; the rest of the ethnic nationalities who formed their own respective National States became almost like "vassal states" of the ethnic Burman or Myanmar. This constitutional arrangement was totally unacceptable to the Chin, Kachin and Shan who had signed the Panglong Agreement on the principle of equality, a view that was shared by the other nationalities.

They therefore demanded at the 1961 Taunggyi Conference the amendment of the Union Constitution and the formation a genuine Federal Union composed of National States, with the full rights of political autonomy, i.e., legislative, judiciary and administrative powers within their own National States, and self-determination including the right of secession. They also demanded separation between the political power of the Burman/Myanmar National State and the sovereign power of the Union, i.e., the creation of a Burman or Myanmar National State within the Union.[36]

The second point they wanted to amend on the Union Constitution was the structure of the Chamber of Nationalities. The original idea of the creation of the Chamber of Nationalities was that it was not only to safeguard the rights of non-Burman nationalities but also the symbolic and real equality envisaged at the Panglong Conference. Thus, what they wanted was that each National State should have the right to send equal representatives to the Chamber of Nationalities, no matter how big or small their National State might be. In other words, they wanted a kind of Upper House similar to the American Senate.

But what had happened, based on U Chan Htun's Union Constitution, was that while all the non-Burman nationalities had to send their tribal or local chiefs and princes to the Chamber of Nationalities; it allowed Burma Proper to elect representatives to the Chamber of Nationalities based on population. Thus, the Burman or Myanmar from Burma Proper, who composed the majority in terms of population, were given domination of the Union Assembly.

In this way, the Union Assembly, according to U Chan Htun's version of the Union Constitution, was completely under the control of the Burman or Myanmar ethnic nationality. Not only did the powerful Chamber of Deputies have the power to thwart aspirations and the interests of non-Burman nationalities, but the Burmans also dominated the Chamber of Nationalities. That was the reason why the total votes of non-Burman nationalities could not block the state religion bill even at the Chamber of Nationalities. Thus, all the non-Burman nationalities now viewed the Union Constitution itself as an instrument for imposing "a tyranny of majority" and not as their protector. They therefore demanded a change from such constitutional injustice at the 1961 Taunggyi Conference.[37] Therefore, the Federal Movement and the Taunggyi Conference can be viewed, as noted by Shan scholar Chao Tzang Yawnghwe, as "a collective non-Burman effort to correct serious imbalances inherent in the constitution" of 1947.[38]

In response to the demand of the 1961 Taungyi Conference, U Nu had no choice but to invite all the political leaders and legal experts from both Burman and non-Burman nationalities to what became known as the Federal Seminar at which "the issues of federalism and the problems of minorities would be discussed with a view to finding a peaceful solution."[39] The meeting opened on 24 February, 1962 in Rangoon while parliament was meeting in regular session. But before the seminar was concluded and just before U Nu was scheduled to speak, the military led by General Ne Win seized state power in the name of the Revolutionary Council. In the early morning of 2 March 1962, he arrested all the non-Burman participants of the Federal Seminar and legally elected cabinet members, including U Nu himself, dissolved parliament, suspended the constitution and thus ended all debate on federal issues.

The Military Coup in March 1962

Brigadier Aung Gyi, the most powerful and second only to General Ne Win in the Revolutionary Council, stated that the main reason for the military coup in 1962 was "the issue of federalism."[40] The Burma Army, which staged the coup d'état, was "the product of Burman nationalism," as Chao Tzang Yawnghwe pointed out, "...a national sentiment revolving around racial pride and memories of the imperial glories of Burinnong, Alaungpaya and Hsinphyusin,"[41] and was very much enraged by the federal movement. They were desperate too, since a successful constitutional reform would also undermine the army's supremacy in non-Burman areas.[42] Moreover, if constitutional reform was carried out successfully, the Burman would be on the same level as non-Burman nationalities and this certainly was unthinkable for Burman national-chauvinists like Ne Win and Aung Gyi.[43]

Although the Burma Army was originally established by Aung San as the BIA (Burma Independence Army) during the Second World War there were two factions from very different backgrounds that had made up the Thirty Comrades - the core of the BIA. "Twenty-two of the young comrades were followers of the old writer and national hero, Thakhin Kodaw Hmaing" and were later known as the "Kodaw Hmaing-Aung San faction". But another eight, including Ne Win, came from the "Ba Sein-Tun Oke faction."[44] As noted already, Ba Sein refused to sign the Aung San-Attlee Agreement, mainly because of the non-Burman nationality issue on which he could not agree with U Aung San.

As a matter of fact, Aung San had officially recognized, by signing that agreement, the pre-colonial independent status of the Chin, Kachin, Shan and other non-Burman nationalities and their right to regain independence directly from Great Britain and their right to form their own respective sovereign nation-states without any mutual attachment to Burma. However, Ba Sein and his fellow U Saw, who later killed Aung San, could not recognize historical truth and refused to sign the agreement in 1947. In addition, they also accused Aung San of being a traitor of Burman traditional nationalism, and went about saying that Burma had been sold down the river by Aung San.[45] Hence, General Ne Win and Brigadier Aung Gyi, as the most faithful disciples of the Ba Sein-Tun Oke Burman national-chauvinist faction, reclaimed their vision of Burma, which in their view Aung San had betrayed. Consequently, they promulgated the Unitary State Constitution in 1974 by force.

Ever since the chauvinistic Burma Army launched a full range of "Myanmarization" measures under the leadership of General Ne Win, the Chin, Kachin, Karen, Karenni (Kayah), Rakhine (Arakan), Shan and other non-Burman nationalities have had no choice but to struggle for their survival by any means, including the use of arms. Today almost all non-Burman nationalities are fighting against the central government in order to gain full political autonomy and self-determination within the Union of Burma. Thus, the civil war in Burma, which began at the time of independence, intensified under General Ne Win's military dictatorship and his successor, the present military junta, which came into power in 1988 in a move to suppress the nation-wide popular uprising for democratic change.

Struggle for the Second Independence

As Daw Aung San Suu Kyi correctly points out, the struggle for democracy, equality and self-determination in present-day Burma is the struggle for the second independence of Burma because what Burma's leaders tried hard to achieve in the first independence movement had all been coercively negated by General Ne Win in the 1962 military coup. Moreover, the 1962 military coup abruptly interrupted the federal movement, which indeed was a struggle for the reformation of a genuine federal union in accordance with the Panglong Agreement and Spirit. Thus, the nation-wide democratic movement in 1988 can be seen as the struggle for the second independence, especially as the revival of the spirit of Panglong. Likewise, the formation of the UNLD can be viewed as the continuation of federal movements, then led by the SCOUHP, in 1950s and 1960s.

In order to achieve the goal of the struggle for the second independence, the UNLD therefore adopted the following policies as its objectives:

1. To establish a genuine federal union.
2. To guarantee democratic rights, political equality, and self-determination for all nationalities of the Union.
3. To build a firm unity of all nationalities in the Union based on the principles of equality and justice.
4. To promote the development of all member states of the Union.
5. To abolish all types totalitarianism in Burma.
6. To establish internal peace and tranquility through dialogue.

The UNLD believes that for building a genuine federal union, the Union constitution must be based on a democratic administrative system, because as noted by a Shan analyst, "....democracy is an essential pre-condition for federalism. Federalism will not work in a polity where there is no democracy because federalism is, at the bottom, about decentralization of power and limits placed on power. In federalism the above is achieved via a set of arrangement that limits and divides or disperses power, so that parts of the whole are empowered and are further enabled to check central power and prevent the concentration of power."[46] In short, democracy and federalism are inseparable, as head and tail of a coin, in a pluralistic and multi-ethnic country like Burma.

The Basic Principles of Federal Union

On the formation of a genuine Federal Union, the UNLD has adopted seven principles of federalism for the future constitution of the Federal Union of Burma, at its conference held in Rangoon, on June 29 - July 2, 1990. These seven principles are:[47]

1. The constitution of the Federal Union of Burma shall be formed in accordance with the principles of federalism and democratic decentralization.

2. The Union Constitution shall guarantee the democratic rights of citizens of Burma including the principles contain in the United Nation's declaration of universal human rights.

3. The Union Constitution shall guarantee political equality among all ethnic national states of the Federal Union of Burma.

4. The Federal Union of Burma shall be composed of National States; and all National States of the Union shall be constituted in terms of ethnicity, rather than geographical areas. There must be at least eight National States, namely, Chin State, Kachin State, Karen State, Kaya State, Mon State, Myanmar or Burma State, Rakhine (Arakan State), and Shan State.

5. The Union Assembly shall be consisting of two legislative chambers: the Chamber of Nationalities (Upper House) and the Chamber of Deputies (Lower House).

    i. The Chamber of Nationalities (Upper House) shall be composed of equal numbers of elected representatives from the respective National States; and

    ii. The Chamber of Deputies (Lower House) shall be composed of elected representatives from the respective constituencies of the peoples.

The creation of a Chamber of Nationalities based on equal representation of the member states of the Union is intended to safeguard the rights of National States and minorities in the Union government. It also intended as a symbol and instrument of the principle of equality among all nationalities of the Union.[48]

6. In addition to the Union Assembly, all member states of the Union shall form their own separate Legislative Assemblies for their respective National States. In Federalism there must be a clear separation of Union Assembly, or Federal Parliament, from the Legislative

Assemblies of the member states of the Union. Moreover, the residual powers, that is, all powers, except those given by member states to the federal center, or the Union, must be vested in the Legislative Assembly of the National State. In this way, the Union Constitution automatically allocates political authority of legislative, judiciary, and administrative powers to the Legislative Assembly of the National States. Thus, all member states of the Union can freely exercise the right of self-determination through the right of self-government within their respective National States.

7. The Sovereignty of the Union shall be vested in the people of the Union of Burma, and shall be exercised by the Union Assembly. Moreover, the central government of the Federal Union shall have authority to decide on action for: (i) monetary system, (ii) defense, (iii) foreign relation, and (iv) other authorities which temporarily vested in the central government of Federal Union by member states of the Union.

UNLD Policies concerning the Power Transition

After the election held in May 1990,[49] the UNLD adopted some policies to be applied during the power transition from an authoritarian military junta to a democratically elected government. Among them: (1) tripartite dialogue, (2) national reconciliation, and (3) national convention. In this paper I shall discuss briefly the need for national convention and tripartite dialogue, the policies adopted by the UNLD at the conference held in Rangoon from June 29-July 2, 1990. I shall, however, omit in this paper the policy of National Reconciliation, the program that is mainly conducted by the UNLD in exile[50] together with other democratic forces, such as NCGUB, NCUB, NDF, and others.

(a) UNLD for Tripartite Dialogue

From the very beginning, the UNLD has opted for a non-violent political transition in Burma, from military dictatorship to a democratic open society. The UNLD believes that Democracy is the only form of sustainable governance which guarantees both individual citizens and national and cultural collectivities in Burma the rights of full participation in the development of social, economic, and cultural resources available to all citizens of the Union. Enduring democracy therefore requires the active participation of all citizens — as individual citizens and as members of an ethnic-cultural collectivity — to build and renovate not only the democratic institutions but also the structure of the Union itself, which shall balance the different interests of nationalities for the common good of all member states of the Union.

As the UNLD believe in democratic principles and the rights of full participation of all nationalities in the process of nation rebuilding, the UNLD demands dialogue as an integral part of the political transition, not only in the process of power transformation from military rule to a democratically elected body, but also in the entire process of democratization, which includes the restructuring of the Union into a federal system. Therefore, in the processes of both power transformation and democratization, dialogue must be the main instrument for bringing all individual citizens and collective members of nationalities of the Union together at all levels.

After the general election in 1990, the UNLD believed that at least two levels of dialogue might be necessary to achieve the goal of the creation of a democratic open society and the establishment of a genuine Federal Union. The first step of dialogue is for power transformation, and the second step, which is more important than the first level, will be for the entire process of democratization and the restructuring of the Union into a federal system.

The UNLD also believes that since the NLD had received the trust of the people in a landslide victory in the 1990 election, a dialogue for a "transformation of power" should be a dialogue between the NLD, led by Daw Aung San Suu Kyi, and the military junta, the *de facto government* of present-day Burma. However, the nature of such dialogue at the first level must focus only on the transition of state powers into a democratically elected body. In other words, it will be a dialogue for administrative power but not for legislative power or constitutional matters. The core of the dialogue at that level therefore is just for a "breakthrough" in political stagnation, which has created a number of political and social crises in today's Burma.[51]

The UNLD strongly believes that the political crisis in Burma today is not just a conflict between dictatorship and democracy. It involves an unmanaged and neglected conflict, including a civil war that has consumed many lives and resources of the country for five decades. The root of civil war in Burma is the conflict over power-sharing between the central government, which so far has been controlled by one ethnic group - Myanmar or Burman, and all National States of the Union. In other words, the root of the problem is, as mentioned already, a constitutional problem or more specifically, the rights of self-determination for non-Burman nationalities who joined the Union as equal partners in 1947. Indeed, most nationalities in Burma are now fighting for rightful self-determination and autonomous status of their respective National States within the Union. Since they were not able to resolve their problems through dialogue, they have had no choice but to attempt to solve their disputes through violent means and civil war.

In order to avoid further bloodshed and violence during the political transition, the UNLD believes that the second level of dialogue must start almost simultaneously with the first level of dialogue. The aim of dialogue at the second level is to solve the entire political crisis in Burma and to end five long decades of civil war through the creation of a genuine Federal Union. The UNLD believes that without a genuine Federal Union there is no means of ending the civil war in Burma. Without ending the civil war, there is no means of establishing a democratic system either. Thus, the participation of all ethnic nationalities in the political transition is the most important element in the entire process of democratization and restructuring of the Union into a federal system. They all have the right to participate in this important process of restructuring the Union. Thus, dialogue at that level must no longer be a two-way dialogue but a Tri-partite dialogue, which shall include three forces, namely the forces composed of the non-Burman nationalities, the democratic forces led by Daw Aung San Suu Kyi, and the military junta.

(b) The Need for a National Convention

From June 29 to July 2, 1990, the UNLD held its conference at the YMCA Hall in Rangoon. At that conference, all the members of the UNLD unanimously adopted a policy on a national convention that states that in order to lay down the general guidelines of a federal constitution which will serve as the foundation on which to build a new democratic society for the future Federal Union, a National Consultative Convention shall be convened, similar to the Panglong Conference.[52] As the UNLD had adopted from the start a policy for the restoration of "internal peace and tranquility through dialogue,"[53] it was envisaged that such a National Consultative Convention would ensure peace, unity and equality for all nationalities of the Union. Alternatively, it could be said that the National Consultative Convention would serve as a kind of peace talks aimed at ending the five decade civil war.

The UNLD consulted on issue of the National Consultative Convention with the NLD, the winner of the general election in 1990. On August 29, 1990, the UNLD and the NLD made a joint declaration known as the Bo Aung Kyaw Street Declaration. Some of the points included in this declaration were:

> After the emergence of the Pyithu Hluttaw (Union Assembly or Federal Parliament), this Hluttaw shall form the elected government at the earliest time, then the Pyithu Hluttaw shall organize to convene a "National Consultative Convention" consisting of the representatives from all the nationalities, and other personages that are deemed necessary to take part in this convention. This convention shall lay down general guidelines for the Constitution of the Union. The Pyithu Hluttaw shall draw up, approve, and enact the constitution of the Union in compliance with above general guidelines.

All nationalities shall have full rights of equality, racially as well as politically, and, in addition to having the full rights of self-determination, it is necessary to build a Union with a unity of all the nationalities which guarantees democracy and basic human rights.[54]

Conclusion

In this paper, I have argued that the democratic movement in Burma since 1962 was the continuation of the federal movement led by the SCOUHP in the late 1950s and early 1960s. At the same time I have highlighted the fact that the role of the UNLD in the struggle for democracy and federalism is the continuation of a political role undertaken by the SCOUHP in the federal movement in the late 1950s and early 1960s. The only difference between the SCOUHP and the UNLD is based not on policy or the goal, but rather the political situation. In the early 1960s, the Federal Movement was seen mainly as a separatist movement by the majority ethnic Burmese (Burman). Thus, the non-Burman nationalities under the leadership of the SCOUHP did not receive enough support from their fellow citizens, the Burman majority. At the Taunggyi Conference, for instance, three delegates who belonged to U Nu's Party were against the move for the formation of a genuine federal union, despite the fact that they all were non-Burman politicians.

By contrast, the movement for federalism is now seen as the movement for equality. The UNLD now enjoys strong support from all the democratic forces in Burma, especially the National League for Democracy (NLD) led by Daw Aung San Suu Kyi, the National Coalition Government of the Union of Burma (NCGUB) headed by Dr. Sein Win, the National Council of the Union of Burma (NCUB), the National Democratic Fronts (NDF), the All Burma Students' Democratic Fronts (ABSDF), and other democratic forces. They all agree that the ultimate goal of democratic movement in Burma is the establishment of a genuine federal union, where all indigenous nationalities can live peacefully together. This unity in the same policy is the best hope not only for the UNLD but also for the future of the entire Federal Union of Burma.[55]

Notes

[1] Ever since the first Myanmar Kingdom of the Pagan dynasty was founded by King Annawrattha in 1044, the term "Myanmar" has been used to denote the ethnicity of the majority ethnic group, which is in turn inseparably intertwined with, as the saying goes: Buddabata Myanmar Lu-myo (broadly, the implication is that to be "Myanmar" is to be Buddhist). The term Myanmar-Buddhist does not include the Chin and other ethnic groups who joined together in a union, the Union of Burma, in 1947 on the principle of equality. Thus, although the present military junta has changed the country name from Burma to Myanmar after the unlawful military coup in 1989, almost all the ethnic groups as well as Burmese democratic forces (led by Daw Aung San Suu Kyi) do not recognize the name, since it was changed by an illegitimate de facto government. I shall therefore use the term Burma to denote the country, and the term Myanmar will be used to denote the ethnic group of Myanmar, interchangeably with the word Burman. It might in parenthesis be noted that there is controversy over the use of the terms Myanmar, Bama, Burman, and Burmese, revolving around the question about whether the terms are inclusive (referring to all citizens of the Union) or exclusive (referring only to the Burmese-speakers).

[2] Maung Maung Gyi, *Burmese Political Value: The Socio-Political Roots of Authoritarianism in Burma*, (New York: Preager Publishers, 1983), p. 3.

[3] Here I use Chinland and Chinram interchangeably. At the "Chin Seminar", held in Ottawa, Canada, on 29th April to 2nd May 1998, Dr. Za Hlei Thang, one of the most outstanding politicians and scholars among the Chin, proposed the word ram in Chin should be used instead of the English word land, as Chinram instead of Chinland. It was widely accepted by those who attended the seminar.

[4] Aung San Suu Kyi, *Freedom from Fear*, (London: Penguin Books, 1991), p. 24.

[5] The White Paper, Part 11, Section 7, cited also in Aung San Suu Kyi (1991), p. 24.

[6] Clive Christie, Modern History of South East Asia (London: Tauris Academic Stdies, 1998), p. 155

[7] Aung San Suu Kyi (1991), op.cit., p. 30

[8] U Maung Maung, *Burmese Nationalist Movements, 1940-1948,* (Honolulu: University of Hawaii Press, 1989), p. 253

[9] Hugh Tinker, *Burma: The Struggle for Independence* (1944-1948), (London:1984) p. 217.

[10] Ibid., quoted also in Maung Maung (1989), p. 257.

[11] See in C. T. Yawnghwe, *The Shan of Burma* (Singapore: Institute of Southeast Asian Studies, 1987), p. 99.

[12] Original document is reprinted in Tinker 1984 and quoted in Maung Maung (1989).

[13] The full text of this document is reprinted in Tinker (1984), pp. 325-328.

[14] In 1938, the Dobama Asi-Azone split into two factions: one faction was led by Aung San and Thakin Kodaw Hmaing, and the other by Tun Ok and Ba Sein. Although each claimed to maintain the Dobama Asi-Azone, they were in reality two separate parties. While Aung San and Kodaw Hmaing opted for the "non-racial, non-religious secular" approach of inclusive secularism, Tun Ok and Ba Sein centered their political conviction on "race" and religion, namely, Burman or Myanmar "race" and Buddhism. As they put it well, to be Myanmar is to be a Buddhist (Buda-bata Myanmar-lu-myo, their creed in Burmese). Moreover, while Aung San stood for democracy and federal Union, Tun Ok and Ba Sein were in favour of totalitarian form of national organization and the restoration of monarchy, a country in which the Burman or Myanmar race would tightly control the entire political system. See in Maung Maung (1989), and Khin Yi, *The Dobama Movement in Burma, 1930-1938*, (Cornell University, 1988).

[15] U Maung Maung (1989), op.cit., p. 255.

[16] Ibid., pp. 20-21.

[17] Aung San Suu Kyi, *Aung San of Burma: A Biography Portrait by His Daughter* (Edinburgh: University of Queensland Press, 1984), p. 46.

[18] Ibid. However, not withstanding the British insistence that tha Frontier Areas people be consulted on their wishes and aspirations, the commitment of the British Labor government to the FA peoples is doubtful. Would the Labor HMG have supported the FA peoples had they opted for independence -- against its treaty partner, Aung San and the AFPFL --is an open question. Besides, the Labor HMG was at the time embroiled in the bloody partition of the Indian subcontinent into two new nation-sates – India and Pakistan. As such, it might not be unfair to say that the Labor

HMG was more than happy to let the FA peoples negotiate on their own their future with Aung San and the AFPFL.

[19] John F. Cady, *A History of Modern Burma*, (Cornell University Press, 1958), p. 539

[20] Maung Maung (1989), op.cit., p. 282

[21] Cited by Aung San Suu Kyi (1991), op.cit., p. 32

[22] The Mon Kingdom was conquered by the Burman King Alaung-paya in 1755, and the Rakhine (Arakan) Kingdom by King Bodaw-paya in 1784.

[23] The Karen National Union (KNU) rejected the terms of the 1935 Burma Act in 1946 because they demanded independence for a separate homeland. They thus boycotted general elections of the 1947 Constituent Assembly, but the Karen Youth Organization (KYO) entered the general elections and took three seats in the Constituent Assembly and even the cabinet post in the Aung San's Interim Government.

[24] My concept of "nations-to-be" can be compared with Benedict Anderson's theory of "imagined political community" and Shamsul's "nations-of-intent". See Benedict Anderson, *Imagined Community: Reflections on the Origin and Spread of Nationalism* (London: Verso (2nd.ed) 1991 and Shamsul A. B. "Nations-of-Intent in Malaysia" in Stein Tönnesson and Hans Antlöv (ed.), *Asian Forms of the Nation* (Copenhagen: NIAS, 1996), pp. 323-347.

25 Lian Uk, "A Message on the Golden Jubilee of National Chin Day" in Chin Journal (February 1998), p. 185

[26] See the resolutions of Chin, Kachin and Shan leaders at SCOUHP's meeting on March 23, 1947 and the memorandum they presented to the FACE (FACE's report 1947).

[27] Ibid.

[28] See *Aung San's speeches: Bogyoke Aung San i Maint-khun-mya*, (Rangoon, 1969); quoted also in Tun Myint, *The Shan State and Secession Issue*, (Rangoon, 1957) pp. 10-11.

[29] Josef Silverstein, "Minority Problems in Burma Since 1962", in Lehman (ed.,), *Military Rule in Burma Since 1962* (Singapore, 1981), p. 51.

[30] Hugh Tinker, *Union of Burma* (London, 1957); quoted also in Tun Myint 1957, p. 13 ; See also my article in Chin Journal (March, 1997) No.5, pp. 84-94.

[31] Josef Silverstein, "Minority Problems in Burma", in Lehman (ed.,), *Military Rule in Burma since 1962*, (Singapore: SIAS, 1981),pp.51-58

[32] Mikael Graver, *Nationalism as Political Paranoia in Burma* (Copenhagen: NIAS, 1993), p. 56 (Emphasis added!)

[33] Those three delegates who did not agree to the idea of a federal Union were Za Hre Lian (Chin), Aye Soe Myint (Karen), and Sama Duwa Sinwanaung (Kachin).

[34] Aung San, *Burma's Challenge* (Rangoon, 1947), reprinted in Josef Silverstein, *The Political Legacy of Aung San*, (New York: Cornell University Press, 1993), cited in Maung Maung, *Burma's Constitution* (The Hague, 1959), p. 169.

[35] Maung Maung (1989), p. 170.

[36] See Documents of Taunggyi Conference, 1961 (Rangoon: Published by the SCOUP, 1961) in Burmese.

[37] See Documents of Taunggyi Conference, 1961 (in Burmese).

[38] Chao Tzang Yawnghwe, "The Burman Military", in Josef Silverstein (ed.), *Independent Burma at Forty Years: Six Assessments* (Cornell University, 1989), pp. 81-101.

[39] Josef Silverstein in Lehman (1981), op. cit., p. 53.

[40] Guardian, March 8, 1962; cited also in Josef Silverstein, Burma: Military Rule and the *Politics of Stagnation* (Cornell University Press, 1977), p. 30.

[41] Those are the Burman or Myanmar Kings who conquered their neighbouring countries such as Mon, Rakhine, Shan and Siam in their past history. But no Burman king ever conquered the Chinland.

[42] Chao Tzang Yawnghwe, *The Shan of Burma: Memoirs of a Shan Exile* (Singapore: Institute of Southeast Asian Studies, 1987), p. 120.

[43] Ibid.

[44] Bertil Lintner, *Outrage: Burma's Struggle for Democracy* (Hongkong: Review Publishing, 1989), p. 34.

[45] Dr. Maung Maung, *Burma's Constitution* (The Hague: Martinus Nijhoff, 1959), p. 80.

[46] Chao Tzang Yawnghwe, "On Federalism", a paper presented at the "State Constitution Seminar", jointly organized by the UNLD-LA and NDF on 20-26 August 2001, at the Lawkhila Camp.

[47] I do not follow the original Burmese version of the UNLD text strictly here, but I am confident that this English translation will not miss the points we have described in Burmese, for I myself drafted the original version in Burmese. See the UNLD documents in Lian H. Sakhong, *Peaceful Coexistence: Towards Federal Union of Burma* (Chiangmai: NPR Program Printing, 1999), pp.94-95 [in Burmese!]

[48] As James Madison once explained regarding the role of the Senate in the USA, the role of the Chamber of Nationalities also will be "first to protect the people against their rulers, and secondly to protect against the transient impressions into which they themselves might be led".

[49] The UNLD and its umbrella parties contested that election and won 69 seats, which is 16% of the parliamentary seats in the Union of Burma. A landslide victory went to NLD, a grand alliance of UNLD.

[50] The UNLD was unilaterally dissolved by the SLORC in 1992. Thus, the UNLD in exile had to be formed in a liberated area in order to carry out its mission until victory comes. An official announcement on the formation of UNLD (exile) was made on Union Day of 1998.

[51] See the protocols of the UNLD's Second Conference, held at the YMCA Hall in Rangoon from June 29-July 2, 1990.

[52] The protocols of UNLD's Second Conference, held the YMCA Hall, Rangoon from June 29-July 2, 1990.

[53] See UNLD's aims and objectives, No. 6.

[54] See also in my book *Peaceful Co-existence: Toward Federal Union of Burma* (in Burmese), the text of "Bo Aung Kyaw Street Declaration" is reprinted.

[55] See such important documents as the Bo Aung Kyaw Street Declaration signed by the NLD and UNLD on August 29, 1990, and the Manerpalaw Agreement signed by NCGUB, NLD (LA), DAB and NDF on July 31, 1992.

BIBLIOGRPHY

Anderson, Benedict. *Imagined Community: Reflections on the Origin and Spread of Nationalism* (London: Verso (2nd.ed) 1991)

Aung San. *Burma's Challenge.* Rangoon, 1947, reprinted in Josef Silverstein, *The Political Legacy of Aung San* (New York: Cornell University Press, 1993)

Aung San Suu Kyi. *Aung San of Burma: A Biography Portrait by His Daughter* (Edinburgh: University of Queensland Press, 1984)

Aung San Suu Kyi *Freedom from Fear* (London: Penguin Books, 1991)

Christie, Clive. *Modern History of South East Asia* (London: Tauris Academic Stdies, 1998)

Cady, John F. *A History of Modern Burma* (Ithaca, New York: Cornell University Press, 1958)

Graver, Mikael. *Nationalism as Political Paranoia in Burma* (Copenhagen: Nordic Institute of Asian Studies, 1993)

Khin Yi. *The Dobama Movement in Burma, 1930-1938* (Ithaca, New York: Cornell University, 1988)

Lian Uk. "A Message on the Golden Jubilee of National Chin Day" in Chin Journal (February 1998)

Lintner, Bertil. *Outrage: Burma's Struggle for Democracy* (Hongkong: Review Publishing, 1989)

Maung Maung, Dr. *Burma's Constitution* (The Hague: Martinus Nijhoff, 1959)

Maung Maung, U.   *Burmese Nationalist Movements, 1940-1948* (Honolulu: University of Hawaii Press, 1989)

Maung Maung Gyi,   *Burmese Political Value: The Socio-Political Roots of Authoritarianism in Burma* (New York: Preager Publishers, 1983)

Sakhong, Lian H.   *Peaceful Coexistence: Towards Federal Union of Burma* (Chiangmai: NPR Program Printing, 1999) [in Burmese!]

Sakhong, Lian H.   *Religion and Politics among the Chin People in Burma, 1896-1949* (Uppsala University: Studia Missionalia Upsaliensia, 2000)

Shamsul A. B.   "Nations-of-Intent in Malaysia" in Stein Tönnesson and Hans Antlöv (ed.), *Asian Forms of the Nation* (Copenhagen: Nordic Institute of Asian Studies, 1996)

Silverstein, Josef.   *Burma: Military Rule and the Politics of Stagnation* (Cornell University Press, 1977)

Silverstein, Josef.   "Minority Problems in Burma", in Lehman (ed.,), *Military Rule in Burma since 1962* (Singapore: SIAS, 1981)

Tinker, Hugh.   *Union of Burma* (London: 1957)

Tinker, Hugh.   *Burma: The Struggle for Independence, 1944-1948* (London:1984).

Yawnghwe, Chao Tzang.   *The Shan of Burma: Memoirs of a Shan Exile* (Singapore: Institute of Southeast Asian Studies, 1987).

Yawnghwe, Chao Tzang.   "The Burman Military", in Josef Silverstein (ed.), *Independent Burma at Forty Years: Six Assessments* (Cornell University, 1989).

Documents of Taungyi Conference, 1961. Rangoon: Published by the SCOUP, 1961. (in Burmese).

FIVE

The Basic Principles for a Future Federal Union of Burma

This is a Concept Paper, initially written in Burmese and edited from the original 48 pages, for a Seminar on the Basic Principles for a Future Federal Union of Burma, held on February 9-12, 2005. The Seminar was attended by more than 106 representatives from 42 organizations, including elected MPs, senior leaders of ethnic nationalities and political parties, and representatives of women and youth organizations; and adopted above 8 principles as the "Basic Principles for Future Federal Constitution of the Union of Burma". Written by Dr. Lian H. Sakhong, General Secretary of UNLD-LA, for the seminar and presented on behalf of the Joint Action Committee of NUGUB, NCUB, NDF, UNLD-LA and WLB. This paper was published as chapter two in the 'Designing Federalism in Burma' edited by Dacid C Williams and Lian H. Sakhong, UNLD Press, 2005

Preamble

The Union of Burma was founded in 1947 at the Panglong Conference by pre-colonial independent nations, namely, Chin State, Kachin State, Federated Shan State and Burma Proper or Ministerial Burma. The peoples of Karen, Karenni, Mon and Rakhine States (Arakan) later ratified the "Panglong Agreement" through the constitutional arrangement of independent Burma. The essence of the "Panglong Agreement" was not only to hasten their own search for freedom but also to establish a new multi-national-state of the Union of Burma for those who struggled together to free themselves from colonial power.

Therefore, based on the "Panglong Agreement", the Constituent Assembly of the Interim Government of the Union of Burma promulgated a new constitution on September 24, 1947, thus paving the way for securing "independence" from Great Britain on January 4, 1948.

Ever since independence, however, the Union of Burma has suffered more than five long decades of civil war, in which thousands of lives have been sacrificed. In the name of suppressing this civil war the successive governments of the Union of Burma have violated not only basic human rights and civic rights but also a variety of collective rights. In the name of national sovereignty, the right of self-determination for the ethnic nationalities who joined the Union as equal partners are rejected; in the name of national integration the right to follow different religions, to practice different cultures, and to speak different languages are deprived; and in the name of national assimilation the rights to up-hold different identities and traditions are denied. As a result, the entire population in Burma has miserably endured fifty years of human rights abuses, seen the demise of democratic principles, and witnessed the collapse of the nation's economy and the attendant poverty and hardship, all due to the authoritarian rule of the BSPP and the present military dictatorship.

In order to redress this, it is imperative to rebuild the "Union of Burma" based on the spirit of Panglong, which General Aung San and ethnic nationalities leaders had anticipated in 1947. The Panglong Spirit is for "democracy, equality and self-determination". Thus, the future "Federal Union of Burma", which shall be built upon the spirit of Panglong, will guarantee the fundamental rights for all citizens including the principles contained in the United Nation's declaration of universal human rights, political and ethnic equality for all nationalities and the rights of self-determination for all member states of the Union.

We, the representatives of the Chin, Kachin, Karen, Karenni, Mon, Myanmar (Burman), Rakhine (Arakan) and Shan, therefore, in the spirit of Panglong, adopted the following "Basic Principles" for the future Federal Union of Burma. These principles, in fact, are the same Basic Principles as when the Union was founded in the first place in 1947. In essence, therefore, what we are putting forward as our vision for the future Union of Burma is the revival of the "Panglong Spirit", which, we hope, everyone in the Union of Burma can agree upon.

The Basic Principles of Federalism at the time of Union Formation

There are ten basic principles that were borne in mind by General Aung San and the Founding Fathers of the Union when they signed the Panglong Agreement for setting up a Federal Union. They are:

1. Sovereign State

The Union of Burma shall be a sovereign multi-national-state, and the sovereign authority shall be rested with the people. General Aung San and the Founding Fathers of the Union particularly emphasized "popular sovereignty", which opposed the concepts of both "the sovereignty belongs to the nation" (the French Revolution's tradition) and "sovereignty is vested in the nation's parliament" (the British system). It was, therefore, assumed that the people of the entire Union of Burma, not merely a people from any particular ethnic group or state, are vested with sovereignty, it shall be exercised on their behalf on the basis of a functional division of powers between the central Federal Government and the member states of the Union.

2. Voluntary Association

The founding members of the Union, who signed the Panglong Agreement in 1947, were leaders from pre-colonial independent "nations". In principle, therefore, they all had the rights to regain their own independence directly from Great Britain, and to form their own respective independent nation-states. However, they all opted to establish a new multi-national-state of the Union of Burma together. The principle for joining the Union, or becoming a member state of the Union, was "Voluntary Association" which was strongly emphasized by General Aung San and the leaders of ethnic nationalities at the

Panglong Conference and also at the Constituent Assembly of 1947, at which the Union Constitution was framed.

3. Equality

In political domain, the term "equality" implies individual rights for all citizens, collective rights for all ethnic nationalities in the Union, and political rights for all member states of the Union. At individual level, every citizen of the country shall enjoy equal rights and equal opportunities before the law; at collective level of ethnicity and nationality, every nationality has equal right to preserve, protect and promote their culture, language, religion and national identity. At political level, all member states of the Union shall enjoy equal political rights and political powers; which mean all political powers of legislative, administrative and judiciary shall be equally bestowed upon all member state of the Union. In order to exercise political powers freely and fairly, all member states of the Union shall be entitled to establish a State Legislative Assembly, State Government, and a State Supreme Court. Moreover, each of all member states of the Union shall elect and send an equal number of representatives to the Chamber of Nationalities (Upper House) of Union Assembly.

4. Self-determination

For the Founding Fathers of the Union, the principle of the right to self-determination was meant to have two aspects; "external aspect" and "internal aspect". External aspect of self-determination implies the colonial situation of being subjected to foreign domination, thereby emphasized as the right of the peoples of the Union of Burma to determine collectively to establish a sovereign multi-national-state and freely determine their international status as an independent country. An internal aspect of self-determination implies the right of all ethnic nationalities and member states of the Union to choose their own system of government and the right to participate in the political process that govern them. An internal aspect of self-determination also implies that all ethnic nationalities in the Union, by virtue of the right to self-determination, have the right to freely determine their political status and freely pursue their economic, social and cultural developments. Moreover, all ethnic nationalities of indigenous peoples in the Union of Burma have the rights to possess their natural wealth and natural resources in their own respective homelands.

Politically speaking, the internal aspect of "self-determination" implies the rights of member states of the Union to exercise political powers of legislation, administration and jurisdiction; and the rights to set up political institutions, namely, State Legislative Assembly, State Government and State Supreme Court, in order to ensure the free practice of political powers in accordance with laws.

Ethnic nationalities leaders who signed the Panglong Agreement with General Aung San took this issue of self-determination very seriously and accordingly made an ardent request for it. They retained the idea of "internal self-determination" in the administration and planning of their own internal affairs of respective states, even though they agreed that the Sovereign Power must be vested in the entire population of the Union in order to be able to set up a Federal Union. In that way they vested sovereign power in the Union while retaining in their hands the right to legislate freely in each of all member states of the Union all legislative, administrative and judicial powers.

5. Federal Principles

One of the most important principles that helps the realization of the above three principles (Principles 2 to 4) at the time of the formation of a Union is the "Federal Principle". In other words, "Voluntary Association", "Equality" and "Self-determination" cannot be materialized in any other constitutional form except for the Federalism. That means the principles of "Voluntary Association", "Equality" and *internal* "Self-determination" cannot be realized in a system of a Unitary State. They can be implemented only through the political system of Federalism.

At the time of Union formation, this fifth principle, i.e., the "Federal Principle", was indeed a fundamental principle because it had to do directly with the constitution of the newly independent multi-national-state of the Union of Burma. Questions like: Shall we set up the new Union in the form of Unitary State? Or shall we set it up in the form of a federal system? etc., were the crucial questions for both General Aung San and the ethnic nationalities leaders at the Panglong Conference. It was General Aung San who first raised and also answered the question. And he said:

> When we build our new Burma, shall we build it as a Union or as a Unitary State? In my opinion it will not be feasible to set up a Unitary State. We must set up a Union with properly regulated provisions to safeguard the rights of the national minorities.[1]

The "Federal Principle" was the corner stone of Aung San's version of a (draft) Constitution of the Union of Burma, which was ratified by the AFPFL convention in May 1947.[2] Moreover, based on the federal principle, Aung San submitted his "Seven Basic Principles", which would form the main components and guidelines in drawing the Constitution of the Union of Burma at the Constituent Assembly of the Interim Burmese Government and which the Assembly duly ratified before he was assassinated.

In his now classic work: *Burma's Constitution*, Dr. Maung Maung mentioned that the intention of General Aung San and the Founding Fathers of the Union at Panglong, was as follow:

> The original idea was that the Union States [member states of the Union, i.e., Chin, Kachin, Karen, Karenni, Mon, Rakhine and Shan States] should have their own constitutions, their own organs of state, viz. Parliament, Government and Judiciary.[3]

The "Federal Principle", therefore, implies the notion of two or more orders of government with combining elements of 'shared rule' and 'self-rule': shared rule through common institutions, and regional self-rule through the governments of the constituent states. The federal principles of self-rule and shared rule, in turn, are based on the fact that all member states of the Union are entitled to exercise legislative, administrative and judiciary powers within their respective states on the one hand, and, on the other, to make sure that at the Union Assembly there must be a bicameral legislature consisting of a Chamber of Nationalities (Upper House) and Chamber of Deputies (Lower House), and each member state of the Union should send an equal number of representatives to the Upper House regardless of its population or size.

This is the main principle of the federal system envisioned by General Aung San and leaders of Chin, Kachin and Shan when they signed the Panglong Agreement in 1947.

6. Minority Rights

As mentioned, the Union of Burma was founded at Panglong by four former British colonies all of which already had their own constitutions. All of these former colonies were territorial states; none of them were ethnically homogeneous. For example, there lived Karen, Mon and Rakhine peoples besides Burmans in the Burma Proper or Ministerial Burma, which was formed according to the 1935 Burma Act. The Chin Hills Regulation, which was promulgated in 1896, represented not only the Chins but also the Naga people living in present India and Burma, the indigenous peoples in present Manipur State in India, and also the peoples in the whole of Magalia State (excluding the Silong municipality). The same can be said about the Federated Shan State where many ethnic nationalities, such as Lahu, Pa-laung, Pa-o and Wa are living side by side with the Shan.

Therefore, for General Aung and the Founding Fathers of the Union, an important issue to be considered seriously was the rights of minority nationalities living in each of the member states of Union when it came to the issue of forming a Union. The rights of the minority nationalities should be protected legally in accordance with laws in many ways.

To well protect legally the minority nationalities in the member states of the Union, General Aung San proposed in his draft of the Union Constitution that those areas where minority groups are living must be designated as Autonomous Regions and National Areas. He proposed that those minorities shall be granted not only the rights to preserve and develop their own culture, religion, language and national identity, but also personal autonomy, which would enable them to ensure their rights by acting themselves within the framework of their own institutions.

7. Fundamental Rights

The 1947 Constitution of the Union of Burma enshrined the fundamental rights, such as freedom of speech and expression, freedom of religion, freedom of association, freedom of movement, and also freedom of voting and contesting in general elections, freedom of holding public office, freedom of pursuing education and professional life, and freedom of pursuing happiness in life. This also included gender equality, equal rights and equal opportunity for every citizen regardless of gender, race, ethnicity, language, religion and age.

8. Multi-party Democracy System

Though this "Multi-party Democracy System" had been an important principle at the time of the Union's formation, this particular principle caused the most heated debate. At that time many Burmese political leaders were more or less under the influence of Marxist-left-wing ideology. Accordingly the extremist left wings and those who were members of the Communist party and the Socialist party did not support a multi-party democracy system. On the other hand, there were some extremist right-wing politicians, that admired Fascism in Japan and Nazism in Germany, who wanted to set up an absolute authoritarian system.

Moreover, the Chin, Kachin, Karen, Karenni, Shan and most of other ethnic groups were still practicing a feudal systems with its attendant titles, such as *Ram-uk, Duwa, Sawke, Saophya* and *Saobwa,* respectively, and thus did not understand much about the multi-party democracy system.

It was due to General Aung San and the Founding Fathers of the Union's far-sighted vision, however, that democratic rights were definitely enshrined in the 1947 Constitution of the

Union of Burma. The multi-party democracy system lasted only 12 years, and General Ne Win, with the support of left- and right-wing politicians, militarists and chauvinists, seized power and established a one-party socialist-military dictatorship. As a consequence the country has witnessed repeated abuse of human rights, the demise of democracy, and bitterly suffered from various sorts of political, economic and social crises including an ongoing civil war that as lasted more than 50 years.

The essence of this basic principle is that there should not be a lasting monopolization of power and bullying hegemony by one ethnic group or one ideology or one organization or one party, but rather a political ideology which envisions peaceful multi-ethnic, multi-ideology and multi-party coexistence. It also envisions peaceful administration of the nation in accordance with the laws for the benefits of all people, and alternative participation in the administration during one's elected term through a free, fair and just process of multi-party election contests.

9. Secular State

Like a "Multi-party Democracy System", the principle of a "Secular State" also received a heated debate among Burmese politicians. Leaders like Dedot U Ba Chu argued that, "if we cannot proclaim Buddhism as a state religion, independence would be a hallow freedom". General Aung San, however, rejected such argument, and said:

> Religion is a matter of individual conscience, while politics is social science. We must see to it that the individual enjoys his rights, including the right to freedom of religious belief and worship. We must draw clear lines between politics and religion because the two are not the same thing. If we mix religion with politics, then we offend the spirit of religion itself.[4]

In his draft constitution, General Aung San clearly stated his policy on religion as follows:

14(1). The abuse of the church or of religion for political purposes is forbidden.

14(2). The state shall observe neutrality in religious matters.

14(3). Religious communities whose teaching is not contrary to the Constitution are free in practice and exercise of their religion and religious ceremonies and are also free to have schools for the education of priests: but schools shall, however, be under the general supervision of the State.

However, after General Aung San was assassinated, U Chan Htun, under the supervision of U Nu, reversed the Union Constitution as follows:

14(1). The State recognizes the special position of Buddhism as the faith   professed by the great majority of the citizens of the Union.

14(2). The State shall not impose any disabilities or make any discrimination on the ground of religious profession, belief, or status.

14(3). The State may extend material or other assistance to any religious institution.

U Chan Htun's version of the Constitution, which was promulgated in September 1947 as the Constitution of the Union of Burma, officially proclaimed a "confessional policy of religion". The reversion of a "secular state" to a "confessional policy of religion" and the promulgation of Buddhism as state religion of the Union of Burma in 1961 was the beginning of religious-oriented ethnic conflict in Burma.

10. Rights of Secession

When the basic principles were laid down at the time of the Union's formation, the "Right of Secession" was included as the principle that safeguards and underlines all the rest of the principles.

The essence of the "Right of Secession" is that the newly formed Union shall be a multi-national-state and be founded on the principle of Federalism; all member states of the Union shall decide for themselves to become a member state and accordingly join the Union in accordance with their own consent. In addition, all the member states of the Union shall enjoy equal rights politically and socially when they decide to join the Union as a member State. The member states of the Union shall also enjoy the right to self-determination in the areas of political, economic, social and cultural affairs. What is meant by this is that all member states of the Union shall be entrusted with legislative, administrative and judicial powers and also that all member states of the Union shall send an equal number of representatives to the Chamber of Nationalities (Upper House) of the Union Assembly. In this way, the essence of a Federal Union formed by member states of the Union that are equally entrusted with the right of self-determination will be realized.

Moreover, the right of minority nationalities in each of all member states of the Union shall be protected legally and constitutionally. Democratic and fundamental rights shall be guaranteed for all citizens, and the Union shall observe neutrality in religious matters. To prevent the emergence of chauvinism and narrow-minded nationalism, clear guidelines for the Form of State and Form of Government must be provided legally and constitutionally in accordance with the above principles.

If it is found that the Form of State and Form of Government do not conform to the principles agreed upon or go astray from the intention of those principles, all member states of the Union have the right to secede from the Union. Thus, it was clearly enshrined in chapter 10, article 201 and 202 of the Constitution of the Union of Burma, adopted in 1947, that:

Chapter (X): The Right of Secession

201. Save as otherwise expressly provided in this Constitution or in any Act of Parliament made under section 199, *every state shall have the right to secede from the Union* in accordance with the condition hereinafter prescribed.

202. The *right of secession* shall not be exercised within ten years from the date on which this Constitution comes into operation.

The above principles were the lifeblood of the Union at the time of its formation. The Union would never be created unless these principles existed. Therefore it is hoped that more or less these basic principles would be of help for the restoration of the Union.

Proposal for the Future:

Basic Principles for the Future Federal Constitution of the Union of Burma

All ethnic nationalities in the Union of Burma have lived together, sharing the fates of each other for more than 50 years. In this period they have faced together five long decades of civil war and have also passed through the bitter experiences of dictatorship and associated persecution of various kinds. Together they have suffered the bitterest severities under military dictatorship. Likewise, they are waiting together for a new light of hope for the future.

Therefore we are now fighting in the hope of creating a situation in which all ethnic nationalities can live together peacefully and fraternally. All ethnic nationalities are still fighting the resistant war against the military regime in Rangoon, in the hope of creating the opportunity for all the peoples of Burma to fully enjoy their human rights, to establish a democratic system, to create a open society, and to materialize the right to self-determination for all member states of the Union. To build up a peaceful Union the following principles are outlined.

These principles are based upon those principles envisioned by General Aung San and the Founding Fathers of the Union at Panglong. In other words, it can be seen as a regenerated policy of national leader General Aung San.

However, due to the experience of 50 years two important principles made at that time are omitted. These two principles are "Voluntary Association" and "Right of Secession". For after 50 years of living together the "Voluntary Association" seems no longer necessary. Though this principle was important at the formation of the Union in the past, it is considered not to be important in the present.

Moreover, another important principle at the time of Union formation, that is, the "Right of Secession" is also omitted. The sole reason for the insertion of "Right of Secession" in the 1947 Constitution was for the protection of the right of non-Burman ethnic nationalities who joined the Union as equal partners in 1947 at Panglong. The "Right of Secession", however, failed to protect the rights of ethnic nationalities on one hand, and encouraged, on the other hand, the emergence of the one-party dictatorship (BSPP) and then the military dictatorship (Revolutionary Council in 1962 to present military junta) to bully the rights of the peoples at their whim. The 'Right of Secession' had been used as a pretext for Ne Win, and the army, to seize political power on March 2, 1962 claiming that the Union would disintegrate without a strong army.

Therefore it is believed that instead of emphasizing the "Right of Secession", making a new constitution that will protect the rights of "democracy, equality and self-determination", which are the very essence of the "Right of Secession" will bring more benefits to the Union and the people and will also guarantee the survival and prosperity of future generations.

Therefore for the attainment of peace and progress for the future Union, the following principles are presented:

1. Popular Sovereignty

The people of the Union of Burma, not a particular ethnic group or state, shall be vested with the sovereign power of the Union.

2. Equality

All citizens of the country shall enjoy equal rights and equal opportunity before the law; all ethnic nationalities shall be granted equal rights to preserve, protect and promote their culture, language, religion and national identity; and all member states of the Union shall be entitled to exercise equal political powers and rights.

3. Self-determination

All ethnic nationalities and member states of the Union shall enjoy the rights to self-determination in the areas of politics, economics, religious, culture and other social affairs.

4. Federal Principle

All member states of the Union shall have their separate constitutions, their own organs of state, that is, State Legislative Assembly, State Government and State Supreme Court. Moreover, the Union Assembly must be a bicameral legislature consisting of a Chamber of Nationalities (Upper House) and a Chamber of Deputies (Lower House), and each member state of the Union shall send an equal number of representatives to the Upper House regardless of its population or size.

5. Minority Rights

The new Federal Constitution of Burma shall legally protect the minority nationalities in the member states of the Union, they shall be granted not only the rights to preserve and develop their own culture, religion, language and national identity, but also personal autonomy, which will enable them to ensure their rights by acting themselves within the framework of their own institutions.

6. Democracy, Human Rights and Gender Equality

Gender quality, democratic rights and human rights shall be enshrined in the new Federal Constitution of the Union of Burma; including, freedom of speech and expression, freedom of religion, freedom of association, freedom of movement, freedom of voting and contesting general elections, freedom of holding public office, freedom of pursuing an education and a professional life, and freedom of pursuing happiness in life.

This includes gender equality, equal rights and equal opportunity for every citizen regardless of gender, race, ethnicity, language, religion and age.

7. Multi-party Democracy System

A Multi-party democracy system shall be applied as the country's governing system.

8. Secular State

The Union Assembly shall make no law that proclaims a state-religion; and the abuse of religion for political purposes shall also be forbidden. Moreover, the Union shall strictly observe neutrality in religious matters.

Notes

On the Union Day of 2005, more than 106 representatives from 42 organizations, including elected MPs, senior leaders of ethnic nationalities and political parties, and representatives of women and youth organizations adopted the above eight principles as the "Basic Principles for Future Federal Constitution of the Union of Burma".

All participants at the conference which adopted the "Basic Principles" unanimously decided to form a "Federal Constitution Drafting and Coordination Committee" (FCDCC), based on National Coalition Government of the Union of Burma (NCGUB), National Council of Union of Burma (NCUB), National Democratic Front (NDF), Nationalities Youth Forum (NY-Forum), Students and Youth Congress of Burma (SYCB), and United Nationalities League for Democracy (UNLD), and Women League of Burma (WLB).

The "Federal Constitution Drafting and Coordination Committee" (FCDCC), therefore, was formed on 19 April 2005. Based on this "Basic Principles", the FCDCC produced the first draft of the "Constitution of Federal Republic of the Union of Burma" in April 2006, and the second draft, which was adopted as an official draft of the democracy movement in Burma, on 12 February 2007 — the Union Day of Burma.

[1] Aung San, Burma's Challenge (Rangoon, 1947), reprinted in Josef Silverstein, *The Political Legacy of Aung San* (New York: Cornell University Press, 1993), cited in Maung Maung, Burma's Constitution (The Hague, 1959), p.169.
[2] U Nu and U Chan Htun changed Aung San's version of Union Constitution after he was assassinated in July 1947.
[3] Dr. Maung Maung, *Burma's Constitution* (1959), p. 170.
[4] Aung San's speech entitled "Problems for Burma's Freedom", delivered on January 20, 1946, in Josef Silverstein (ed.), *Political Legacy of Aung San* (Ithaca, New York: Cornell University Press, 1993), p. 96.

SIX

Dialogue:
Non-Violent Strategy for the Democracy
Movement in Burma

This paper was first published as chapter eight in the 'The New Panglong Initative: Rebuilding the Union of Burma' *edited by Chao Tzang Yawnghwe and Lian H. Sakhong, UNLD Press, 2004*

Introduction

"Dialogue" in popular usage simply means "conversation or talk". The original Greek word for "dialogue" meant "a form of literally expression in the form of a conversation between two or more people". In Greek culture, dialogue was usually expressed in a "literary or philosophical work, written in the form of conversation". One of such examples is the "Platonic Dialogue" which revealed the "antiquity, dignity and seriousness of the term dialogue and what it implied." In fact, the word dialogue was one of the fundamental terms at the root of Greco-Roman world, Judeo-Christian traditions and Western cultures. Sakowicz, therefore, claims that "at the start of civilization there was conversation, and there was dialogue"[1]

In today's world, the concept of dialogue is no longer contained within Western civilization; it has become a global phenomenon within the civilization of humanity, a civilization without any boundaries between East and West, North and South. Dialogue challenged "religions and cultures to come out of security of their yards" in order to overcome distrust and to attain liberation from fear. It has challenged all kind of political doctrines which built "walls of prejudice" and created a culture of "monologue". The task of dialogue in such context is to "oppose any form of injustice" imposed upon society by dictators. In a democratic open society, on the other hand, dialogue between political powers is necessary for the normal functioning of a nation, since it keeps government from abusing its powers.

As Pope John Paul II teaches us, "society cannot give its citizens happiness which they expected from it, unless it is based on dialogue."[2] Dialogue also enables one to understand the past as well as the future marked by a spirit of openness, and the "fruit of dialogue always is reconciliation between people."[3]

Dialogue in a Burmese Political Context

In a new Burmese political culture, the term "dialogue" becomes the key word to express the nature of the democracy movement and the meaning of the freedom struggle, especially after 1994 when the United Nations General Assembly passed a resolution, which called for a "Tripartite Dialogue".

"Tripartite Dialogue" in a Burmese political context means a negotiation amongst three parties: the military government known as "State Peace and Development Council" (SPDC), the 1990 election winning party, the National League for Democracy (NLD), and the ethnic nationalities, the founding nations or national groups of the Union.

The essence of tripartite dialogue is "inclusiveness" and "recognition" which includes all the major political stakeholders, or conflict parties in Burma: the military junta, the democratic forces led by Daw Aung San Suu Kyi, and the ethnic nationalities. Moreover, the UN's tripartite dialogue resolution recognizes the 1990 election results which have been denied by the military government for 14 years, and also recognizes the indispensable participation of ethnic nationalities in the political transition and national reconciliation process in Burma.

The UN resolution also acknowledges the very nature of the political crisis in Burma which, conceptually speaking is a "constitutional problem" rather than solely an ideological confrontation between democracy and military rule or totalitarianism. It is not a "minority" problem, or even an ethnic problem which some Burman or Myanmar[4] politicians argue can be solved later once democracy is established. The question of democracy, military rule and the constitutional arrangement with special reference to the non-Myanmar (non-Burman) ethnic nationalities[5] are intrinsically intertwined and cannot be solved individually. This is the meaning behind the call for a "tripartite dialogue".[6]

Ever since the United Nations General Assembly passed the resolution calling for a "tripartite dialogue" in 1994, "dialogue" has become the grand strategy of the democracy movement in Burma. However, this also raises the question of how does Burma's "armed resistance movement" fit within the call for dialogue? Armed resistance has been the main strategy, a self-defence response, and a reaction to the repression and the atrocities experienced by the ethnic nationalities of Burma in their struggle for self-determination and political equality for over 50 years.

In this paper, I will argue that adopting dialogue as a "grand strategy" does not mean the rejection of armed struggle or "people's power", the latter being advocated so dearly by some elements of Burman/Myanmar politicians in exile. Both armed resistance and "people's power" are still important but they now play different roles. The crucial point, however, is this: strategy may change as the changing situation demands, and the tactics may change in accordance with the changing internal and external politics but the ultimate goal shall not be changed until and unless the goal itself is achieved. A strategy is adopted in order to achieve a goal, and tactics are applied in order that the strategy works; but changing strategy and tactics shall not affect the ultimate goal.

The Ultimate Goal of the Democracy Movement in Burma

What is the ultimate goal of democracy movement in Burma?
The answer to this question depends on how we analyse the nature of political crisis in Burma. How do we perceive and analyse the nature of Burma's political crisis, and how do we intend to solve its problems? Should Burma be a unitary state or a federal union? How shall we deal with the problem of power sharing and division of powers between the central government and states? In short, how do we avoid Burman/ Myanmar domination and ethnic separation, which are two very crucial issues that has dominated and shaped politics in Burma, especially since 1962? Are there any means to live peacefully together in this Union? If the answer is yes, then the next question is: how are we going to build a peaceful nation together?

Different actors answer this question differently, for their goals are fundamentally different in nature. For the military junta, the answer is *"total* domination" even "ethnic Myanmar domination of Burma". For them, politics is nothing but power—i.e. power as a means of "domination". In their attempt to achieve their goal, they have opted for a strictly centralised government based on a unitary constitution, where the Armed Forces, dominated by the Burman/Myanmar ethnicity, can play a central role in governing the state by, as they proposed at the National Convention in 1995, controlling 20 percent of the national parliament and as well as state and divisional assemblies.

The politics of "ethnic domination" is not a new phenomenon in Burmese political culture; it has long been associated with Myanmar ethnic nationalism that emerged from within the Myanmar nationalist movements in the colonial period. As U Maung Maung observes in his book *From Sangha to Laity: Nationalist Movement in Burma, 1920-1940*, a main source of inspiration for the early Burman/Myanmar nationalist movement was religion oriented, as noted in Nationalist slogans such as, *"Buda-Bata Myanmar-lu-myo"* (To be a Myanmar is to be a Buddhist), in which Myanmar ethnicity and Buddhism were inseparably blended together. When the *Dobamaa Asi-Azone*, one of the earliest anti-British national organizations, was founded, ethnicity (Myanmar identity), religion (Buddhism) and language (*Myanmar-sa*, the language of the Myanmar or Burman) played the central role: Nationalism was conceived in terms of ethnicity and religion.[7]

Aung San, however, challenged such an ethno-religious brand of nationalism when he became Secretary General of the *Dobama Asi-Azone* in 1938. He criticized the notion of religious-oriented traditional Burmese nationalism of "our race, our religion, our language", which he said "have gone obsolete now". And he clearly states "religion is a matter of individual conscience, while politics is social science. We must see to it that the individual enjoys his rights, including the right to freedom of religious belief and worship. We must draw clear lines between politics and religion because the two are not the same thing. If we mix religion with politics, then we offend the spirit of religion itself."[8]

Although Aung San claimed that the *Dobama Asi-Azone* was the "only non-racial, non-religious movement that has ever existed in Burma", some elements of traditional nationalism, which blended Myanmar (Burman) ethno-nationalism with Buddhism remained, it being the founding principles of the organization when it was established in the 1930s. This stream was represented by such prominent figures as Tun Ok and Ba Sein. Thus, while Aung San's policy, defined by an inclusive radical secular approach, allowed a certain level of inclusiveness towards the non-Burman nationalities, this very same policy caused *Dobama Asi-Azone* to split into two factions in March 1938. A group opposed to Aung San's policy of inclusion and secularism was led by Tun Ok and Ba Sein, and was thus known as the "Tun Ok–Ba Sein" faction. The remaining majority faction was led by Thakin Kodaw Hmaing and Aung San. Although each claimed to be *Dobama Asi-Azone*, "they were in reality two separate parties".[9]

While Kodaw Hmaing and Aung San opted for a "non-racial, non-religious secular approach", Tun Ok and Ba Sein's political convictions were centred on ethnicity and religion, namely the Myanmar ethnicity and the religion of Buddhism. Moreover, while the former pair advocated democracy and a Federal Union, Ba Sein and Tun Ok were in "favour of a totalitarian form of national polity,"[10] and declared that "totalitarianism would benefit Burma".[11] They also "favoured the restoration of the monarchy", an institution which was inseparably associated with the state religion of Buddhism.[12] Buddhism for them was not just a religion but a political ideology as well. Thus, they could not conceive of religion without a defender of the faith, i.e. the "king who appointed and ruled the Buddhist hierarchy".[13] They proposed the revival of the monarchy as the best means of achieving independence.

As Tun Ok and Ba Sein had opted for the exclusion of non-Buddhists and non-Burman/Myanmar ethnicities, under such slogans as "one race, one blood, one voice," and "a purer race, a purer religion and a purer language,"[14] they not only excluded non-Burman nationalities, such as the Chin, Kachin and Shan, they even ignored the existence of these nationalities and peoples. That was the reason why Ba Sein and his fellow U Saw refused to sign the "Aung San – Attlee Agreement" and rejected the result of the 1947 Panglong Agreement. U Saw was later executed for killing Aung San, who had invited Chin, Kachin, Shan and other ethnic nationalities to join the Union of Burma as equal partners.

After Aung San's assassination, Ba Sein and Tun Oke buried Aung San's policy of pluralism, ethnic equality and the secular state. The legacy of "Ba Sien – Tun Oke" which advocates ethno-religious oriented Myanmar domination in Burmese politics was kept alive by General Ne Win and Brigadier Aung Gyi in the 1950s and 1960s. It continues with the current military junta. In addition to General Ne Win and his military successors, there are elements who even now maintain that non-Myanmar ethnic nationalities claim for self-determination should be considered *only* after democracy is restored. For them "democracy is first, democracy is second, and democracy is third": so, the non-Myanmar ethnic nationalities must "keep silent, follow the leaders, and obey the order".

It seems that history is repeating itself. During the independence movement, the "Tun Oke – Ba Sein" faction of Burman/Myanmar nationalists claimed that "independence is first, independence is second, and independence is third" and they ignored non-Burman/Myanmar issues completely. In contrast, Aung San came to Panglong in 1947, and invited Chin, Kachin, Shan and other ethnic nationalities to jointly form the Union, a year prior to independence. In this way, Aung San created a political atmosphere in which all of Burma's nationalities could feel that they were the founding members of the Union of Burma.

During the 1988 democracy uprising, while Brigadier Aung Gyi and other leaders rejected the ethnic nationalities demands for self-determination and federalism, Daw Aung San Suu Kyi, like her father, met with non-Myanmar ethnic leaders, and a meeting at the UNLD office, on 15 July 1989. They agreed to work together for "democracy and to resolve the ethnic issues". Thus, the position of Aung San Suu Kyi and the ethnic nationalities was that the questions of "democracy and the ethnic issues", which are inseparably linked with the "constitutional problems", and must be addressed together in order for democracy to be restored. They cannot be separated for they hold the same value like two sides of the same coin.

Currently, Burman/Myanmar ethnic politicians in exile say that "to solve these two problems [democracy and ethnic issues], we need different approaches." Accordingly, they say: "we need to establish democracy in the country first." They impatiently asks, "Why [can't we] wait until we have democratic government? Why do we have to insist on addressing the ethnic issue under a repressive military regime rather than waiting to do so under a democratic [government]? Do the ethnic nationalities believe that demanding their rights under military rule is easier than under a democratic government?"[15]

The main problem with such an argument is that they cannot definitely proclaim their ultimate goal, and the sort of democracy that they want to restore is unclear. For example, a former Burman student leader has said, "We already have the 1947 constitution, which guarantees democratic rights". A counter question that may be posed in response is: do they want to restore the semi-unitary arrangement of the parliamentary democracy system of the 1950s? Democracy can be, as Tocqueville warned us a century ago, a "tyranny of majority" which only encourages the politics of "ethnicity and ethnic domination".

For the non-Burma/Myanmar ethnic nationalities, though they want democracy, the typical Westminster-style majoritarian system of governance is simply not an option. They have had enough negative experiences of the tyranny of Westminster-style majoritarian rule during the so-called parliamentary democracy era of the 1950s and early 1960s under the 1947 Constitution, especially when the central government promulgated Buddhism as a state religion in 1961. For them, the only option is federalism with strong emphasis on self-determination, decentralization, and inclusive representative system of all the people at local, state and federal levels.

Similar to the ethnic nationalities' position, Daw Aung San Suu Kyi's stand is that the current democracy movement is "the struggle for second independence". In this way, she links current struggle for democracy with the first struggle for self-determination - for both of them are rooted in the "Spirit of Panglong" upon which the Union of Burma was founded at the first place. Under her leadership, the NLD (National League for Democracy) and UNLD (United Nationalities League for Democracy, an umbrella political organization of all the non-Myanmar or non-Burman political parties in Burma), issued a statement which read:

> All nationalities shall have full rights of equality, ethnically as well as politically, and, in addition to having the full rights of self-determination, it is necessary to build a Union with a unity of all the nationalities which guarantees democracy and basic human rights.[16]

Thus, we can conclude by saying that for the NLD under the leadership of Daw Aung San Suu Kyi and ethnic nationalities, as represented by the UNLD, the ultimate goal of the democracy movement is to establish a genuine federal union based on the principles of political equality for all member states of the union, the right of self-determination for all ethnic nationalities, and democratic rights for all citizens of the union. This policy was adopted also by the Ethnic Nationalities Solidarity and Cooperation Committee (ENSCC) when they launched the policy of "The New Panglong Initiative: Re-building the Union of Burma" in 2001.

Dialogue: Grand Strategy for Democracy Movement

As mentioned above, dialogue has become the grand strategy for Burma's democracy movement since 1994. However, we must remember that "dialogue strategy" is derived from the notion of a non-violent struggle for democratic change, a concept advanced by Daw Aung San Suu Kyi in 1988. "Dialogue strategy" cannot be separated from the "non-violent movement" — for the two hold the same value together.

The purpose of "dialogue strategy" is not only to achieve the ultimate goal of the democracy movement, that is, to establish a genuine democratic federal union through a peaceful transition without bloodshed. It is believed that through dialogue competing interests can interact in a non-adversarial way. In countries like Burma that are or have been engaged in serious conflicts, dialogue can also act as a mechanism to help prevent, manage and resolve conflict:

- *As a mechanism for the prevention of conflict.* By bringing various actors together for structured, critical and constructive discussions on the state of the nation, dialogue can result in a consensus on the reforms that are needed to avoid confrontation and conflict.

- *As a mechanism for the management of conflict.* Dialogue can help put in place democratic institutions and procedures that can structure and set the limits of political conflicts. Democratic institutions and procedures provide mechanisms for political consultation and joint action that can peacefully manage potential conflicts.

- *As a mechanism for the resolution of conflict.* Furthermore, political dialogue can defuse potential crises by proposing appropriate peaceful solutions. Democratic institutions and procedures provide a framework to sustain peace settlements and prevent the recurrence of conflict.[17]

Likewise, the UNLD also adopted the non-violent strategy when it was formed in 1988, and they declared that "democracy is the only form of sustainable governance which guarantees for all members of various nationalities, both individually and collectively, the rights of full participation in their social, economic, and cultural development and as well the ownership of resources available to all citizens of the Union."[18] Stable and enduring democracy therefore requires the active participation of all citizens, both as an individual citizen and as collective members of ethnic communities, to build and renovate not only the democratic institutions but also the structure of the Union itself which shall balance the different interests of nationalities for the common good of all member states of the Union.

Since they believe in democratic principles and the rights of full participation of all nationalities in the process of rebuilding the Union of Burma, both ethnic nationalities and democratic forces demand *dialogue* as an integral part of political transition, not only in the process of power transformation (from a military-controlled and monopolized kind of power to a democratically ordered one), but which also includes the restructuring of the Union into a federal system. Therefore, in the processes of both power transformation and democratisation, dialogue must be the main instrument for bringing all individual citizens and collective members of ethnic nationalities of the Union together at all levels.

After the general election in 1990, it was generally accepted that at least three levels of dialogue might be necessary to achieve the goal of the creation of a democratic open society and the establishment of a genuine federal union.

The first step of dialogue is for a "breakthrough" which will break the stagnant political deadlock; and the second step, which is more important than the first level, will be not only for power transformation but also to find a solution to the entire political crisis and to end the civil war in Burma; and the third step will be concerned with the entire process of democratisation and the restructuring of the Union as a federal system.

Conceptually the three levels of dialogue that will be needed are:

- Pre-negotiation Talk or Talk about Talk.

- Tripartite Dialogue (for power transformation/power sharing, and to lay the foundation of the future federal union).

- National Consultative Convention (for consolidating democratic federal system).

The First Level: Pre-negotiation Talk

At the first level, Pre-negotiation Talk is needed for the first contact between opposite parties (directly or through negotiator/mediator) to discuss the "process" of negotiation, without mentioning the "substance" or the "outcomes".

In any kind of negotiation for a transition plan, there are always two components: the "process" and the "substance". The "substance" is concerned with what the conflicting parties want to achieve? What kind of outcome do they want to see through this negotiation? What sort of political structure should be negotiated for during the "process"? In short this is the substance of the solution itself, or the goal of the struggle. "Process", on the other hand, is the business of negotiation and dialogue, which focuses on the elements of the solution, that is, how to reach a solution? Both are important: without the substance, process is worth nothing and without a good process the substance cannot be achieved.

Pre-negotiation Talk, therefore, is needed to set up the framework within which the "process of negotiation" is going to be designed. Thus, the "Pre-negotiation Talk" should be chiefly concerned with:

(i)   Where and when the negotiation will take place (time and venue)?

(ii)   How to choose the representatives: that is, who will participate in the process, and what shall be the method of representation?

(iii) Agreeing on basic rules and procedures;

(iv)   Dealing with preconditions for negotiation and barriers to dialogue;
       - A nation-wide ceasefire
       - Freedom of assembly and meeting
       - Free passage for non-ceasefire groups (for example!)
       - Re-instatement of banned political parties
       - Release political prisoners, especially Daw Aung San Suu Kyi.

(v)   Communication and information exchange;

(vi)   Managing the proceeding;

(vii) Time frames;

(viii) Decision-making procedures;

(ix)   The possible assistance of a third party;

(x)   Resource and financial assistance that will be needed during the negotiation, etc.[19]

The Second Level: Tripartite Dialogue

As mentioned above, political crisis in Burma today is not just a conflict between totalitarianism and democracy. It involves a protracted civil war that has consumed many lives and much of the resources of the country for five decades. The root of civil war in Burma is the conflict over power arrangement between the central government, which so far has been controlled by one ethnic group called Myanmar or Burman, and all the non-Myanmar (or non-Burman) ethnic groups in the Union. In other words, it is, as mentioned earlier, a problem of constitution, or more specifically, the rights of self-determination for non-Burman nationalities who joined the Union as equal partners in 1947. Indeed, most nationalities in Burma are now fighting against the military monopolized central government for self-determination and autonomous status of their respective National States within the Union.

In order to avoid further bloodshed and violence during the political transition, the second level of dialogue must start almost simultaneously with the first level of dialogue. Dialogue at the second level shall be concerned not only with power transformation and sharing but also with solving the entire political crisis in Burma. It should end the five long decades of civil war by laying down the foundation of a genuine Federal Union. The non-Myanmar (non-Burman) ethnic nationalities' position is that without a genuine Federal Union there is no means of ending the civil war in Burma. Without ending the civil war, there is no means of establishing a democratic system. Thus, the participation of all ethnic nationalities in the political transition is the most important element in the entire process of democratisation and restructuring of the Union into a federal system. Alternatively, it could be said that tripartite dialogue will serve not only as a platform for power transformation but also as a means to end the civil war.

Thus, dialogue at that level must be a three ways negotiation, or a *tri-partite dialogue*, which shall include three forces, namely the forces composed of the non-Myanmar nationalities, the democratic forces led by Daw Aung San Suu Kyi, and the military junta. To fulfil the demand for a tripartite dialogue, as called for by successive United Nations General Assembly resolutions since 1994, the participants must include in equal proportions the representatives of the 1990 election winning parties, representatives of the SPDC, and representatives of ethnic nationalities.

The Third Level: National Consultative Convention

As a tripartite dialogue is needed for power transformation during the process of democratisation, another level of dialogue is needed for "consolidating" a democratic federal system and "ensuring" peace in Burma. That stage of dialogue can be called the "National Consultative Convention".

Regarding this, the UNLD had adopted a policy of establishing a national convention at the conference held in Rangoon, on June 29 to July 2, 1990. At that conference, all the members of the UNLD unanimously adopted a policy of national convention that stated "in order to lay down the general guidelines of a federal constitution which will serve as the foundation on which to build a new democratic society for the future Federal Union, a National Consultative Convention shall be convened, similar to the Panglong Conference."[20]

The UNLD consulted on the issue of the National Consultative Convention with the NLD, the winner of the 1990 general election. On August 29, 1990, the UNLD and the NLD made a joint declaration known as *Bo Aung Kyaw Street Declaration*, which called for a "National Consultative Convention".

Similar to the *Bo Aung Kyaw Street Declaration* (but within a different political context due to fourteen years of political deadlock), the ENSCC called for the "Congress of National Unity" which would produce a "Government of National Unity", when they produced the "Road Map for Re-building the Union of Burma" in the beginning of September 2003.

The ENSCC's political "Road Map" stated: "in the spirit of Panglong, we are committed to national reconciliation and to the rebuilding of the Union as equal partners in the process. We believe that in order to establish a stable, peaceful and prosperous nation, the process of rebuilding the Union must be based on a democratic process which includes the following basic principles:

1. A peaceful resolution of the crisis in the Union,
2. The resolution of political problems through political dialogue,
3. Respect for the will of the people,
4. The recognition and protection of the rights of all citizens of the Union,
5. The recognition and protection of the identity, language, religion, and cultural rights of all nationalities,
6. The recognition and protection of the rights of the constituent states of the Union through a federal arrangement."[21]

In line with the above principles, the ENSCC's political "road map" recommended "a two-stage process to generate confidence in the transition to democracy": A Congress for National Unity (two year term) and Government of National Unity (four year term). The Congress for National Unity, which in fact is a "Tripartite Dialogue", will draft a "National Accord", according to which, the "Independent Constitution Drafting Commissions" (for the Federal Constitution and State Constitutions) and the "Government for National Unity" will be formed.

At a second stage of the third level, the "Government of National Unity" will conduct "a referendum", to be monitored by the international community to ensure that the will of the people is reflected in the new National Constitution. Following a successful referendum on the new National Constitution, "general elections" monitored by the international community will be held to establish a democratic federal government at the end of the four years.[22]

Some Obstacles to Negotiation and Dialogue Strategy

Since Burma's democracy movement, under the leadership of Daw Aung San Suu Kyi, has chosen dialogue as the main strategy; negotiation and compromise will become the methods that are employed to achieve the objectives of the struggle. It is clear from the onset that negotiations will undoubtedly require compromise on many issues in order to achieve a peaceful settlement. Actually, in a democratic culture, politics itself is a "process of compromise". However, a successful negotiation can be defined as "compromise" without losing one's position, compromise without sacrificing the "ultimate goal".

The leaders of both democratic forces and ethnic nationalities should, therefore, mentally prepare for difficult and painful compromises at tripartite negotiation, in order to solve the political crisis in Burma in a sustainable manner. At Tripartite Dialogue, at least three challenges can be foreseen:

(i) The role of the Armed Forces in a future democratic Union of Burma: The SPDC's Generals are demanding, as they have proposed at the National Convention in 1995, that they should control at least 25% of parliamentary seats, and also in state and division assemblies. Can such an undemocratic demand be accepted?

(ii) The 1990 election result: Can the NLD compromise their hard won victory in order to form a Transitional Authority, in which they need to include military and ethnic nationalities?

(iii) Federalism: The establishment of a Federal Union is the ultimate goal, especially for the ethnic nationalities. But, the SPDC Generals maintain that Federalism equals "disintegration of the Union", which they oppose. How could agreement be reached on this particular issue? Is there any compromise possible with such opposing views?

In addition to the challenges that will be faced at the dialogue table, there are a number of obstacles, partly because of the misconception of dialogue itself. Some people think that a dialogue strategy means only a "tripartite dialogue", which for the Myanmar ethnic group in exile is too complicated and should therefore be bypassed altogether. Htun Aung Kyaw, for example, said "tripartite dialogue at this point in time will not offer the solution. Instead it will complicate a situation."[23] On the other hand, most ethnic nationalities leaders envision "tripartite dialogue" as similar to the negotiation at the 1947 Panglong conference. It might be suggested that dialogue as a strategy should not be seen as a "One Time Event", but rather should be seen as a long term process, in which "tripartite dialogue" is only one step in a very long process.

A single main obstacle to dialogue, of course, is the SPDC's unwillingness to engage in dialogue with democratic forces and ethnic nationalities. Since they first came to power in 1962, General Ne Win and his successors have never believed in a peaceful political settlement. Their strategy has always been one of violent suppression, for they only believe in power that comes from the barrel of a gun. The most effective tactics they

125

employ are those of violent confrontation including civil war and urban killings. And they want their opponents to play along accordingly, as they are masters of violence. In fact, violent confrontation is the name of their game which they want to deploy at any cost. On the other end, they refuse to engage dialogue because they know and think that they are going to lose if they do.

One of the most disturbing excuses for the unwillingness among some in the movement to accept the dialogue strategy is that the "SPDC is not sincere, and they are not going to enter into a dialogue". Sincerity seems an inappropriate word in this regard, because one cannot expect "sincerity" from one's opponent. It is obvious that the Generals are going to use every brutal means that they can in order to keep their power intact. Holding on to power at any cost is their ultimate goal, and ethnic Myanmar domination through the *Tatmadaw* is their dream; violent suppression is the strategy they employ to achieve their goal, torture and killing are the tactics they use, deception is the method they apply, and avoiding dialogue is their escape.

Surely, the junta is buying time and weapons to keep their power. However, democratic forces and ethnic leaders should know that therein lay their strengths and weaknesses. Thus, it is essential to study their strengths and weaknesses, and analyze why they refuse to engage in dialogue. What is needed, therefore, is to create a situation—through coordinated local, national and international efforts—whereby the junta will have to come to the negotiating table, to see dialogue not as a danger but as a way to resolve the conflict in Burma that has plunged the country into crisis.

Some Tactics for Non-violent Actions

The term "tactics" is seldom used in this movement. Instead, "strategies" is used interchangeably with "tactics". The misuse of terminology can cause a lot of confusion and misunderstanding, as observed by a Shan politician and leader, "A lot of time has been wasted in the meeting debating which strategy to recognize and support and which to discard or abandon, without a practical acceptable outcome for all the groups because each group has its own strategies [tactics?] based on its own political role, status and space which are different from one another."[24]

As a matter of fact, terms like "strategy" and "tactics" are dynamic words, not static or rigid, in terms of both theory and practice. Armed Struggle, for example, can be the main "strategy" of certain ethnic armed groups, but it has become a "tactic" for the entire movement. Likewise, "economic sanction against the regime" can be the main "strategy" of certain international Burma support groups, but they should be only one of the "tactics" in terms of the entire democracy movement in Burma. It is essential to look at the big picture of the entire movement, in which all "strategies" and "tactics" are integrated in to a "Grand Strategy". As has been pointed out, "the strategies of ENSCC, Daw Aung San Suu Kyi's NLD, UNA and other democratic forces should be considered as part of the Grand Strategy of the movement."[25] The understanding of "the Grand Strategy will create cohesion among the groups, who could independently carry out their own strategy [tactics?], having in mind that one's strategy is complimentary to others in the integrated '*Grand Strategy*' form, because all are striving towards the same accepted aims."[26]

1. Popular Uprising as Non-violent Action

Since the 1988 popular uprising for democracy, the struggle for freedom in Burma has usually been described as a "non-violent movement". The notion of a "non-violent movement" was strengthen when Daw Aung San Suu Kyi was awarded Nobel Peace Prize in 1991. Indeed, the non-violent actions in the 1988 popular uprising represented the finest hours of Burma's democracy movement, which remains today its greatest strength for the struggle. Moreover, "popular uprising" is the most relevant tactic of non-violent action, which can easily translate into the grand strategy in order to produce a final victory.

The basic theory of non-violent action is that the "political power of governments or dictators disintegrates when the people withdraw their obedience and support". Based on this simple theory that the political power of governments may in fact be very fragile, Mahatma Gandhi challenged British colonial power, saying that:

> You have great military resources. Your naval power is matchless. If we wanted to fight with you on your own ground, we should be unable to do so, but if the above submissions be not accepted to you, we cease to play the part of the ruled. You, if you like, cut us to pieces. You may shatter us at the cannon's mouth. If you act contrary to our will, we shall not help you; and without our help, we know that you cannot move one step forward.[27]

Gandhi's theory of non-violent action is based on the fact that "if the maintenance of an unjust or undemocratic regime depends on the cooperation, submission and obedience of the populace, then the means for changing or abolishing it lies in the non-cooperation, defiance and disobedience of the populace." Applying Gandhi's theory of non-violent action, Gene Sharp outlines the main characteristics of non-violent action as follow:

> In political terms non-violent action is based on a very simple postulate: people do not always do what they are told to do, and sometimes they do things which have been forbidden to them. Subjects may disobey laws they reject. Workers may halt work, which may paralyze the economy. The bureaucracy may refuse to carry out instructions. Soldiers and police may become lax in inflicting repression; they may even mutiny. When all these events happen simultaneously, the man who has been "ruler" becomes just another man.

And he concludes, by saying that:

> The human assistance which created and supported the regime's political power has been withdrawn. Therefore, its power has disintegrated.[28]

The movement applied non-violent actions in various means and ways from the very beginning and it will continue to do so. The important factor, however, is that the tactic of non-violent actions needs to be able to translate into a grand strategy, which will bring the final victory for the movement. During the 1988 uprising, the movement employed the best tactic of non-violent action but did not have a grand strategy. The movement, therefore, needs to learn lessons from both its successes and failures.

2. The Armed Resistance Movement as a Tactical Means of Pressure

Carl von Clausewitz, in his classic work *On War*, wrote, "War is the continuation of politics by other means". His famous quote leads to the discussions of those of "other means", that is, the military strategy of winning war through force, but "it does not say how to achieve the state's goal without war."[29] In contrast to the Western concept of war, ancient Chinese philosopher Sun Tzu in his *The Art of War* suggested that military strategy should be integrated into domestic policy and foreign policy in a form of "state craft", which includes "looking beyond conflict to its resolution, ensuring peace and system of interstate relationships more profitable to one's nation."[30]

The Armed Resistance Movement that all the non-Burma/Myanmar ethnic nationalities in Burma engage is, in essence, different from waging offensive war. The difference is that in offensive war, military strategy is deployed in order to win the war by force. The Armed Resistance Movement of Burma's ethnic nationalities have never applied such a strategy, but holds arms only for defensive purpose. The similarity, however, is that ethnic nationalities in Burma engage in civil war only because they are unable to resolve the conflict through peaceful means. The Armed Resistance Movement, therefore, is, like any war, "the continuation of politics by other means".

None of the non-Myanmar ethnic nationalities in Burma believe that the armed struggle or Armed Resistance Movement is the end game. It is only for self-defence. However, "as long as SPDC wages war on us", as one of the Chin National Front (CNF) leaders said, "killing our children in order to wipe out our future generations, using rape as weapon of war against not only the Chin but all ethnic minorities in the country, and applying religious persecution as the method of destroying ethnic identities, especially against Chin, Kachin and Karen Christians; our hands will be forced to hold arms in order to protect our children, to defend our mothers, our sisters and our homeland, and to uphold our dignity and identity intact."[31]

It is, therefore, very clear that the dialogue strategy does not reject the Armed Resistance Movement altogether. It encourages Armed Resistance Movement as an important "tactical means" for the movement, as part and parcel of the pressures that should be put on military junta to bring it to the dialogue table.

In order that the Armed Resistance Movement becomes an effective tactical means of pressure for dialogue, it is essential to build unity among ethnic armed groups, and support the efforts of the National Democratic Front (NDF), the largest alliance of Ethnic Armed Groups in Burma, and the "Five Nations Military Alliance". However, as Sun Tzu suggested, the long term goal of an Armed Resistance Movement should be "to subdue the enemy without fighting", which he said is "the acme of skill". The best military "strategy is not only to achieve the nation's aims through controlling or influencing its sphere of influence, but to do so without resorting to fighting."[32]

According to Sun Tzu, the best military strategy is the one that can subdue the enemy through negotiation and talk without fighting; that is what we call in our context "dialogue" which will bring a "win-win" solution to the establishment of a democratic government in Burma.

War, including an Armed Resistance Movement, may sometimes be a necessary evil. But, as Jimmy Carter said, "no matter how necessary, it is always an evil, never a good. We will not learn how to live together in peace by killing each other's children."[33] That's the reason why dialogue, not war, is called for by all.

3. International Pressures

As mentioned above, "dialogue" was adopted by the democracy movement as a grand strategy, and it was based on the United Nations General Assembly resolution of 1994. This indicates the fact that international pressure is viewed as a very important strategic and tactical factor.

From the very beginning, the movement has adopted at least three international pressure tracks, to exert strong pressure on the military junta to get it to the dialogue table. They are, One, lobbying the UN, governments, regional blocs, neighboring countries such as China, India, Japan, to bring about diplomatic pressure for dialogue; Two, undertaking international campaigns, calling for sanctions, exposing and condemning human rights abuses by the regime, exposing forced labor practices, highlighting the plight of political prisoners, and so on; and Three, calling for international mediation.

The role of International Mediation has been highlighted by the ENSSC's Road Map (2003), saying that "to ensure that the transition progresses smoothly and on schedule, we request that the international community under the leadership of the UN, Thailand, and ASEAN continue to assist in the transition process". It is, therefore, very clear that the "third party" involvement in this process is more than welcomed. However, the exact role of third party intervention or involvement still needs to be clarified, that is what kind of third party involvement will be needed: Arbitration? Facilitation? Pure Mediation? Or Power Mediation?

Conclusion

In this paper, I have explored: What is the ultimate goal of the democracy movement in Burma? What is the grand strategy that the movement has adopted to achieve its goal? And what are the tactics that the movement has applied? I have argued that the strategy and tactics may change in accordance with the changing political situation has demanded, but changing strategy and tactics shall not affect the ultimate goal.

The main argument, which runs throughout this paper, is that the chronic problems of Burma will not be solved by merely changing the government, for the fundamental nature of political crisis in Burma is not ideological confrontation between democracy and totalitarianism, but a constitutional problem rooted in the question of self-determination for non-Myanmar (non-Burman) ethnic nationalities who joined the Union as equal partners in 1947 at Panglong. The ultimate goal of the democracy movement in Burma, therefore, is not just changing the government but to establish a genuine democratic federal union, where various ethnic nationalities from different backgrounds (ethnically, culturally, religiously, linguistically, and historically, etc.,) can live peacefully together.

I have highlighted in this paper that since 1994, the movement has adopted "dialogue" as the main strategy based on the United Nation General Assembly's resolution. The main source of "dialogue strategy", however, is derived from non-violent actions which the movement has taken since 1988, under the leadership of Daw Aung San Suu Kyi. As such, non-violent actions and international pressure has become the most important tactics in this movement to bring the military junta to a dialogue table.

I also argued that adopting "dialogue" as a "grand strategy" does not undermine the "Armed Resistance Movement" which most of the non-Burman/Myanmar ethnic groups are engaging in order to defend themselves for more than five decades. As a matter of fact, the armed resistance that all the non-Burman/Myanmar ethnic nationalities in Burma engage in is a defensive war. Moreover, they carry arms and wage armed struggle only because they are unable to resolve the conflict through peaceful means. None of the non-Burman/Myanmar ethnic nationalities in Burma believe that armed struggle or armed resistance is the end game. It is only for self-defence.

Strategically speaking, armed resistance, or struggle, constitutes only a tactical means, part and parcel of the pressures that should be put on the military junta in order to bring them to the negotiating table.

Since the military junta is refusing to engage in dialogue, it is essential to employ several tactics at once, to make sure that the strategy works properly. All kinds of tactics, such as, Non-violent Actions, including Internal Pressures and the so-called "People's Power", Armed Resistance Movement and

International Pressures, etc., should be integrated into the Grand Strategy of the entire movement in order to produce a final victory.

Notes

1 Eugeniusz Sakowicz, "Dialogue and Identity" in David W. Chappell (ed.), *Socially Engaged Spirituality* (Bangkok: Sathirakoses-Nagapradipa Foundation, 2003), pp. 435-447.
2 Cited by Sakawizc, ibid., p. 440
3 Ibid, p. 436.
4 Ever since the first Myanmar Kingdom of the Pagan dynasty was founded by King Annawrattha in 1044, the term "Myanmar" has been used to denote the ethnicity of Myanmar, which in turn is inseparably intertwined with their state religion of Buddhism as the saying goes: Buddabata Myanmar Lu-myo (To be a Myanmar is to be a Buddhist). The term Myanmar therefore is very exclusive, which does not include the Chin and other ethnic groups who joined the Union of Burma in 1947 on the principle of equality. Thus, though the present Military Junta had changed the country name from Burma to Myanmar as a result of the unlawful military coup in 1989, almost all of the ethnic groups and democratic forces of Burma led by Daw Aung San Suu Kyi do not recognize the name, for it was changed by an illegitimate de facto government. I shall therefore use the term Burma to denote the country, and the term Myanmar will be used to denote the ethnic group of Myanmar interchangeable with the word Burman.
5 Comprising close to 40 percent of the total population
6 See "Tripartite Dialogue" in *The New Panglong Initiative: Re-building the Union of Burma* (Chaing Mai: ENSCC Publication, 2002), pp. 5-6.
7 See Khin Yi, *The Dobama Movement in Burma, 1930–1938* (Cornell University, 1988), p. 255.
8 Aung San's speech entitled "Problems for Burma's Freedom", delivered on January 20, 1946, in Josef Silverstein (ed.), *Political Legacy of Aung San* (Ithaca, New York: Cornell University Press, 1993), p. 96.
9 U Maung Maung, *Burmese Nationalist Movements 1940–1948* (Honolulu: University of Hawaii Press, 1989), pp. 20–21.
10 Ibid.
11 Ibid.
12 Ibid.
13 Cf. Jerold Schector, *The New Face of Buddha: The Fusion of Religion and Politics in Contemporary Buddhism* (London: Victor Gollance, 1967), pp. 105–127.
14 See Khin Yi, *The Dobama Movement in Burma, 1930–1938* (Cornell University, 1988), p. 255.
15 Htun Aung Kyaw, "Searching for the Common Ground" in Mizzima News, http://www.mizzima.com , September 18, 2003.
16 "Bo Aung Kyaw Street Declaration" issued jointly by NLD and UNLD on August 29, 1990.
17 *Dialogue for Democratic Development: Policy Options* (Stockholm: International IDEA, 1999), p. 40
18 See "Democracy Movement towards Federal Union: The Role of UNLD in the Struggle for Democracy and Federalism in Burma" in Peaceful Co-existence: Towards Federal Union of Burma, Volume Two, Collection of Papers from UNLD-LA Conference, 2001.
19 Cf. Peter Harris and Ben Reily, *Democracy and Deep-Rooted Conflict: Options for Negotiators* (Stockholm: International IDEA, 1998), pp.66-69.
20 The protocols of UNLD's Second Conference, held the YMCA Hall, Rangoon from June 29-July 2, 1990.
21 See ENSCC's Road Map for Re-building the Union of Burma (2003-09-01)
22 ENSCC's Road Map for Re-building the Union of Burma (2003-09-01).
23 Htun Aung Kyaw, "Searching for the Common Ground" in Mizzima News, http://www.mizzima.com September 18, 2003.

[24] Sao Seng Suk, e-mail communication posted on Internet on September 17, 2003.
[25] Ibid.
[26] Ibid.
[27] Larry Collins and Dominique Lapierre, *Freedom at Midnight* (New York: Avon Books, 1975); cited also by Gene Sharp, p. 84
[28] Gene Sharp, ob.cit., pp.63-64
[29] Mark McNeilly, *Sun Tzu and the Art of Modern Warfare* (Oxford and New York: Oxford University Press, 2001), p.14
[30] Ibid.
[31] Interview conducted by the author but his name is withheld.
[32] Cited in Mark McNeilly, *Sun Tzu and the Art of Modern Warfare* (2001), p.13
[33] Jimmy Carter's speech, delivered upon receiving the Nobel Peace Prize on December 10, 2002.

SEVEN

Road Map for Rebuilding the Union of Burma

This paper arose out of a 2003 seminar to formulate a roadmap for transition in Burma jointly organized by the ENSCC and the Euro-Burma Office. It was first published as chapter three in the 'The New Panglong Initiative: Rebuilding the Union of Burma' *edited by Chao Tzang Yawnghwe and Lian H. Sakhong, UNLD Press, 2004, and revised the text in 2006.*

The Burmese military regime has always claimed that there are 135 national races in the Union, and that it must remain in power to prevent a break up of the country.

We dispute this. The founding fathers of the Union were Chin leaders, Kachin leaders, Shan leaders and Aung San. We created the union of Burma through the 1947 Panglong Agreement.

The ethnic nationalities took up arms only because all attempts to solve problems by political means were blocked. We were forced to defend ourselves against military aggression.

But in the spirit of Panglong, we are committed to national reconciliation and to the rebuilding of the Union as Equal partners in the process. We believe that in order to establish a stable, peaceful and prosperous nation, the process of rebuilding the Union must be based on a democratic process which includes the following basic principles.

1. A peaceful resolution of the crisis in the Union
2. The resolution of political problems through political dialogue

3. Respect for the will of the people
4. The recognition and protection of the rights of all citizens of the Union
5. The recognition and protection of the identity, language, religion and cultural rights of all nationalities,
6. The recognition and protection of the rights of the constituents states of the Union through federal arrangement

Therefore, in the interest of the nation, we recommend a two-stage process to generate confidence in the transition to democracy:

STAGE – I(2 years)

i. Dialogue

The current administration will immediately enter into negotiation with

- Representatives of the 1990 election winning parties, and
- Representatives of the ethnic nationalities

During the two years negotiation period while the details of the national Accord are worked out, the following will take place

i. The SPDC will continue to govern the country:

- The Commander-in Chief of the Defence Services will remain a military man,
- The Tatmadaw will retain its military Command Structures,
- The Tatmadaw will retain its economic interest such as the UMEHC,
- Individual Tatmadaw personnel will retain their economic interests,
- Security laws that affect the national reconciliation process will be repealed,

ii. Daw Aung San Suu kyi will be freed,
iii. Other political prisoners will be freed,
iv. Political parties will be allowed to function freely
v. The media will be allowed to function freely,

vi. Peacemaking process: A cessation of hostilities will be negotiated between the Tatmadaw and the ethnic nationalities, a mutual withdrawal of forces will be negotiated where applicable,

vii. A general amnesty will be mutually declared to enable all parties in the conflict to participate in the national reconciliation process without fear of retribution,

viii. Inter-party, inter-ethnic, and inter-religious consultations will take place in-country, and abroad to build confidence, trust, and understanding, to facilitate the national reconciliation process,

ix. Humanitarian assistance: A country-wide program to assess humanitarian needs will be carried out by local communities with technical and financial assistance of international non-government organizations and the international community, Immediate humanitarian assistance to the most affected communities will be implemented directly by international non-government organization together with local communities,

x. Various joint bodies will be established to determine how to alleviate the suffering of the people. These could include:

- HIV – AIDS,
- Internal displacement,
- Refugee repatriation and resettlement
- Border area development,
- Drug eradication,
- Economic reform,
- Civil service reform,
- Public health reform,
- Legal reform,
- Security integration,
- Local government

II. National Accord

The negotiation team will draft, in two years, a National Accord under which a transitional Government of National unity will be formed.

The procedural codes of the SPDC's National Convention and the one hundred and four articles for the constitution proposed by the Burmese Military in the past do not reflect democratic principles and cannot by their implementation lead to a democracy.

Therefore, the National Accord will recognized the results of the 1990 general elections, a political role for the military and the rights of the ethnic nationalities.

III. International Mediation

Decisions during the negotiations will be made by consensus. International mediation will be sought to break any deadlocks.

To also build confidence and ensure that a transition progresses smoothly and on schedule, it is **absolutely crucial** that the international community under the leadership of the United Nations continue to assist in the transition process. An international team or forum made up of representatives of the following nations is proposed:

Neighbours –

1. ASEAN
2. Bangladesh
3. India
4. China

Friendly Nations –

1. Australia
2. Canada
3. EU
4. Japan
5. Norway
6. USA

Objectives of the international team/forum:

a. Agreement that the crisis in the Union of Burma must be resolved by the people of the union – the military, the election-winning parties, and the ethnic nationalities;

b. Agreement on the role of the international community – coordination and facilitation of the national reconciliation process including financial support and sanctions - if agreements are violated or not implemented on schedule;

c. Agreement on the purposed time framed for the two stage process to democracy;

d. Facilitate inter-party, inter-ethnic, inter-religious consultations by hosting and/or financing meeting, providing visas, security, and space for consultations. Training in Negotiation Strategies and Conflict Resolution, as well as Capacity Building may be necessary;

e. Monitoring and mediating the national reconciliation process

The immediate task of the international team / forum would be to persuade all parties in the conflict to agree to a national reconciliation process with UN-led mediation.

International monitoring/mediation team

To effectively monitor and mediate the process, an in-country international monitoring team will be necessary. The team can be headed by the representative of the UN Special Envoy for Burma, and the resident ambassadors of the countries included in the international team/forum. In the case of the USA, it will be the charges D'Affaires, and in the case of the EU, it may be appropriate to have the British Ambassador. The exception would be Australia, Canada, and Norway whose ambassadors reside in Bangkok.

IV. Independent Consitution Drafting Commissions

The National Accord will constitute independent National Constitution Drafting and State Constitutional Drafting Commissions.

The composition of the Constitution Drafting Commissions will be as broad-based as possible but will reflect the tripartite nature of the negotiating team.

It is envisioned that the decision-making in the commissions will be by consensus and that international mediation will be sought for a deadlock

The State and national Constitution Drafting Commissions will ensure that structures at the national and state levels are compatible.

V. Humanitarian Aid

With the successful initiation of the dialogue, the international community is called upon to increase humanitarian aid to the people of the Union.

Programs to alleviate the suffering of the people and address the problems of HIV – AIDS, internal displacement, refugee repatriation and resettlement, border area development and drug eradication should also be launched in consultation with effected local communities.

STAGE – II (4 YEARS)

VI. Transition Government

At the end of the two-year negotiation period, a transition government will be established as per the National Accord.

VII. Lifting Of Sanctions

With the successful establishment of the transition government, economic sanctions including import bans and the ban on new investments could be lifted.

VIII. Funding For Development

At this point, the International community is called upon to provide development aid to fund economic reform, public health and educational programs hat will facilitate a transition to democracy.

IX. Referendum

A referendum monitored by the international community will be conducted to ensure that the will of the people is reflected in the New National Constitution

X. General Elections

Following a successful referendum on the new National Constitution, general elections monitored by the international community will be held to establish a democratic federal government at the end of the four years.

PROPOSED PLAN OF ACTION

Having agreed on the basic objectives for the Union of Burma, it is proposed that the following steps be taken to promote national reconciliation –

1. ENC invites international involvement

    *   ASEAN (China)
    *   Six Nations (Korea)
    *   UNSC

2. Agreement to talk

3. Pre-conditions:

    i.   The State Peace and Development Council releases Daw Aung San Suu Kyi, Hkun Htun Oo and all other political prisoners that agree and are committed to the six common objectives;
    ii. The State Peace and Development Council rescinds SLORC Law No. 1/95 that restricts discussion of the constitution, and other repressive security laws;
    iii. End of hostilities, nationwide ceasefire/withdrawal of forces;
    iv. Stop violence/human rights abuses against civilian population;
    v.   Freedom for all parties to travel, meet and consult anybody (inside and outside) including international experts;

    vi.   Media freedom

   vii.   Political Party freedom to function

  viii.   Mutual Amnesty

4.   Pre-negotiations talk – Talk for Talk – AGENDA

    i.   Transition Agreement

   ii.   Transition Period Time Frame

  iii.   Humanitarian Aid

5.   Dialogue

6.   Transition Agreement

    i.   Lifting of sanctions

   ii.   Development Aid

7.   Interim government (3-5 year) – End of de facto SPDC Government

8.   Drafting of Constitutions

9.   Referendum

10. Elections

11. New Democratic Government

Conclusion:

This is only a very roughly sketched preliminary Plan of Action for the future Union of Burma. However, such a plan which spells out the possibilities of building on existing realities could be very attractive to the ruling SPDC, democracy advocates, the ethnic nationalities and even the international community, especially neighbouring countries.

If a similar plan can be developed in more detail, it may be the catalyst that is needed to solve the current political deadlock in the Union of Burma

EIGHT

In Defence of the ENSCC Road Map

This is in reply to Kanbawza Win's critique of the ENSCC roadmap that was posted on the internet and widely distributed in Kao Wao and Chinland Guardian on 9 September 2003

Ever since the ENSCC Road Map for democratic transition in Burma was released, a number of reactions from both friends and foes alike have been received, some are very positive but some are quite critical. Both are welcomed. Since the ENSCC has taken a big step for a big mission, it was realised from the very beginning that not every one would agree or understand the idea behind the proposal, which suggests a peaceful democratic transition in Burma.

We all love our country and our people, and we believe that Burma deserves peace and democracy, freedom and prosperity, justice and equality for all who reside there. We want to end the oppressive regime, we want to end a five-decade civil war, we want to end human rights abuses, and we want to end any kind of injustice in Burma.

We want to see all of our beloved friends who are held unjustly in prisons become free, we want to see all refugees return home safely, we want to see all who are in exile reunite with their love ones and we want to see our country become free.

We want to see our country no longer as a big prison but as a free and open society where the various ethnic nationalities can live peacefully together.

We want to solve our country's problems but we don't believe in violent means. Violence only begets violence, and there is still no solution after fifty years of violent conflict in Burma. If violent means was a solution, the military regime would have been a solution already, for they have opted for such a solution ever since they first came to power in 1962. We don't believe in a zero-sum game, which will lead our country into a lose-lose situation.

In a nutshell, we want to solve our crisis through a peaceful means where the biggest winner will be the people, the ordinary folks. We believe that we follow Daw Aung San Suu Kyi's method of non-violent strategy, for she herself is opting to solve our country's problems through dialogue. And we obey the United Nations General Assembly's resolution which calls for a "tripartite dialogue."

Critics like Kanbawza Win claims that the ENSCC Road Map "does not call for immediate release of all political prisoners, glosses over the crimes against humanity such as the 1988 massacre and the latest butchering at Depayin." He made his point quite clearly but he failed to see the very nature of ENSCC Road Map. Theories say that there are at least three different kinds of political transition road maps; 1) Demanding Road Map, 2) Process Inviting Road Map, and 3) A Comprehensive Transition Plan. Ours is not a "demanding road map" nor a "comprehensive transition plan" but "process inviting road map" through which we invite our conflict partners (whom we want to turn into our peace partners) to join hands. We are not going to shy away from the method that we have chosen, because we dare to make peace with our enemy. After all, peace is made with an enemy not with a friend.

Secondly, Kanbawza Win failed to differentiate "road map" from "blue print". Any kind of political transition "road map", even "a comprehensive transition plan", is not a "blue print". A "Blue print" is not easily changeable but a "road map" is. In a normal situation, a "road map" should be produced after discussion with opposite party or parties. That's why pre-negotiation talks are needed in a transition to democracy, as we have seen in South Africa and elsewhere. Unfortunately, we are not in a normal situation; our opposition does not believe in a peaceful means of conflict resolution but violent oppression.

However, we should carefully avoid playing the games our enemy wants us to play, that is., any kind of violent confrontations. They know that they going to win if we engage in the games they set, because they are masters in dealing with violence. Violent confrontation is the name of their game, which we should avoid. On the other end, they refuse to engage in dialogue because they know and think that they are going to lose if they attend a dialogue table. So, we should know what are our strong points and our weak points, and turn our weak points into strong points. This simple method will be helpful, if we apply it properly.

We believe in "tripartite dialogue"; not only because it is called for by the UN, as it also reflected the very nature of the political situation in Burma. The essence of "tripartite dialogue" is "inclusiveness" and "recognition", which includes all major conflicting parties in Burma and at the same time recognizes the 1990 election result, recognizes the SPDC as the de facto government in Burma (not as de jure government, Kanbawza Win is just twisting the word in order to lay blame), and recognizes ethnic nationalities as the founding members of the Union, and thereby one of the major political actors in Burma.

This is unfortunate that although the UN and international community recognize ethnic nationalities, through a UNGO resolution, as major political actors in Burma, Kanbawza Win plays down the role of ethnic nationalities merely as "pressure groups" or "activist groups", by comparing them with Burmese in the Diaspora and international NGOs. And he wants us to follow the "Lion" like "hyenas". It reminds me of Ne Win's exhortation of *"nout-like kaung hmah khong-soung-kong peta-de"*, literally, "You must be a good follower in order to become a good leader". The simple reason for creating such a saying is that they want us to "keep silent, follow the leader, and obey the order", as successive military regimes have, since Ne Win's, wanted us to do. And they are always the "Lion" and we merely the "hyenas".

Let me be very frank: without the ethnic nationalities participation in this transition process, you might be able to change the government in Rangoon but you will never be able to solve the political crisis in Burma. I am sure Kanbawza Win can see the difference between changing the government and solving the political crisis in Burma. Let me put in a different way: the political crisis in Burma today is not merely ideological confrontation between democracy and dictatorship which can be solved through changing the government, but this is also a constitutional problem rooted in the question of the rights of self-determination for ethnic nationalities who joined the Union of Burma as equal partners and co-founders in 1947. So, if you do not recognize ethnic nationalities as one of the main actors and equal partners in Burma's politics, there is no way to end 50 years of civil war in Burma. I sincerely think that we should learn lessons from fifty years of civil war in which we lost too many lives already. If we try to learn this lesson, Kanbawza Win should appreciate it, instead of blaming the ethnic nationalities initiative.

Finally, I would like to clarify that in any political road map or transition plan there are always two components: the "process" and the "substance". The "substance" is a matter of what we want to achieve. What kind of outcome we want to see through this road map? What sort of political structure will be the component of the solution over which we are going to negotiate during the "process"? In short, this is the substance of the solution itself, and the goal of our struggle. "Process", on the other hand, is a business of negotiation and dialogue, which focuses on the elements of the solution but not the solution itself, that is, how to get to a solution? As such, one can clearly see that the ENSCC Road Map is for "process initiative" not a comprehensive transition plan with details of account of the "substance". We only produce a road map for "process initiative", or "process inviting", because we think that it is unwise to put everything on the table at once.

NINE

Ethnic Nationalities Council Policy Statement

This statement was first published as chapter one in the 'ENC Policy Papers, Letters and Statements' as number 12 of the series 'Peaceful Co-existence: Towards a Federal Union of Burma' edited by Lian H. Sakhong, UNLD Press, 2006, and revised the text in 2009.

Introduction

The Ethnic Nationalities Council (ENC) was originally established as the "Ethnic Nationalities Solidarity and Cooperation Committee" (ENSCC) in August 2001. It was entrusted with the task of fostering unity and cooperation between all ethnic nationalities in preparation for a 'Tripartite Dialogue" and a transition to democracy in Burma. The 'ethnic nationalities' from Seven States in the Union of Burma together represent more than 40% of the 50 million people residing there, and their combined homelands cover 60% of the territory bordering Bangladesh and India to the west; India and China to the north; and China, Laos and Thailand to the east.

The National Democratic Front (NDF) and the United Nationalities League for Democracy – Liberated Area (UNLD-LA) who co-founded the ENSCC, resolved that the ENSCC would:

1.   Undertake pro-active and constructive actions to bring about a peaceful resolution to the political conflict in Burma through a dialogue process involving the SPDC, the NLD, led by Daw Aung San Suu Kyi, and the ethnic nationalities, as dialogue partners;

2. Consult widely, cooperate, and work closely with all stakeholders in Burma and with the international community, international bodies and agencies, the United Nations, and humanitarian organizations, to resolve the grave humanitarian crisis in Burma, which most seriously affect the ethnic nationality populations;

3. Strive to facilitate an orderly and peaceful democratic transition in Burma, and to rebuild the country in accordance with the spirit of Panglong, based on the principle of Equality, Self-determination, Democracy, and Justice.

At the 3rd Ethnic Nationalities Seminar in January 2004, the ENSCC was transformed into the Ethnic Nationalities Council (ENC) with a broader mandate. At that time, the ENC represented non-Burman political fronts, parties and organizations such as the United Nationalities League for Democracy - Liberated Areas (UNLD-LA) and its 11 member political parties; the National Democratic Front (NDF) and its 8 member organizations; other ethnic nationality organizations like the Karenni National Progress Party (KNPP) and others who are not members of either the NDF or the UNLD-LA; and some ethnic nationality organizations that have cease-fire arrangements with the Burmese military regime.

At the 4th Ethnic Nationalities Conference in April 2005, a new structure for the ENC was adopted. The ENC became State–based. In this new structure ethnic representation to the ENC was reconstituted based on Arakan, Chin, Kachin, Karen, Karenni (Kayah), Mon and Shan States. This decision was taken to facilitate the establishment of a future Federal Union of equal states and also to ensure the participation and representation of all parties and all ethnic nationalities within each state.

It was also decided at this meeting that each of the seven states should send 7 representatives to the ENC

i. Five State representative elected to represent all political parties, groups and peoples within the State;

ii. A woman State representative elected to represent all women within the State and;

iii. A youth State representative elected to represent all youth within the State.

To ensure its goal of bringing genuine peace and democracy to the country the Ethnic Nationalities Council coordinates the efforts of non-Burman Ethnic Nationalities to bring about a 'Tripartite Dialogue' to resolve the problems of the Union of Burma. In doing so it cuts across organizational and ethnic lines to build a common inclusive consensus among all relevant ethnic actors. These include Political Parties; Ethnic Organizations; Armed Groups; Women's Groups; Youth Organizations; Community Based Organizations; and Religious Organizations. The ENC recognizes, and believes that all vested parties should acknowledge the fact, that unless the grievances of the ethnic nationalities are addressed, there can be no lasting peace.

To realize this goal, the ENC has been preparing for a transition to democracy and future constitutional arrangements by drafting federal and state constitutions. It has been at the forefront in endeavors to strengthen capacity through the promotion and development of civil society and grassroots organizations and, as the 2010 election approaches, it is actively engaged in ensuring that the voice of the ethnic nationalities is not stifled in any future political process.

Background to the conflict in Burma

British Burma

The ethnic Burman/Myanmar and the many other peoples who constituted the Myanmar Kingdom of the Konbaung Dynasty were the victims of a three staged colonial annexation that lasted over 70 years. The first Anglo-Burmese war lasted from 1824 to 1826 and saw the annexation of Arakan, bordering British India, and Tennesserim, the lower part of Burma which borders both Thailand and what was then Malaya. A further war, the second Anglo-Burmese War lasted from 1852 to 1853 and saw the annexation of Rangoon and Pegu and all the areas became known as Lower Burma and became part of, and were governed from, British India. The third and final war, from 1885 to 1886, would see the total annexation of the Burman/

Figure 1 - Burma under British India showing ethnic states
under indirect and self rule

Myanmar Kingdom of Konbaung Dynasty and the joining of both upper and lower Burma.

However, the occupation of the Burman/Myanmar Kingdom, which was recognized and governed by the British as 'Burma proper', did not include the Chin, the Kachin, the Karen from the Salween Hills, the Karenni, and the Shan. These peoples were recognized as being completely independent due to the fact that they had never been conquered by the Burman/Myanmar King. The British gradually conquered the ethnic peoples separately during different periods of time and ruled them on an individual basis. The Chin country was the last to be occupied, in 1896, and the British promulgated for them a separate constitution known as the "Chin Hills Regulation". The Karenni, however, were never occupied but recognized as an independent people during the entire colonial period.

It was this separate recognition of the peoples of the borderlands that would result in the division of the country into two distinct entities and the granting of authority to the Chin, Kachin, Karenni, and Shan to maintain their feudal administrations in what became known as the frontier or excluded areas. The frontier areas were comprised of what is now Karen State (then known as the Karen Salween Hill tracts), Chin State (Chin Hills), Kachin State (Kachin Hills) and Shan State (Federated Shan States).

After the First World War the British moved to introduce a number of reforms for its colonies. In 1917 a meeting, the Chelmsford-Montague hearings, took place in India. The Burman delegates, represented by the Young Man's Buddhist Association, sought to seek seperation from British India and the crown while the Karen sought to retain links to the British. In 1920, the Greater Council for Burmese Associations (GCBA), an alliance of Buddhist groups, was formed. The GCBA embarked on a number of anti-colonial policies including advocating the boycott of foreign goods. A year later, in 1921, the Whyte Commission was formed to look into communal representation and the country's first parliament was finally established in 1923.

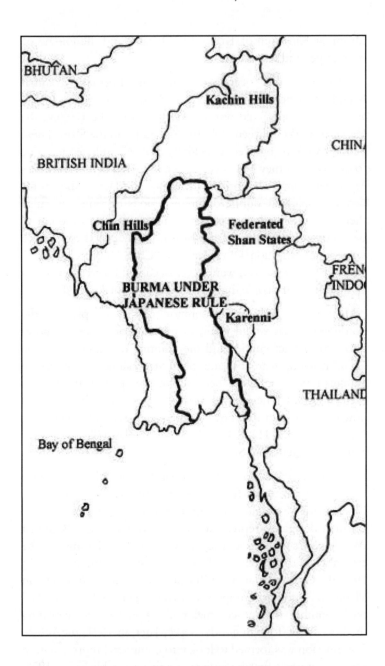

Figure 2 - Burma under Japanese rule

By the early 1930s the country was facing an economic and political crisis and a populist peasant rebellion, led by Saya San, spread throughout the country. Amidst the turmoil of 1930, the Dobama Asiayone (We Burmans Association) was founded. The Dobama Asiayone, which also became know as the Thakin movement, was to hold the mantle of Burman nationalism. Its main objective was total independence of the country from the British but also the impostion of Burman values on an independent Burma - as noted in its slogan:

> 'Burma is our country; Burmese literature is our literature; Burmese language is our language. Love our country, raise the standards of our literature, respect our language.'

Second World War and Japanese Occupation

The Burman nationalists continued to demand independence and members of the Thakin movement, led by Aung San, contacted the Japanese and received training to fight the British. In 1942, the Japanese, supported by the Thakin led Burma Independence Army, invaded the country forcing British forces to retreat to India. Many of the ethnic groups, including the Karen, Kachin and Chin, continued to support the British and fought against the Burma Independence Army and their Japanese allies.

Unhappy with the limited authority given to the Japanese installed Burmese government, the Thakins finally made an agreement with the British to fight against their former allies and the Japanese were soon forced to retreat. After the war, Aung San formed a provisional government, the Anti-Fascist People's Freedom League (AFPFL), which included among its members a number of ethnic representatives.

Aung San – Attlee Agreement

After assuming office in September 1946, the newly appointed Governor, Sir Hubert Rance, entered into discussions with political leaders to form an Executive Council containing members of all the leading parties. Aung San, and the AFPFL, soon dominated the council and an AFPFL delegation led by Aung San, and minus any ethnic representation, was warmly welcomed by British Premier Clement Attlee on 19th January 1947.

On the 27th January 1947 the Aung San-Attlee agreement was signed. The agreement provided for elections within four months to set up a constituent assembly, recognition of Aung San's Cabinet as an interim Dominion Government, British nomination for Burma's membership of the United Nations, and British loans and support. It also stated that a conference to discuss ethnic representation must be arranged by the AFPFL. However, the path to independence was not to be an easy one. Former Prime Minister U Saw and Thakin Ba Sein refused '... to associate themselves with the conclusions of the agreement.' While in Rangoon, Thakin Than Tun and Thakin Soe denounced it primarily due to it allowing too much British influence.

The Panglong Conference

Precolonial independent peoples of the Chin, Kachin and Shan held a conference to decide their own future in March 1946, which was known as the First Panglong Conference. The Second Panglong Confernce was held in Shan State on the 12th of February 1947, resulted in the signing of what became known as the "Panglong Agreement". This agreement provided the basic founding principles of the Union of Burma, and guaranteed the autonomy for the Chin, Kachin and Shan who signed the agreement, and other ethnic nationalities that will eventually joined the Union as equal partners, and became the member states of the Union of Burma.

Since the conference was initated by precolonial independent peoples from "Frontier Areas", it was not inclusive. Although both the Karen and the Karenni sent observers to the conference there were no representatives from the Arakanese, Mon or other ethnic peoples. The Karen representatives, under the political leadership of the Karen Central Organization, refused actual participation in the Panglong conference due to the fact that it's own AFPFL members had not been included in the London delegation.

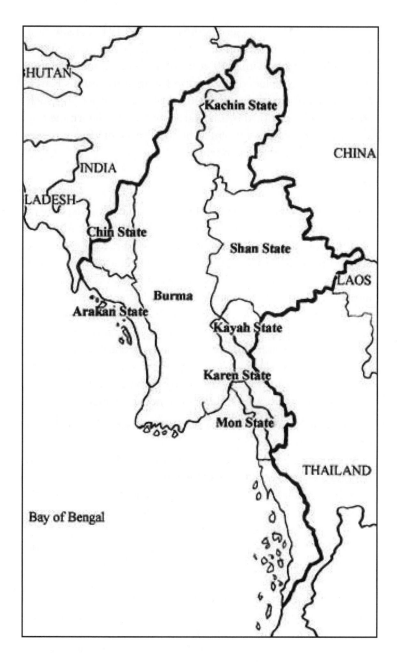

Figure 3 – Seven Ethnic States in the Union of Burma

The ethnic issue was also addressed in the 1947 constitution which included a provision that ethnic states could secede from the Union but not within 10 years of the constitution coming into law. It also included a provision for an autonomous Karen State or Kaw-thu-lay based on the 'Salween district and such adjacent areas occupied by the Karens as may be determined by a special commission appointed by the President.' But this was to be decided after independence.

Independent Burma

On the 4th January 1948, Burma became an independent republic outside of the commonwealth under Prime Minister, U Nu. Not long after independence was granted the country erupted into civil war as communist and ethnic armies fought for their individual goals. U Nu's government was able to stay in power and by 1958 began to reestablish government control over the many areas of the country that had been lost to the various factions. In 1958, disunity among the various members of the AFPFL resulted in the government's collapse. Although U Nu won a new election, it was by such a small margin that he resigned and instead asked the head of the army, General Ne Win, to take over power and organize new elections.

General Ne Win held power for 16 months before U Nu once again was elected to the position of Prime Minister. Throughout the period the relationship with the various ethnic nationalities in the country had been tenuous at best. A number of ethnic armies, especially the Karen and Kachin, had won major gains and were still in open rebellion. In addition to the armed conflict, the government was also facing the prospect of the Shan and Karenni states seeking the right to secede as allowed for in the 1947 constitution. To address these issues U Nu arranged a federal seminar to take place on the 25th of February 1962 to amend the constitution and give greater rights to the ethnic minorities. Fearing the country's collapse, Ne Win seized power on the 2nd March and detained U Nu and over thirty Karenni and Shan leaders. The 1947 constitution, and the rights of the minorities to secede, was suspended.

Shortly after seizing power, General Ne Win established the Revolutionary Council (RC) and replaced the federal parliamentary system with a military dictatorship. The Revolutionary Council then created it owns political party, the Burma Socialist Program Party (BSPP), and published its ideology as the 'The Burmese Way to Socialism' on the 30th April 1962. To further establish control over the political processes of the country, the RC issued a decree entitled 'The Law Protecting National Unity' on March 23, 1964, whereby all political parties with exception of the BSPP, were abolished. The BSPP soon embarked on a policy of nationalization and the military assumed direct control of the economy. In 1971, the BSPP attempted to transform itself into a civilian administration; however, it was still primarily comprised of retired military officers. In 1974 a new constitution was adopted which further entrenched the BSPP as the only legal political party in the country.

Throughout the seventies the BSPP's failed economic policies wreaked havoc within the country. Workers staged violent strikes and student demonstrations in 1974 were bloodily repressed. After years of mismanagement and repression Ne Win finally stepped down from the presidency in 1981, but he still held the reins of power of the BSPP. In 1987, as the country continued to face economic disintegration, the BSPP demonetized three currency bank notes and refused to reimburse those who had lost most of their savings. The move resulted in over 70% of the currency in circulation becoming worthless and as a result mass protests were organized.

The 8-8-88 Democracy Movement

In March 1988, a brawl in a tea shop, which led to the death of a student at the hands of the Police, resulted in violent campus wide disturbances. The government responded by closing all the universities and in an attempt to calm the situation promised an inquiry. Believing the environment to be more stable, universities were reopened in June. However, violence once more broke out at the failure of the government to bring to justice those responsible for the student's death. Unrest soon spread nationwide and martial law was declared. A general strike on the 8th of August 1988 was bloodily suppressed with thousands of demonstrators and students gunned down in the streets. On the 18th September student led demonstrations were once again brutally crushed and soon gave way to an army staged coup.

The army, under the guise of the 'State Law and Order Restoration Council' or SLORC, led by General Saw Maung, abolished the Pyitthu Hluttaw and quickly moved to assure the public of it intentions. On the 21st of September the government promulgated the 'Multi-Party Democracy General Elections Commission Law No. 1/88' and six days later 'the Political Parties Registration Law'. On the same day the National League for Democracy (Ah-myo-tha Di-mocray-si Ahphwe Choak) was formed with the aim of 'establishing a genuine democratic government.' The NLD was led by Chairman U Aung Gyi; Vice Chairman, U Tin Oo, and General secretary Daw Aung San Su Kyi. Altogether 233 parties were registered to contest the 27 May 1990 election.

To participate in the election the BSPP changed its name to the National Unity Party (Taing-yin-tha Nyi-nyutyay Party) and also began to canvass. However, it soon became evident that the NUP was losing to the National League for Democracy, especially due to the popularity of Daw Aung San Suu Kyi. After slanderous attacks on her in the media had failed, the government had both Aung San Suu Kyi and U Tin Oo arrested on the 19th July 1989. Despite the fact that two of its main leaders were under house arrest and disqualified, the National League for Democracy was still able to win 392 of the 485 seats.

The Bo Aung Kyaw Street Declaration

Despite the party's clear victory, the SLORC refused to hand over power to the NLD claiming that a constitution needed to be drafted first. The NLD and the newly formed United Nationalities League for Democracy (UNLD), an umbrella group of ethnic party representatives, issued a joint statement:

1. Calling on the State Law and Order Restoration Council (SLORC) to convene the Pyithu Hluttaw in September, 1990, in accordance with Article (3),Chapter(2) of the Pyithu Hluttaw Election Law

2. Calling for a speedy dialogue between the authorized representatives from the National League for Democracy, which won by a substantial margin in the Multi-Party Democracy General Election, and the authorized representatives from the SLORC

3. Calling on the State Law and Order Restoration Council, concerning the current interests and long-term interests of Burma, to free expeditiously Chairman U Tin Oo ,Secretary-General Daw Aung San Suu Kyi of the National League for Democracy and all of the political prisoners

4. Calling on the State Law and Order Restoration Council to lift the restrictions on the democratic rights and people's rights.'

Despite such calls the SLORC refused to honour the election result and instead sought to hold on to power claiming that a National Convention would need to be convened to write a new constitution.

The SLORC National Convention

After two years of political impasse, and with members of the NLD still in jail or under house arrest, the SLORC announced, on the 23rd of April 1992, that it would hold a National Convention - the six main objectives would be:

1. Non-disintegration of the Union;
2. Non-disintegration of national unity;
3. Perpetuation of national sovereignty;
4. Promotion of a genuine multiparty democracy;
5. Promotion of the universal principles of justice, liberty and equality;
6. Participation by the Defence Services in a national political leadership role in the future state.

On the 28th May 1992 a National Convention Steering Committee was formed to write the new constitution. The committee included 14 junta officials and 28 people from seven different political parties. The committee named 702 delegates. Of these only 99 were elected Members of Parliament and seventy percent of the delegates were township level officials handpicked by the military.

After constant suspensions and reopening, delegates had agreed 104 principles with ethnic representatives still attempting to secure a federal system. In an attempt to ensure that Aung San Suu Kyi would have no political role in the government of the country the convention law stated, despite opposition from many of the delegates, that the president of Burma must have been a continuous resident for more than 20 years, have political, administrative, military and economic experience and not have a spouse or children who are citizens of another country.

By September 2004 the convention had agreed that at least a third of the seats in any new parliament would go to the military. On 29 November 1995, in response to criticism from the National League for Democracy, the Military regime expelled all of the NLD delegates from the assembly resulting in the number of MPs elected in 1990 becoming less than three percent of all delegates. The SLORC then passed a law which made it illegal to make speeches or disseminate written statements criticizing the National Convention – offenders faced 20 years in jail.

The SPDC Seven Steps Road Map

The convention was once again suspended and the constitutional process stalled until the appointment of new Prime Minister Khin Nyunt in 2003. The new premier unveiled what he called a seven point road map. The points made were:

1. Reconvening of the National Convention that has been adjourned since 1996.
2. After the successful holding of the National Convention, step by step implementation of the process necessary for

the emergence of a genuine and disciplined democratic system.

3. Drafting of a new constitution in accordance with basic principles and detailed basic principles laid down by the National Convention.

4. Adoption of the constitution through national referendum.

5. Holding of free and fair elections for Pyithu Hluttaws (Legislative bodies) according to the new constitution.

6. Convening of Hluttaws attended by Hluttaw members in accordance with the new constitution.

7. Building a modern, developed and democratic nation by the state leaders elected by the Hluttaw; and the government and other central organs formed by the Hluttaw.

In the face of open criticism from a number of parties, both within and outside of the country, including Kofi Anan, The U.N. Secretary General, the National Convention reconvened on the 17th May 2004 with 1,076 invited delegates including representatives from 25 ethnic ceasefire groups. The National Convention concluded, after 14 years of deliberation and several sessions, on the 3rd of September 2007. On the 9th of February 2008, the SPDC stated that a National Referendum to adopt the constitution would be held in May 2008. In spite of the fact that Cyclone Nargis struck the country on the 2nd and 3rd of May 2008 causing widespread devastation, the regime insisted on continuing with its plan to hold the referendum, including in areas where the destruction occurred most. There were widespread reports of coercion, including voters being given ballots that had already been ticked and voting closely monitored by Government officials. After voting was conducted on the 10th of May 2008, the regime announced that the draft Constitution had been overwhelmingly approved by 92.4 per cent of the 22 million eligible voters, stating that there had been a turnout of more than 99 per cent. They later announced that elections would be held in the year 2010.

The Current Problem

The political crisis in the Union of Burma today is not just an ideological confrontation between democracy and a military dictatorship. The problem is rooted in a constitutional crisis which was created due to the 1947 Panglong Agreement not being fully implemented. The 1994 U.N. General Assembly Resolution noted that to resolve Burma's problems and to build a sustainable democracy, there should be a 'Tripartite Dialogue', amongst:

1. The military led by the SLORC / SPDC
2. 1990 Election-winning Parties led by the NLD
3. The Ethnic Nationalities

It must be realized that Tripartite Dialogue is not just a "Three-party talk" but consists of "Three-Issues" represented by three conflict partners:-

The State Peace and Development Council

The SPDC's Road Map ignores the result of the 1990 elections and excludes the election winners, including the NLD & UNLD. It also ignores constitutional recommendations made by the ethnic nationalities. The military's constitution concentrates power in the hands of the president and the army chief. No decentralization of administrative powers. No independent judiciary. The military remains above the law and is independent from the government that will be elected in 2010. The military constitution will not lead to democracy, peace and justice. It will only legitimize military dictatorship and continue the problems the country currently faces i.e. militarization, economic mismanagement, humanitarian crises and civil war.

The National League for Democracy and Aung San Suu Kyi

The NLD seeks a democracy which the people of Burma had already expressed their willingness to have a in the 1990 Election.

Ethnic Nationalities

Face a constitutional crisis that deny them their inherent rights and are forced to continue a sixty years old conflict.

Solution:

- To establish a Democratic Federal Union of Burma, which will guarantees,

    i. Democratic rights for all citizens of the Union of Burma,
    ii. Political equality for all Ethnic Nationalities, and
    iii. The rights of self-determination of all Member States of the Union of Burma through Federal arrangement.

Strategy:

- Solving political problems through political means, that is., through a negotiated-settlement
- United Nations General Assembly Resolution since 1994, which called for a 'Tripartite Dialogue', amongst:

    i. The military led by the SLORC / SPDC;
    ii. 1990 Election-winning Parties led by the NLD, and
    iii. The Ethnic Nationalities.

Tripartite Dialogue:

Tripartite Dialogue is not just "Three-party Talk" but "Three-Issues", represented by three conflict partners:-

1. The SPDC (Military Junta): the problem of De-militarization of Burma, how to transform the Armed Forces into a normal civil servants (civil-military relation);
2. NLD and Aung San Suu Kyi: Democratization, the people of Burma already expressed their willing to have a democratic government in 1990 Election;
3. Ethnic Nationalities: Constitutional Crisis and Sixty Years of Civil War

The SPDC Road Map and 2008 Constitution:

1. SPDC's Road Map ignores the result of 1990 elections, and excludes the election winners. It also ignores

constitutional recommendations made by the ethnic nationalities.

2. The military's constitution concentrates power in the hands of the president and the army chief. No decentralization of administrative powers. No independent judiciary. The military remain above the law and is independent of the government that will be elected in 2010.
3. The military constitution will not lead to a democracy, peace and justice. This will only legitimized military dictatorship.

ENC Position on 2010 Election

- The ENC cannot endorse the election in principles, it will support the people.
- This means that if the ceasefires and other organizations, decided to contest the ENC will not oppose their decision.
- The ENC strongly believes that 2010 election will not give legitimacy to the SPDC.
- Truly legitimate government must be of the people, elected by the people, and work for the people.

Some ceasefire Groups Position on 2010 Election: Gradual Transition

- 2010 election as a "Stepping Stone" by applying "South Korea Model";
- Reason: Had the NLD stayed at the convention until the end, they think that Burma might have experienced at least three elections in 12 years (since 1996);
- If that was the case, the country might already have moved towards change, instead of remaining under the military regime.
- Thus, no matter how flawed the constitution is, and how imperfect the process may seem, the people of Burma should take a chance on the 2010 election in order to start a gradual transition.

- Gen Saw Maung said that the SLORC was merely a transitional authority, and should not engage dialogue with oppositions;
- Gen Khin Nyunt reaffirmed the SLORC/SPDC position, and told the ceasefire groups that "political negotiation should be left for a new government"
- ceasefire leaders believe that "in order for a new government to emerge", the SPDC should be allowed to hold election in 2010;
- The Ethnic Nationalities, especially ceasefire groups, will engage meaningful dialogue with a new government and democratic forces.

Why some ceasefire groups are opting for the election:

- For the ethnic ceasefire groups, gradual transition is a lesser evil compared to the status quo maintained by the military dictatorship.
- If the regime, even after the 2010 election, remains unopposed, it will be very difficult for them to protect and promote their culture, their language and their identity through a unitary form of nation-building.
- If the regime remains unopposed, they may forever lose what they have been fighting for all these years.
- Thus, they are opting to contest the election; even though they know that the SPDC's Constitution is not perfect.

The Role of the International Community:

- The international community through the United Nations Security Council should pass a binding resolution which will guarantee the roles of the NLD and the ethnic nationalities;
- The UN and the international community should insist on the inclusion of "Tripartite Dialogue" among the new government, elected in the 2010 election, but still under the control of SPDC, involving the NLD, led by Daw Aung San Suu Kyi, and the ethnic nationalities.

- The UN and the international community should seek to support the following conditions:

    i.   All the political prisoners, including Aung San Suu Kyi and Hkun Htun Oo, should be released;

    ii. The NLD and UNLD/UNA should be allowed to function freely, even if they are opting to stay away from 2010 election;

    iii. Ceasefire groups should not be forced to transform into Border Guard Forces.

- The main purpose of a "Tripartite Dialogue" should be to see an end to the 60 years of civil war by guaranteeing the rights of ethnic nationalities and to review the constitution to ensure that it will guarantee democratic rights and the rule of law, create the conditions for a peaceful existence among different ethnic groups and different religious groups in the Union of Burma.

Post-Election Scenarios:

Continued Deadlock

The military will remain in power and continue their attempts at Myanmarization of the country. In recalling the Myanmar/ Burman nationalist sloganeering of 'one blood, one voice, one command' and 'one religion, one language, and one ethnicity' the regime will continue to subjugate the ethnic peoples and seek to remove all vestiges of their cultures, languages, separate identities and ways of life. Such a process has been well documented in the past.

People's Uprising

Burma has experienced people's uprisings twice: the 1988 Democracy Movement and the 2007 Saffron Revolution. Both of them ended in bloodshed and without any significant change.

- If another people's uprising occurs without change, what will be next?

- Even if such uprisings can topple the SPDC and its top generals, what will happen with the regional commanders?
- Some pessimists suggest that Burma will have 14 military dictators instead of the current one, if such a scenario is realized.

Further Ethnic Armed Struggle

- The emergence of 14 warlords created by the ensuing chaos is not purely hypothetical but a very likely scenario that can happen anytime if the current status quo is prolonged any further.
- If such a situation becomes an eventuality, further chaos can be envisioned especially in ethnic areas.
- Instead of living under Myanmar-ethnic regional warlords, or a consolidated military dictator from Naypyidaw, the non-Burman/Myanmar ethnic nationalities may prefer to join their respective brothers who are living on the other side of international boundaries.

Disintegration of the Union

- It is important to note that most of the ethnic nationalities in Burma transcend international boundaries and as such can easily adapt to any country so long as they can identify where they live as their homeland.
- Such a scenario could result in the Chin State and Upper Chindwin becoming part of Mizoram State and North East India; Kachin and Shan States become part of Yunnan Province in China; and the Karen, Karenni and Mon States becoming part of Thailand where most of their blood-brothers live.
- This scenario will leave Burma in its original form - the Myanmar Kingdom prior to the colonial period.

What We Want for the Future?

- We don't want to see the disintegration of the Union of Burma.

- We are willing to rebuild the Union of Burma based on the principles of Panglong Agreement in 1947.
- We want to solve our country's problem through a negotiated-settlement.
- Though we think that the negotiated-settlement is the best means to solve the problem of Burma, we shall never negotiate with the SPDC because of our fear. But we do not fear to negotiate with them either.
- Ethnic leaders, especially in ceasefire groups, see the 2010 election as a stepping stone towards democracy; even though they know that the SPDC's Constitution is not perfect they see it as the only way forward.

Conclusion

The Ethnic Nationalities Council does not want to see the disintegration of the Union of Burma. It is willing to rebuild the Union of Burma based on the principles of the 1947 Panglong Agreement and solve our country's problem through a negotiated-settlement.

Some Ceasefire groups have suggested that the 2010 Election can be seen as a "Stepping Stone" towards a gradual transition similar to that of the so called "South Korea Model." They have also argued that "had the NLD stayed at the National Convention until the end it is believed that Burma might have experienced at least three elections in 12 years (since 1996)". If this had been the case, the country might have already moved towards change, instead of remaining under the military regime. Therefore, no matter how flawed the constitution is, and how imperfect the process may seem, the people of Burma should take a chance on the 2010 election in order to start a gradual transition.

Burma has experienced widespread people's uprisings twice. In 1988, there was the Democracy Movement followed by the 2007 Saffron Revolution. Both of these ended in bloodshed and without any significant change. Even If a future uprising is successful in toppling the SPDC and its top generals, it would not remove the military's grip on the country. Regional commanders would still remain. Some pessimists have suggested that Burma would have 14 military dictators instead of the current one.

In addressing the issues affecting the country, it is important to note that most of the ethnic nationalities in Burma transcend international boundaries and as such they can easily adapt to any country so long as they can identify where they live as their homeland. Failure to correctly address ethnic aspirations could result in the Chin State and Upper Chindwin becoming part of Mizoram State and North East India; Kachin and Shan States becoming part of Yunnan Province in China; and the Karen, Karenni and Mon States becoming part of Thailand where most of their blood-brothers live. This scenario will leave Burma in its original form - the Myanmar Kingdom prior to the colonial period.

Despite claims to the contrary, ethnic armed forces can continue their struggle for another 60 years, but is not a valid solution. Such methods are purely for the defence of the ethnic population against Burma Army aggression. Armed struggle will not end until, and unless, the political crisis, including the aspirations of the ethnic peoples, is settled. To achieve peace in Burma the Ethnic Nationalities Council believes that a negotiated-settlement through tripartite dialogue is the only means to solve the problems of the country.

TEN

ENC Mission Statement
Washington DC, USA
4-9 June 2007

The following Mission Statement was presented to various concerned parties in the U.S. Government during the ENC advocacy mission from 4-9 June 2007. As a consequence the ENC delegation was invited to speak at the White House by the first lady Laura Bush.

We, the delegates of the Ethnic Nationalities Council of the Union of Burma, are here in Washington DC, the capitol of the United States of America, to express our sincere thanks to the people of the United States of America and its government for their support for our struggle for democracy, human rights and freedom in the Union of Burma. We particularly thank the government of the United States for its effort to bring Burma's problems to the United Nations Security Council on 12 January 2007. Although the draft resolution, sponsored by the United States of America and the United Kingdom of Great Britain and Northern Ireland, was vetoed by China and Russia along with South Africa, we still believe that there must be a way and means that the international community can help the peoples of Burma through the United Nations, such as the good offices of the Secretary-General under the mandate of the General Assembly.

We, therefore, come here to seek further assistance and support from the United States. We particularly request the government of the United States to take the initiative for

"Multi-party Talks on Burma", which would put strong pressure on the military regime (called the State Peace and Development Council or SPDC) to engage in a meaningful political dialogue with those seeking to bring democracy to Burma. The Ethnic Nationalities Council (ENC) believes that the best means to solve the political crisis in Burma, including more than five long decades of civil war, is a negotiated settlement brought about by dialogue and compromise.

Since 1994, successive United Nations General Assembly resolutions have called for a "tripartite dialogue" in Burma between the military government, the National League for Democracy (the political party led by Daw Aung San Suu Kyi that won the 1990 election) and the ethnic nationalities, who were founding partners in the creation of the Union of Burma in 1947. We strongly endorse these resolutions. The call for a "tripartite dialogue" reflects the tripartite nature of the political crisis in Burma. The crisis in Burma is not merely an ideological conflict between democracy and a military dictatorship. Instead, the crisis comes from a constitutional problem: Burma's governments have always denied the right of self-determination for ethnic nationalities who joined the Union of Burma as equal partners at the 1947 Panglong Conference. That denial brought on civil war even before the military came to power; indeed, the military seized control as a result of the unrest bred by the underlying constitutional problem. Merely to restore democracy without addressing the deeper causes of conflict will not lead to long-term peace. Burma's problems can therefore be solved only through a federal constitution of the sort agreed by General Aung San, the leader of Burma's independence movement, and the leaders of the ethnic nationalities at Panglong.

We are hopeful that China and Russia will be able to collaborate with the United States, the United Kingdom and other members of the international community in organizing "Multi-party Talks on Burma" under UN auspices. Although both countries vetoed the draft resolution on Burma at the UN Security Council, they acknowledged that Burma is "facing many political, economic and social challenges and that some of its problems are quite serious." They further acknowledged that Burma, indeed, is "faced with a series of grave challenges relating to refugees, child labor, HIV/AIDS, human rights and drugs," and suggested that the UN should address those problems through the good offices of the Secretary-General under the mandate of the General Assembly.

We, therefore, request the United States to take the initiative for "Multi-party Talks on Burma", which may include the United States, China, Russia, India, Japan, the EU and ASEAN, under the aegis of the United Nations. We are aware that unless our neighboring countries, especially China, India, Japan and ASEAN, are involved in solving Burma's problems together with the USA and EU, the suffering of the peoples of Burma will unnecessarily be prolonged. We, therefore, need "Multi-party Talks on Burma" (similar to the Six Party Talks in Korea) in order to find common ground that will allow a democratic transition and national reconciliation to begin.

To solve our own problems, the ENC and other democratic forces have prepared ourselves in many different ways. We have drafted a federal constitution for the Federal Republic of the Union of Burma and, within that federal framework; we have also developed state constitutions for the seven ethnic states that have been the traditional homelands for many ethnic minorities. We also prepared a "Road Map for Rebuilding the Union of Burma" which has been generally accepted by all ethnic nationalities and democratic forces. However, we are unable to find common ground for a democratic transition with the military regime, for they still refuse to engage in a meaningful political dialogue. We, therefore, need the assistance of the international community to start the transition process in Burma.

While we need "Multi-party Talks on Burma" to find a long term solution, we also need humanitarian assistance in order to relieve the suffering of the peoples of Burma. We, therefore, request such assistance from the United States and the international community, especially cross-border assistance to ethnic areas where the suffering is more acute. We also need financial and technical assistance for capacity building, especially in the fields of health and education. We need to train and empower our people, especially youth and women, in order to rebuild our country and lay a solid foundation for future generations!

ELEVEN

Negotiated Settlement, Not Violent Confrontation

The following text is an interview given to the Chinland Guardian on the 17 May 2009

Chinland Guardian: The SPDC has shocked the world once again by transferring Aung San Suu Kyi from her house arrest to Insein Prison to "face charges". It seems justice has been badly humiliated under the watchful eyes of the world's civilized community and it surely is disheartening for those who advocate for democracy and human rights in Burma.

Dr. Lian: Yes, this really is disheartening! Things keep going from bad to worse in our country. As you said, the whole justice system has been humiliated in Burma since the military dictators first came to power in 1962. The latest episode is just a reminder of the true nature of the current military regime, the SPDC. By transferring Daw Aung San Suu Kyi to Insein Prison, they openly declare that under this regime, there is "no law at all, but the use of force", as General Saw Maung once admitted.

The intention of the military regime, of course, is clear: they want to extend Daw Aung San Suu Kyi's thirteen years house arrest, which is set to end on 27 May. But the bizarre coincidence is that the regime founded the intrusion of an American man who sneaked into her compound as a scapegoat. And now, she is transferred to the notorious Insein Prison, and is going to face a mockery of a trial. If she is convicted, she can face up to an additional seven years of incarceration.

We should not forget the fact that Daw Aung San Suu Kyi is not alone. She will be joining another 2,000 political prisoners in Insein Prison, who committed no sin but wanted to live a peaceful life and enjoy freedom. What Daw Aung San Suu Kyi and all these political prisoners in Burma are sacrificing for is nothing but freedom.

And, we have to remind ourselves that freedom transcends all the boundaries of nations, race, ethnicity, religion, and culture. If we see freedom as a transcendental phenomenon, we then realize that what Daw Aung San Suu Kyi is fighting for is not only for Burma but for the entire humanity. So, I would like to request the international community: who loves freedom, who stands for freedom, and who lives in the free world; please try to identify yourselves this time —just this moment— with Daw Aung San Suu Kyi, and do something to free Daw Aung San Suu Kyi.

For those of us who are fighting for freedom in Burma, Daw Aung San Suu Kyi is more than a leader; she is our icon for democracy and the symbol of our struggle for freedom. So, when she is sitting in prison, or under house arrest, we feel like part of our life is imprisoned. What I am trying to say is that to free Daw Aung San Suu Kyi for us is identical to freeing ourselves and our country.

Chinland Guardian: The SPDC is determined to go ahead with their election plan in 2010. What is the ENC's Stance in that regard?

Dr. Lian: The ENC issued a statement in August 2008, saying that, "the SPDC's Seven Step Road Map, including the 2008 military's constitution and 2010 general elections, will not bring peace and democracy to the country". Our reason is quite simple: if you look back at the way they conducted the "national convention", the whole process was totally unacceptable. It was not inclusive: they even excluded the winners of the 1990 elections. The delegates were merely hand-picked by the SPDC: so where is the legitimacy of the "national convention".

The term "national convention" is very important. Since the term itself reflects the very nature of the entire nation and the people, the "national convention" should be the place where the people, with whom sovereign power of state actually belongs, can freely discuss and decide their own future: what kind of political system they want to establish and what kind of constitutional system they want to adopt. So, the delegations at the national convention must genuinely represent the people. They should not be chosen by one group or one person.

What I am trying to say here is that the process of the regime's seven step road map, especially the way they conducted the national convention, is not only flawed but missing its legitimacy — the most essential element of conducting a national convention. For this simple reason, we cannot accept it.

Secondly, if you look at the "substance", I means, the result of the national convention: this is not just flawed but dangerous for the future of the Union of Burma, especially for ethnic nationalities. This is dangerous because the military's constitution concentrates power in the hands of the president and the army chief. So, what will happen under this constitution is that Burma will becomes a country where the Army own the State, not the other way round: because the Army will stay above the law, and they will control the entire country.

Actually, this "process" began in 1962 but the difference this time is that the Army will legally own the State in accordance with the highest law of the land. Since the constitution allows the Army to stay above the law, people cannot expect the rule of law, and there will be no independent judiciary. The whole judicial system, including the courts, will simply be a mockery.

And there is no decentralization of administrative powers in this constitution, which is very dangerous for ethnic nationalities. The danger is not only centralization of powers but a unitary form of nation-building. The combination of centralization and a unitary form of nation-building, which is blended into the model of "one language, one ethnicity, and one religion", is designed for forced-assimilation in imposing the language of *Myanmar-ska*, the ethnicity of *Myanmar-lumyo*, and the religion of Buddhism, in order to build a homogenous *Myanmar-naingngain*, and fulfil the dream of *"Buddha-bata Myanmar-lumyo"*, which means., "to be a Myanmar is to be a Buddhist". For us, nation-building process through the model of "one language, one religion and one ethnicity" is nothing but ethno-cultural genocide which we cannot accept.

But, as you said, the regime will go ahead with their own roadmap because this is the only way they can transform themselves from a *de facto* government to a *de jure* government. They will control and own the country legally according to the law that they promulgated, and thus complete a unitary form of the nation-building process. This is what they want, and this is what we oppose.

Chinland Guardian: It seems that you are still insisting on tripartite dialogue in spite of the fact that the possibilities of the talks seems very slim looking at how unfruitful the several UN Special Envoy's missions to Burma during the past several years, including the present UN Special Envoy Mr. Gambari, have been.

Dr. Lian: I sincerely think that a negotiated-settlement is the best means to solve political crisis in Burma. If we abandon a negotiated-settlement through dialogue, then the only option left for Burma will be a violent confrontation. If violent confrontations and suppression are the solution, then General Ne Win would have solved all the problems of Burma in 1962 when he came to power through a military coup and suppressed all the oppositions. But it was not the solution.

For me violent confrontation is not the solution for Burma, and fighting on battle grounds is not the end game for the ethnic nationalities. That's why we are opting for a negotiated-settlement, although most ethnic nationalities are still fighting a six decade long civil war. The ethnic nationalities are holding arms only for self-defense purposes and we know that armed-struggle is not the solution. That is the reason why we endorse the United Nations General Assembly's resolution that called for a "tripartite dialogue" with the regime, the 1990 election winning party, led by Daw Aung San Suu Kyi, and the ethnic nationalities.

The essence of "tripartite dialogue", for us, is not just three-party talks but solving three essential problems of today's

Burma. The first problem is military dictatorship, represented by the SPDC. Burma has been under military dictatorship for almost half a century, and we, ethnic nationalities, have been engaging in civil war for sixty years now. So, if we want to transform our country into a normal peaceful country; we have to solve this problem first. How are we going to transform the SPDC's Armed Forces and ethnic fighting forces into normal civilians? We simply don't need such a big army.

The second problem that we need to solve is democracy and democratization. The people of Burma already expressed their willingness to have a democratic government, and live their life peacefully and enjoy fundamental rights. But, after twenty long years, the military dictators are still in power while leaders of the democracy movement are either in jail or in exile, and in the case of Daw Aung San Suu Kyi, she has spent 12 years of the past 18 of her life under house arrest. This is a big problem that Burma is facing, and it cannot be ignored. We must solve it, but not through a zero-sum game. We need to find a win-win solution. That's why we are calling for a dialogue.

Thirdly, there is an ethnic problem. We, ethnic nationalities, are here in this country only because of the fact that we joined the Union of Burma as equal partners in 1947 at the Panglong Conference. We expected to enjoy autonomy in our homeland, the rights to protect and promote our culture, our language, our religion, our identity and our ways of life. And we also envisioned equal opportunities and equal rights among the member States of the Union. But what happened to us is, in the name of civil war, that successive governments of the Union of Burma have violated not only basic human rights but also our collective rights; in the name of national sovereignty the rights of "self-determination" and autonomy status for the ethnic nationalities are rejected; in the name of national integration the right to follow different religions, to practice different cultures, and to speak different languages are deprived; and in the name of national assimilation the rights to up-hold different identities and traditions are denied.

So, our conviction is that so long as Burma is under military dictatorship, so long as the peoples of Burma are demanding democracy and human rights, so long as we, ethnic nationalities, are engaging in civil war and fighting for our rights; we will still be calling for a negotiated-settlement no matter what kind of international situation present themselves to us. We must end this conflict, and we must find a solution. And we are opting to find the solution on a dialogue table not on the battle field. We have already sacrificed enough blood and lives. We also deserve a peaceful life, and we have to remember — and remind ourselves all the time that our blood is not cheaper than anyone else's.

Chinland Guardian: Some people say that the United Nations, the United States and the European Union's approach to the SPDC has had little or no impact at all in terms of the restoration of democracy and human rights in Burma. And it looks like what they are saying is true the fact remains that the number of political prisoners has been increasing so as the lengths of the sentences. What is your opinion on that?

Dr. Lian: The problem seems to me is the fact that that the international community does not have a common policy towards Burma. While Western countries prioritize restoration of democracy in Burma, our neighboring countries, especially China, India and ASEAN countries, are concerned more about stability in the country and the region. So, the SPDC plays a game between the differences of the East and the West. Sometimes they are hiding behind the back of China; sometimes they use India when they want to play games with the USA and EU, and so on.

My point here is this: so long as the international community applies different policies, the pressures from outside, including sanctions, will not be effective. That's why we are calling for a "Multi-party Talks on Burma" under the UN mechanism in order that the international community can adopt a common policy towards Burma. Such a process and mechanism are needed because the members of the international community who are dealing with Burma should consult each other, so that they can take concerted actions.

We are seriously concerned about the issue of "stability" because this is a matter directly related to us. Unfortunately, our neighboring countries have been buying the propaganda of the country's military dictators since 1962. The generals are saying that if democracy comes to Burma, all ethnic nationalities will secede from the Union, and the Union will disintegrate, and this will cause instability in the country and the region. So, what they are saying is that Burma needs a strong government with a strong army, not democracy.

We are saying that we are not separatists; what we are demanding is a Federal Union where all ethnic nationalities can live peacefully together, and enjoy autonomous status in our respective homelands. Federalism, as we all know, is not separation or independence. But there is a complication of the federal issue in Burma because the right of secession was included in 1947 Constitution. Actually, the reason for including the secession clause was nothing to do with federal principles. It was due to different historical and political backgrounds of the ethnic nationalities when they joined the Union at Panglong in 1947. For that reason, when ethnic nationalities and democratic forces together drafted the Constitution of Federal Republic of the Union of Burma [in 2006], we omitted the right of secession.

So, what we have been telling our neighboring countries is that democracy and federalism will bring peace and stability not only to Burma but also to the region, which is good for all of us.

Chinland Guardian: Many people said that former President Bush and first lady Laura championed Burma's cause. You have visited the White House and had lunch with President Bush in Bangkok during his Asia tour. Now it is said that the Obama administration is reviewing the US policy on Burma. What kind of policy change would you like to see from the Obama administration?

Dr. Lian: I agree. President Bush and the former first lady Laura Bush are among the best friends that we have had for the democracy movement in Burma. For activists like me an invitation from the White House and luncheon with the President of the United States was a great inspiration, and the impact was huge because of the media coverage. Such events sent a strong message to the generals that the democracy movement has some good friends sitting in the White House, and also gave hope and encouragement to the people of Burma that they have not been abandoned by the American people and the international community, and also that the suffering that they are enduring under this military regime is unjust but worth fighting for. So, we do greatly appreciate what the former President Bush and the First Lady Laura Bush have done for us.

I do hope that President Obama will follow the Bush Administration's policy towards Burma, and continue the same commitment to the people of Burma. But, on the other hand, I want to see the new administration's approach more "pragmatic" than the previous one. The Bush's policy was based on "moral principle", which is good but it takes time to materialize in reality. And I also want to see a more "multi-lateral approach" in which the USA, EU and other western countries are closely working together with China, India, Japan, and ASEAN countries under the UN mechanism. So, we will request President Obama to organize "Multi-Party Talks on Burma".

The ENC has been proposing "Multi-Party Talks on Burma" since 2007. Our proposed model is based on a combination of the "Six-Party Talks on North Korea" and the "Quartet of International Mediators for the Middle East" because we want the involvement of the USA, the UN, China, and the SPDC. Unless these four are involved, we cannot go forward.

I sincerely think that it is not too late to organize "Multi-Party Talks on Burma". With the right policies, Burma can become a model democratic nation that respects the rich diversity of its peoples. With freedom, our country can also become the gateway to the world markets for both China's southwest and India's northeast, which will bring greater prosperity and stability to Burma and the region.

Chinland Guardian: Do you think the National League for Democracy (NLD) and the United Nationalities League for Democracy (UNLD), especially the NLD, failed the people of Burma to restore democracy in the country in spite of your overwhelming victory during the 1990 election and their continue support?

Dr. Lian: Well, you see, our movement is not just for changing the government in Rangoon, or in Naypyidaw. If our goal then, was to change the government, maybe, we failed. But, I don't see it that way. This is a long struggle: a struggle for rebuilding the Union of Burma based on the spirit of Panglong where the Union was founded in the first place.

A lot of people fail to see the nature of our movement, and they don't really know what the root course of political crisis in Burma is. They see our struggle as a kind of saga similar to "beauty and the beast", which makes them think that the movement has failed because the beauty is still under detention and the generals are still in power. To me, this is not just a beauty and the beast drama. Not even ideological confrontation between democracy and military dictatorship. We must try to see a wider picture. If we do, we realize that the root course of political crisis in Burma is the constitution: a constitutional crisis that is rooted in the problem of the denial of the rights of ethnic nationalities who joined the Union of Burma as equal partners in 1947 at Panglong.

Since I see the whole process as a long struggle, I do not admit that we have failed. So long as the people are with us, and as you said they are still supporting us, we are still alive and kicking. But I agree that we have to evaluate the whole thing: despite winning the election, why the junta is still in power and democracy forces and ethnic nationalities are either in jail or in exile or in the jungle. What went wrong? Who lost the 1990 election result?

There are many factors involved in losing the 1990 election result. But since your question focuses on the NLD and UNLD, let us speak about the factors related only to these two parties. I must say that the NLD won the election without any hard campaigning. People simply voted for the NLD in order to free Daw Aung San Suu Kyi from house arrest. In my judgement, the NLD leadership, without Daw Aung San Suu Kyi, was not prepared to lead the country. It was obvious when the NLD convened the post-election convention in July 1990 at the Ghandi Hall in Rangoon. The expectation, of course, was high; and people expected that the NLD would form a government and come out from the convention with an agenda for transition, including a list of cabinet members and a date for convening the new Parliament, and so on.

I still remember the atmosphere of the moment: most of us felt a sense of loss when the NLD ended their convention without any agenda for transition, no cabinet list, and no specific resolution. They merely declared that they would draft a "temporary constitution" in order to take over power from the SLORC. It made many people appalled: A temporary constitution! What for? The power had already been given to them by the people.

Before the NLD's Ghandi Hall Convention, we, the UNLD, also held our convention at the YMCA Hall in Rangoon, and demanded from the regime that power should be transferred to the election winning party without any delay. We argued that power can be transferred to the election winning party without a written constitution. I wrote an article in the UNLD's *Equality Journal* and argued on the same line, giving England and Israel as an example where there is no written constitution.

After the Ghandi Hall Convention, the NLD and UNLD issued a joint-statement, known as the *Bo Aung Kyaw Street Declaration*, on 29 August. Before we issued the statement, we formed a Joint-Action Committee, composed of five members from each party. If I remember correctly, U Kyi Maung, U Khin Maung Shwe, U Kyaw Thein, U Soe Thein (Maung Wun Tha) and U Chain Aye (Maung Soe San) represented the NLD, and Naing Khin Maung, U Aye Pe, U Tha Ban, Naing Ngwe Thein, and I myself represented the UNLD. We conducted a series of meetings in July and August.

The irony was that we, the UNLD, pushed so hard for the issue of handing over power to the election winning party, that is, the NLD, but the NLD emphasized more the need for a National Convention in order to draft a new constitution. Actually, we had already highlighted the need for a National

Convention and a new constitution in our election manifesto. So, we liked the idea of having a National Convention but we also felt that after the election, the transfer of power was a more urgent need for the country in comparison to convening a National Convention. But we purely ended up, in the Bo Aung Kyaw Street Declaration, demanding the SLORC to convene the Pyithu Hluttaw in September 1990, and also calling for the need of National Convention. Not a single word about the transfer of power was mentioned in the declaration.

I bring up this issue here because we need to re-evaluate the reasons or the factors behind losing the 1990 election result. In my humble view, the main reason was nothing but the "thought form" or the "thought pattern": what I am trying to say is the reason behind the way we conducted politics in that particular moment — soon after election. I sincerely think, in retrospect, that both the NLD leadership and the SLORC's generals conducted politics within the same "thought pattern" and both sides played a power game within the same paradigm of an old power structure.

Since they were adhering to the same paradigm, both the regime and the NLD leaderships believed that sovereign power of state can only be handled either by the junta who came to power through a military coup, or a civilian government that is formed under a written constitution. So, they both believed that state power cannot be handed over to a civilian government without a written constitution.

So, what happened? Since they realized power within the same paradigm, they seemed to agree, without saying so, that the only solution for the country was to draft a new constitution first, as such power could then be retained by the military junta so long as there was no written constitution in the country. So, what happened after the Ghandi Hall Convention was that the battle ground for the power struggle between the NLD and the SLORC shifted to the National Convention and the focal point centred on who would convene the National Convention in order to draft a new constitution.

Looking back, I think it was the turning point of the movement. The turning point, unfortunately, was not positive for the country and the people. I wish we could have done better or differently at that time, but what can we do now? We have to learn a big lesson from our own experiences and move on, but never give in.

LHS - General Secretary of Chin Cultural & Literature Committee,
Rangoon University (1981)

Before 8888 Movement at Rangoon Univesity: L to R: That Cit became Deputy Army
Chief of the CNF and was killed by Burma Army. Sang Hlun became Vice Chairman of
CNF and was killed in India. LHS, and Salai Ceu Mang is now in exile in Norway

LHS - General Secretary of CCLC, the only student organization BSPP
regime allowed to form at Rangoon University (1982)

Chin Cultural & Literature Committee (CCLC),
Rangoon University (1983)

LHS - Presenting Policy Paper at the UNLD Conference (1990)

The UNLD trip to Arakan State: Saw Than Sein, Aye Tha Aung and
Salai Lian Hmung Sakhong (1990)

CNLD and NLD Meeting: Salai Ngai Sak, Lian H. Sakhong, Ram Ling Hmung, Daw Aung San Suu Kyi, and U Tun Oo (1989)

Salai Ngai Sak, Daw Aung San Suu Kyi, Ram Ling Hmung, U Tin Oo, and Lian H. Sakhong (1989)

LHS Presenting a Policy paper at the UNLD & Ethnic Nationalities Conference:
Hkun Tun Oo is chairing the conference (YMCA Hall, Rangoon, 1990)

Salai Ngai Sak, Thakhin Chit Maung, Ram Ling Hmung, ex-PM U Nu,
Lian H. Sakhong, and Moe Thee Zone (1989)

LHS and Harn visiting to Loitaileng, the RCSS HQ. (2006)

ENC Advocacy trip to USA, (2007)

Uncle Eugene - Lighting Candle on the Tree of Reconciliation
at Uppsala Cathederal (2003)

Pu Lal Thanhawla, Chief Minister of Mizoram at the Book Launch of Chin
History, Culture and Identity (Aizawl - 2009)

To Lian H. Sakhong
With best wishes,

Dr. Lian H. Sakhong and President George W. Bush (White House Photo, 2008)

ENC Delegation with the First Lady Laura Bush and Congressman Joseph Pitt
at the White House (2007)

PART THREE

CHIN HISTORY AND IDENTITY

TWELVE

Chin National Day: The Celebration of the Right to Exist

This is the speech that I gave as the Chief Guest of Chin National Day in Melbourne, Australia, in 2009. I spoke in Chin, English and Burmese simultaneously. This is the English text, and more or less, the same lines were repeated in Chin and Burmese.

Today, in the midst of our struggle for freedom, we are celebrating the 61st Anniversary of Chin National Day in exile.

A celebration in any sense is for joy and happiness! But, today, our feelings are mixed: joy and happiness with sadness and loneliness. As we celebrate with joy this most auspicious day as the self-evident truth of our existence, our heart is saddened by the fact that we are not able to celebrate our national day in our homeland, which reminds all of us of our reality of living in exile. We are longing for our homeland; we sorely miss the sight and sound of our homeland: the mountains, the hills, the valleys, the rivers, the sun shine, the rain, the flowers and even the smell of the grass there!

But, please remember that those of us who are able to celebrate our national day with song and dance, even in exile, are luckier than our people who remain in our homeland. Please remember that our people are not able to celebrate our national day as "Chin National Day" in Burma. The military regime in Burma has prohibited celebrating the 20th of February as Chin National Day.

By prohibiting the celebration of our national day, they refuse to recognize the existence of the Chin people as a legitimate and a distinct ethnic nationality in Burma.

By denying the celebration of our identity, they refuse to recognize the existence of our homeland, our culture, our history and our ways of life because all of these are part and parcel of our identity which makes us - the Chin - a distinctive people.

By prohibiting the celebration of our national day, the military regime is trying to destroy our identity. Knowing that identity is the soul of the people and the nation: they are trying to kill our soul first, and then they will slowly exterminate our existence. After all, without the soul - how could the body survive?

So, this celebration is nothing but defending our national soul.

By celebrating Chin National Day, we are defending our national identity.

By celebrating Chin National Day, we are defending our right to exist as a people.

So, you can see that the celebration of Chin National Day, even in exile, is part of our struggle for freedom: the celebration for our right to exist as a people. This is part of the struggle for democracy, which is an unfulfilled dream of our forefathers.

As we all know the origin: Chin National Day is the celebration and commemoration of the day that the Chin people chose "democracy" as our national political system. After long debates and deliberations at the first Chin National Assembly in Falam, the then capital of East Chinram, known then as Chin Special Division, on 17-22 February 1948, the Chin people democratically decided and chose "democracy" above our own traditional political system called *Ram-uk*, which in fact was a feudal system. The decision was made on the third day of the conference, the 20th of February, and almost all of the delegates, more than 5,000 leaders of *Ram-uk* themselves, or feudal lords, democratically cast their votes. While the vast majority of delegates voted for democracy, only seventeen delegates cast their votes in favour of the *Ram-uk* system.

This is how we, the Chin people, opted for democracy as our national political system. But, as you all know, the dreams of our fathers are not yet fulfilled. That's why you and I are in exile: fighting for democracy and freedom. So, remember that the celebration of Chin National Day in exile is a combination of defending our identity and fighting for democracy and freedom. And, in this struggle, we are not alone!

For the past sixty years, almost all of the ethnic nationalities in Burma have been fighting for freedom and identity, engaging in one of the longest civil wars in modern time. We have sacrificed so many lives in this on-going civil war, including the most venerable and innocent lives of women and children. It has destroyed countless human and natural resources and disturbed so many generations' livelihoods, especially in ethnic areas. While our villages are demolished, our home are burnt, our farms and fields ruined and our farmers are forced to work as porters in the battle fields instead of tending to their fields. Ordinary villagers are accused of being terrorists and killed; women and girls are raped in order to terrorize the entire community of ethnic minorities. This is what we are fighting against, and this is what we are fighting for! We are fighting to defend ourselves and we are fighting for our survival.

We signed the Panglong Agreement in 1947 in order to form a new multi-national-state of the Union of Burma. We wanted to build —and still want to rebuild—the Union of Burma where many different ethnic groups can live peacefully together. We wanted—and still want—the Union of Burma to be a country where many different language groups can speak their own languages freely yet understand each other; We wanted—and still want—our country as a Union where different religious groups can practice their religious teachings, and worship their own different gods or God, and yet follow and promote the essence of all religions, that is, to love one another and live in peace and harmony!

The essence of the Panglong Agreement is for togetherness yet allows the existence of our differences; it is for coming together but not for absolute integration; it is for unity but not for ethnic assimilation. So, the essence of the Panglong Agreement, or what we call the "Panglong Spirit", can best be summed up as "unity in diversity": the spirit of unity to build the Union of Burma together, but recognize and respect our diversity.

In the notion of "unity in diversity": unity is only a means, not the goal to build a country together. We should also be very careful that "togetherness" is not "sameness". If "unity" is the goal of a nation-state, then this country is heading towards "sameness"; and "sameness" is a very dangerous political ideology, especially in a plural country like the Union of Burma. In a plural society where many different ethnic groups and many different religious groups, each practicing different cultures and speaking different languages, are living side by side: then "sameness" as a political ideology is dangerous because the essence of "sameness" is "intolerance", "coercion", and "forced-assimilation".

It is "intolerance" because "sameness" as a political ideology does not allow the existence of any differences: whether the difference is ethnicity, religion, language or culture. When "sameness" becomes state policy it does not allow the speaking of different languages, especially in official functions, such as those at courts, and schools. It does not allow the practice of different religions and cultures or they become subordinate to the state religion.

When "unity" is adopted as the goal of the state, and where "sameness" is practiced as political ideology, "coercion" becomes an inevitable state policy blended into a state coercive mechanism. Consequently, different ethnic and religious groups are forced to speak the national language adopted by the government, they are forced to practice the faith of the state religion and in certain extreme cases they are forced to convert to the state sponsored religion.

The "sameness" as political ideology is for "forced-assimilation" because the politically dominant ethnic group, who also controls state power, uses state mechanisms as a means to force other ethnic groups, religious groups, cultural and language groups to assimilate into the dominant culture, language, religion, and even ethnicity. This is exactly what has happened in Burma during the past sixty years, and this is what we are fighting against.

We all know that the military regime in Burma is launching a "scorched earth" campaign against ethnic nationalities. The "scorched earth" campaigned started in late 1960s, and after forty years of the campaign, we ethnic nationalities are being pushed to the edge of our survival; thus our survival as distinctive ethnic groups is seriously under threat.

In this "scorched earth" campaign, the military regime is applying the "four-cuts strategy": one: to cut off food supply, two: to cut off information and intelligent, three: to cut off recruitment, and finally: to cut off the funding supply.

In order to cut off the "food supply": the military regime has not only destroyed fields, farms, and barns; they have also refused to construct roads and highways to the ethnic areas so that rice and other food supplies from the delta areas cannot reach ethnic homelands. More than that, they also disturb farmers' lives in various ways, the most common practice being forced-labour for regime projects and as porters when government troops launch military offensive against ethnic groups.

In order to cut "information" off in ethnic areas, successive military regimes in Burma have, since 1966, prohibited the publication of any information in ethnic languages. So, there is no independent newspaper, no independent radio station and no printing house for any ethnic language. This strategy is implemented hand in hand with the government policy of "national language": through which ethnic languages are systematically eliminated. While ethnic languages are systematically destroyed, the national language of *Myanmar-ska*, the dominant Myanmar language, is protected and promoted by using state mechanisms. The regime also forced all non-Myanmar or non-Burman ethnic nationalities to speak the *Myanmar-ska* and forced them to learn the *Myanmar-sa*, which is the only official language in the country.

Another aspect of the four-cuts strategy is to cut off "recruitment" for ethnic resistance armies and groups. Here we face a huge problem! How do you differentiate between ethnic resistance soldier and an ordinary villager? They are all just farmers normally but automatically turn themselves into resistance soldiers when the Burma Army comes and attacks their villages. They are just the defenders of our communities, neither an army nor soldiers in a formal sense.

In ethnic areas, we are all the defenders of our village, our children, our homeland, and our ways of life. As we collectively defend our homeland, we also suffer collective punishment: our homes are demolished, our villages are burnt, our farms and fields are destroyed, and our women and girls are raped. Killing and dying have been part of our life for the past sixty years.

As part of the strategy of cutting off "recruitment": the regime has forced thousands of ethnic villagers to relocate to government army controlled areas, resulting in millions of internally displaced-persons and refugees and migrant workers in neighbouring countries. In this long struggle, we have lost countless lives; and the highest cost of civil war is always human life. The costs are too much already for us and we want to stop it!

The final aspect of the "scorched earth" campaign against ethnic nationalities in Burma is to cut off "financial resources" for ethnic freedom fighters. To cut off funding from ethnic areas, the successive governments of the Union of Burma prevent long term investment in ethnic states and prevent the construction of infrastructure including schools, universities and colleges for higher education, hospitals, highways, roads and bridges. Worst of all, in order to cut off financial sources to ethnic armed groups, the government demonetised twice in late 1987 and early 1988 which eventually led to the student-led popular uprising in 1988.

While the regime was launching its "scorched earth" military campaign as a short-term strategy against ethnic nationalities in the country, they also adopted a long-term strategy to build a "homogenous" country through a so called "nation-building process". In this process of "nation-building", the successive governments of the Union of Burma, which is always dominated and controlled by ethnic Myanmars, have been trying to build an ethnically homogenous "national state" of *Myanmar Naing-ngan* or Myanmar Empire. Here the language of *Myanmar-ska* will be the only official language of the country and Buddhism will be the state religion. As the saying goes '*Buddha-bata Myanmar Lu-myo*' which means "to be a Myanmar is to be a Buddhist".

The unitary process of "nation-building" in Burma has, since independence, been based on the notion of "one religion, one language, and one ethnicity". They started the promulgation of Buddhism as a state religion in 1961, this was followed by declaring *Myanmar-sa* as the only official language of the Union of Burma in 1966. Finally, the current military regime changed our country name from Burma to Myanmar, based simply on the name of ethnic Myanmar in 1989. As we see, in this process of nation-building, they have used religious conversion into Buddhism as a means of cultural and religious forced-assimilation. The national language of *Myanmar-ska* is a means of exterminating other ethnic languages and identities. The ethnicity of Myanmar is a means of total domination through a policy of "sameness" to create an ethnically homogenous country of *Myanmar Naing-ngan*.

In this unitary form of "nation-building" the existence of other ethnic languages, cultures and identities are neglected and unrecognized. Instead, all forms of our identities: religious, cultural, linguistic and ethnic are forced to assimilate into the Myanmar ethnicity. In other words *Myanmar-ska* and Buddhism is used as a state mechanism in the name of "nation-building". Our religion, our language, our culture, and our entire way of life are not protected nor promoted. Our life and our whole existence are assaulted by the very government —the government of the Union of Burma— which we expected to be our protector.

So, what we are fighting in this struggle is not only the enemy that we have been confronting during the past sixty years on the battle fields; it is also the enemy that comes in the name of civil war. The most dangerous enemy that we ethnic nationalities in Burma are facing today is the enemy that kills our souls; that destroys our identities, that assaults our ways of life; and that tries to exterminate our existence. And this dangerous enemy also comes in the name of "nation-building".

Today! By celebrating Chin National Day, we are engaging in the battle for identity - the war for our survival. We are confronting the enemy that is trying to kill our national soul and our identity. We are defending ourselves to prevent the extermination of our existence. This is the celebration of our right to exist. And this is not just a celebration but an act of political defiance. We are declaring to the world that we the Chin people still exist, and under the protection of our everlasting God, we will exist until the end of the world as a people!

May God bless the Chin people and our homeland, Chinram!

THIRTEEN

Chin: History, Culture And Identity

The following speech was given at the book release of 'Chin: History, Culture and Identity' on the 16 November 2009 at Mizoram University, Aizawl.

His Excellency Pu Lal Thanhawla, Chief Minister of Mizoram; Sao Harn Yawnghwe, Executive Director of Euro-Burma Office; Distinguished Guests [I can see at least three MPs from Burma and India on the front row]; Ladies and Gentlemen; and Dear Friends;

This is a great pleasure and honour for me to say a few words of thanks on behalf of the Chin National Council, the Chin Forum, and the Euro-Burma Office (EBO).

Ladies and Gentlemen:

I do not know how history will remember what we are doing here today; I do not know how many words spoken here will be remembered and recorded in history books; but I do hope that one day in the future: people will remember that the children of this homeland, although they were still divided by three international boundaries, come here and gathered together in Aizawl, in the *Mizo hnathlak te innpui*, on the sixteenth of November 2009, in order to find their own origins, to remember their own history, to embrace their culture, and to celebrate their common identity.

We are here to release this book, a result of the International Chin Seminar entitled "Exploring the History, Culture and Identity of the Chin", which was held here in this *Chin Khuapui* in

October 2008. The seminar itself was a milestone for the entire Chin people who are still divided over three countries, namely, India, Burma and Bangladesh. The seminar was attended by more than 150 scholars from around the world, and at least 36 papers were presented, which are all put together and printed in this book, *Chin: History, Culture and Identity.*

I sincerely believe that what we are doing here today is a historic moment for the Chin people because the 2008 Chin Seminar was comparable to other historical landmarks in our history, such as the 1892 Chin-Lushai Conference in Calcutta, and the 1947 Panglong Conference in Shan State, but for different reasons.

The significance of this book's release is what we are celebrating: it is not just the result of an academic venture. This is a celebration of the brotherhood of the children of this homeland.

As I mentioned in my opening speech at last year's seminar, the very purpose of the seminar was searching for our origins, our history, our identity and our culture so that we will be able to call ourselves, to declare ourselves once again as brothers and sisters. No matter which side of international boundaries we happen to live, no matter where we are, we are still brothers and sisters of the same ancestors and we are the children of this homeland.

Our homeland may still be divided and known in many different names: Chinram, Lairam, Zoram, Zogam, Maraland, and Mizoram; and our people may also be known by many different names, such as: Asho, Cho, Khumi, Laimi, Kuki, Zomi, Mizo, and Chin; but we all are the descendent of *Chin-lung* and the brothers and sisters of the same *Chinlung-chuak kan ni ta a*; *Zofate, Mizo hnamte kan ni bawk a*, we all are the same *Lai hri tlai "Chinmi" unau kan si.* We are all the same Chin people.

As we are celebrating this joyful event and historic moment, our joy, our gratitude, and our thankfulness are graced and complimented by the presence of His Excellency Pu Lal Thanhawla, the Chief Minister of Mizoram.

Kapu, your presence at this ceremony for us is like fulfilling our dreams. Your presence makes what we are doing here more meaningful and also legitimizes the fact that we all are the same children of this homeland. I say this because you are the democratically and legitimately elected Chief Minister of Mizoram, elected by our brothers and sisters in *Khua-thlang*. Since we cannot have such democratic elections in *Khua-chak*, you are the only democratically elected leader that we all have in this homeland, so you are like the father to all of us, and you are *Kanpa bik na ni a; Kanpu bik pawh na ni e!*

Secondly, I would like to give a word of thanks to Sao Harn Yawnghwe, Executive Director of the Euro-Burma Office. Sao Harn, welcome to Aizawl, *Chin Khuapui* in *Khua-thlang!* Perhaps you are more familiar with the terms like Chin State in Burma and Mizoram State in India, but for us this is just our homeland with two connotations, *Khua-chak,* and *Khua-thlang*. So, welcome to the *Khua-thlang* side of our homeland.

I sincerely believe that what Harn has done for us, not only the 2008 Chin Seminar, but also the publication of this book, is a landmark in our history. So, at this auspicious moment, I would like to say a few words about what Harn has been doing for us, not only for the Chin but also for all ethnic nationalities in Burma through the Euro-Burma Office, and under the National Reconciliation Program.

In the name of national reconciliation, peace, justice and harmony, the EBO has been organizing a series of seminars for all the ethnic nationalities in Burma. We started with the Arakan Historical Workshop in 2006, which was organized together with the Chulalongkorn University in Bangkok, and in 2007, we organized the Mon Historical Seminar in Bangkok, again with Chulalongkorn University.

As we all know, the International Seminar on Chin History was organized here, together with the Mizoram University. And very recently, in October 2009, we organized another seminar for the Shan in Bangkok, and we do hope that, in the coming years, we will be able to organize similar seminars for the Kachin, Karen and Karenni peoples as well.

We sincerely hope that a series of these seminars will bring peace and harmony, and it will create a better understanding between peoples and also between nations. It will also empower local peoples and ethnic groups so that they will appreciate and be proud of their own culture and identity - the very being of who they are!

We do hope also that a series of these seminars will build a bridge between Burma and our neighbouring countries, a bridge between South East Asia and South Asia, and between South Asia and China. The reason is quite simple. If you look at all these ethnic groups and their homelands, you realize that they all are transcending current international boundaries. The Arakan people are living in both Burma and Bangladesh, we the Chin people are transcending the three international boundaries of Burma, India and Bangladesh, the Kachins do the same: they are living in Burma, India and China; and the Shan are in Burma, India, China, Thailand, Laos and in Vietnam. Again, if we look at the Karen, Karenni and Mon peoples, they also are living on both sides of the boundary of Thailand and Burma.

So, if we approach such ethnic complexities in Burma as a positive contribution to the regions in Asia and even to the international community, ethnic groups in Burma can play an important role as bridge builders of the regions between South and Southeast Asia, and between Burma and its neighbouring countries; and they will all become actors that can contribute to peace and harmony in the region.

Unfortunately, for the past sixty years, it was not the case to be! Ethnic differences were seen as the basis for ethnic conflicts and the on-going civil war, not as the strength of the country and the region. Cultural differences were seen as the root cause of division not as the beauty of a plural society. Religious diversities were exploited for hatred, conflicts and violations. Religions, all religions, should be the foundation for love and tolerance in every human society.

These are the reasons for sixty years of civil war in Burma, which negatively impacts on our neighbouring countries. We send you many thousands of refugees and illegal migrant workers. There is drug trafficking, human trafficking, all kind of diseases and social problems. We do sincerely apologize for all these problems that we are creating for you, including here in Mizoram.

On the other hands, we are so thankful, and deeply appreciative for your understanding and your tolerance to our people. We know, and we admit, that thousands of our people are living illegally here in Mizoram, and they create so many problems for you. Despite all these problems that we create for you, you understand us, and still call us as your brothers from *Khua-chak*. We thank you for that! Kan lawm e; *Pathian in malsawnnak in pek rawh seh!*

The series of these seminars that the EBO has been organizing is a sincere and humble attempt to solve the conflict in Burma through dialogue and through people to people relations, which will eventually create a better understanding and peace and harmony not only in Burma but in the entire region. We sincerely hope that the seminars that we have organized here were helpful for you as well, especially for your 'Look East Policy' and for the regional stability and peace that we all want and desire.

This is what the EBO, under the leadership of our Executive Director Sao Harn Yawnghwe, is trying to achieve though the National Reconciliation Program.

Thirdly, I would like to express our sincere thanks to the Mizoram University, which hosted both our seminar last year and today's function. We are so grateful to all the professors and faculty members and the students at the MZU. Whenever we mention Mizoram University, it will not be complete without mentioning one particular name: Dr. K. Robin. Dr. Robin coordinated the seminar for us last year, and he is still running around all over Aizawl, so that we are all safe and sound during our stay here in Mizoram. Above all, Robin is the one who put all these papers from the seminar together and edited this book.

Robin, I can assure you that the book that you have edited will remain as one of the most reliable sources, even indispensible sources, of the future of Chin study. Thank you for what you have done for us and congratulations for your achievement in editing this magnificent book.

Last, but not least, I would like to thanks also to our Chairperson, Mr. Joseph Lalzarliana, and Mr. Lallianchunga, who present this book review for all of us. We would like to express our sincere thanks to all of you who are here today; and the scholars who contributed their papers for this volume!

Thank you so very much to all of you!

FOURTEEN

Exploring History, Culture and Identity of the Chin

The following is a presentation given on the "Origins of the Chin" at the seminar 'Exploring History, Culture and Identity of the Chin' organized by Mizoram University and the Euro-Burma Office, October 2008.

This is a great opportunity for me to present my paper: "the Origins of the Chin" at this historic seminar. As I mentioned in my remarks at the opening session yesterday, this seminar is a historic event for the Chin people who are still divided over three countries. As a divided people who lost our birth right of self-determination, *exploring our history* in order to find our own origins, to embrace our *culture*, and to celebrate our common *identity* are the most important tasks for the survival of our people and our future generations. I therefore say that this seminar is a historic moment for our people and will remain as a landmark in our history.

Talking about the "Origins of the Chin", of course, is very much about searching for our identity: Who are we? Where do we come from? What makes us Chin a Chin? What are the chief features which distinguish the Chin people as an ethnic nationality from other human collectives or ethnic groups? And which criteria make it possible for us to be recognized as a distinctive people and nationality? Why are we in different countries though we are all still living in the same homeland of our forefathers?

But before I touch upon the topic of my presentation, I would like to request one thing: please bear with me that I am standing before you as an activist and an historian. As an historian, I am engaging in a dialogue between the past and the present; and when I look at the future I look backwards, that is.., I first look backwards in order to look towards the future. And the future that I can see as historian is defined not only by how deep we know our own past but by how well we understand and make use of that past. The future, in any case, is partly conditioned by the past: it is not entirely predictable but equally it is not the outcome of pure chance.

And as an activist, I'm currently engaging in dialogue between the present and the future. But an activist's approach is quite opposite to that of a historian: When I look at the past I first look towards the future. For activists like me, the future is not the end of time but the fullness of time, not the transcending of the world and mankind, but the fulfilment through the world and through mankind, that is., through the fulfilment of human actions. The record of such human actions in the past is what we called "history".

So, as an activist, learning history for me is not just looking into the past but looking forwards to the future in order to see whether there is any opportunity for me to create the present more positively. Victor Hugo once said, "the Future has many names; for the weak it is unattainable, for the fearful it is unknown, for the bold it is opportunity". But without knowing the past and without understanding the present, the future cannot be an opportunity even for the bold. As Herbert Butterfield once stated, "a people that lived without the knowledge of its past - without serious attempt to organize its memory - would hardly be calculated to make much progress in its civilization". A Roman historian Cicero also said, "If you don't know what happened before you were born, you then remain forever a child". As a people, and as a Chin, we don't want to remain forever a child. And that's the reason why we want to re-organize our past memory in order to preserve, protect and promote our identity, our culture and our ways of life so that we would be able to create a vibrant and admirable future for the next generations to come.

The very purpose of this seminar is looking back into the past in order to understand the present and look forwards to the future. As a matter of fact, the Euro-Burma Office has organized a series of historical workshops and seminars for all the ethnic nationalities in Burma under the title of "Knowing the Past and Understanding the Present". We conducted the Arakan Historical Workshop in 2006 and the Mon Historical Workshop in 2007; now is the time for the Chin, and next year we will be organizing a seminar for the Shan in Shih-song-panna in Yunan Province of China. Shih-song-panna, like Aizawl for the Chin, is the largest city of the Shan homeland.

The paper that I present to you is entitled: "Origins of the Chin". Before we look at the "Origins of the Chin", I would like to explain why we need to look at the origins at all, which as you all know is much obscured, this I must also admit. But, by studying the "Origins", we are hoping to know our own past more objectively and understand our present more clearly. My purpose, therefore, is quite simple: by studying the "Origins of the Chin" we hope to better understand what happened to us: Why are we divided by so called international boundaries? Why do we live in different countries yet still in the same homeland? What do these international boundaries mean to us? Why we are known and called by many different names though we are the sons and daughters of the same ancestors? In order to understand what happened to us during the past few centuries, we must look back to our past and try to see the "Origins of the Chin" through the lens that transcends outside intervention in our history and which will hopefully give us a clearer picture of what happened to us.

I must confess that we have very little knowledge about our own history after 1896, and also after 1948. This is not our fault: the reason simply is we did not have the right of self-determination. Until recently, history was mostly written by the people who obtained the right of self-determination, that is, the people who were able to build or re-build their own sovereign nation-state. I think such practices of writing history from above are still the norm here in India and in Burma. In such a case, the writing of history is a national project as part of nation-building process. We have to challenge such an old notion of writing history from above, along with many schools of thought, including "*Annales*" school of historians. History should not be written only by those people who have the right of self-determination, in which the term self-determination is interpreted so narrowly as "sovereignty" or "sovereign state". History can also be written by the people from below, people like us, those who lost the fundamental right of self-determination, while challenging at the same time the very notions of "self-determination" and "nation-state". What I am trying to say is that by writing history from below, we can challenge the very notions of "self-determination" and "nation-state".

My point here is not to talk about the right of "self-determination" and the concept of "nation-state" but try to point out why we do not understand our own history. We don't know who we were before 1896. We don't know what happened to us between 1896 and 1948, and after 1948. We don't know why we are now in different countries although our homeland is still the same as before. Why? I think we should ask the Question of "Why" very boldly. After all, you and me who are here in this room today claim ourselves to be scientists, or at least social scientists, because we ask the question of why? Without asking the question of why, we are neither scientists nor historians: we would merely be collectors of facts. I understand that we are here today not as collectors of facts but as scientists who ask the question WHY?

In order to ask the question "Why": Let me tell you about my own experiences in 1991. It was when I first came here to Aizawl: the *Zo Khuapui*, or now I call the *Chin Khuapui*. After being a while in Aizawl, one evening, my friends and I decided to go to the theatre to watch a movie. But while on the way to Mizoram the police arrested us. I strongly protested my arrest not on legal grounds, after all I was the one who had illegally entered into another sovereign country, but I protested my arrest on the grounds of the term that they used when I was arrested: *"Burma ho!"*. I said, *"Burma ho ka ni lo"*. And they asked, *"Tung nge ani, Burma ttong na ttong miah ko"*. The words that they used *"Burma ttong"* made me more angry, and I said, *"Tung nge ka ni, Khua Chak ka ni mei. Burma ttong ka tong miah lo. Lai ttong ka ttong. Poih tong nan ti mi kha ka ttong."* And I tried to explain to them that Lai dialect is the same as Poih dialect, which is part of the Mizo language. And I told them not to call me *"Burma ho"*, and even challenged them: "If you call me *Burma ho*, I would call you *Vai ho*, or Indian *Kala ho*. But you and I are not *Burma ho* nor *Vai ho*. You and I are just brothers from *Khua Chak* and *Khua Thlang*. Our differences are only *Khua Chak* and *Khua Thlang*, not *Burma ho* and *Vai ho*". But, poor me! My Mizo dialect was not enough to convince the angry police. Luckily, before I was brought into the lock-up, my aunty Kheng Hrang nu, Mrs. Hi Phei, came to my rescue.

That incident in 1991 makes me think to myself: If you and I were born before 1896 when the Chin Hills Regulation was promulgated or even before the First Anglo-Chin War of Annexation in 1872, then there would be no such terminology as *"Burma ho"* to denote your brother from *Khua Chak* like me. Before 1896, there would be no such thing as international boundaries that divide us today as an Indian citizen, a Burmese citizen and a Bangladeshi citizen, and there would be no such immigration laws applicable between brothers and sisters. There would be no such thing as India Standard Time, Burma Standard Time and Bangladesh Standard Time, which divides the same time zone of our homeland into three pieces and makes us different in the ways we manage our time and our lives. Gradually, such simple facts as different time zones lead us into different life styles, different ways of life, and different thought pattern, which eventually would become different traditions, customs and cultures. This is part of the destruction of primordial identity that originally bound us into a distinctive ethnic group with a clearly defined territory and homeland.

Our forefathers in this homeland woke up every morning at Cock crow and when the Sun rose from the East. The Cock still crows at exactly the same time as in our forefather's days, and the Sun also rises the same every morning. But, because of different time zones, while we, your brothers and sisters in the so called "Burma side and Bangladesh part", are more or less wake up at the Cock crow as our forefathers did; you, my brothers and sisters in Mizoram, Manipur and Nagaland are still sleeping, waiting for a new and artificial time that has been given to you by the Government of India from New Delhi. You no longer value the dutiful Cock that crowed at the rising of the Sun. You are still sleeping and looking at your watch, which runs according to the Delhi Government's order. I thought you were Christians who worship the Supreme God, *Pathian,* who created the Sun, the Moon and the Universe but it seems to me that you do not obey Him.

At the opening ceremony of this seminar, students from Mizoram University rendered a beautiful choir for us. If I understood correctly, the song was about the "Second Coming" of Jesus Christ. But the problem for us is that even if Jesus Christ makes an appointment for His Second Coming with us here in Aizawl, we will all miss him because we do not follow God's given time in Mizoram. If Jesus makes an appointment with us at the Sunrise, let's say 6 AM in the morning, we all will miss Him because, my brothers and sisters in *Khua-thlang;* you are still sleeping waiting for an artificial time given to you by the New Delhi's government. You simply disobey God's given Natural Law.

God has given a different time zone for us: the Sun rises at a different time for this homeland, the Cock crows in the morning to wake up the children of God in this homeland. But you simple disobey the Natural Law of God, and you worship the time of New Delhi. By doing this, how many hours do you waste every morning, every day, every week, every year, and in your life time.

I sincerely think that you do this because you don't know that you disobey the Law of God, or maybe you don't ask why you do this. Maybe you never ask the question of "Why" very seriously and scientifically. The question of "Why" is very important here!

If you ask the question of why seriously and claim your right of self-determination, then you should follow the Natural Law which is given to us by God, rather than following an artificial time from New Delhi. After all, in the global era, the world has standardized the Natural Law of God into many different time zones, not necessarily following the boundaries of the so called sovereign nation-states. Simply, Mizoram should have a different Standard Time from New Delhi. If you, my brothers and sisters from *Khua-thlang*, are aware of the fact that God has given us different time zones for this homeland, then you should demand the New Delhi Government through the Mizoram Legislative Assembly to pass a law that declares a Chin Standard Time, or if you so wish, just call it a Mizoram Standard Time. This is what we call practicing the right of self-determination.

Let me tell you one thing. Although we are still in the midst of our struggle: We, your brothers from *Khua-chak*, already exercised our right of self-determination by adopting the Chin Standard Time when we held the First Chin National Assembly at Victoria Camp (on Indo-Burma Border) in 2004. As I said, the right of self-determination should not be narrowly interpreted as a sovereign nation-state because there are many levels of self-determination, especially in federal countries like India. That is the good part of a federal system, a system which we also are advocating for the future of Burma.

Let me go now back to my experience in 1991 and ask myself a few more questions. If you and I were born before 1896, then there would be no such names with suffix "a" for male and "i" for female in this room and in Mizoram. Your name would just be Biak Lian, instead of Biakliana, or if you happened to be a female, your name would just be Dar Duh, not Darduhi. Please look back at our past and you will find that in history records there is no such name with the suffix "a" or "i". This is just a new identifier that was imposed on us by outsiders because they didn't know the beauty of our language and our culture. When the British conducted the first census among the Chin in *Khua-thlang* soon after they occupied our homeland they did not know how to differentiate the genders of our grand-grandparents.

To solve their lack of understanding of the language, they just added the suffix "a" for all the males, and suffix "i" for all the females by applying the gender characteristics of the word for "chicken" in Bengali as in "murka" and "murki". In this way, a chicken's identifier has become our gender identity in Mizoram till this day.

In order to reclaim our identity and declare that we are brothers and sisters from the same ancestors who proclaimed this land as our homeland, *Kan Ram*, by their lives and their destiny, in order to reclaim our homeland, in order to embrace our common identity, and in order to declare that we are brothers and sisters, we have to look back at our past and ask the question of "Why" very boldly.

Asking the question of "Why" in history is very much related with the question of change and continuity: what has change brought to us, like different time zones, international boundaries, and our names with suffix "a" and "i", etc.., etc.., and what still remains with us continuously, such as the Sun still rises, the Cock still crows every morning at exactly the same time, and the bamboo still flowers every fifty years bringing much hardship and hunger to our people and to our homeland all as they did in our forefather's time. We all know that we human beings are very much conscious about change: because everything in the social or natural world is subject to change with the passage of time. It is this process of change that influences our day-to-day behaviour, our ways of life and our thought patterns which then eventually creates our new identity.

Through change, we have created a socially constructed identity, but continuity has allowed us to preserve our primordial identity. If changes occurred on a constant basis and if we didn't realize what had happened to us, then we wouldn't be able to freeze the reality, and we would all become strangers in the midst of our brothers and sisters, yet still living in our homeland. That's what happened to me in 1991, and I do not wish such an incident to happen again to my fellow brothers and sisters from *Khua Chak*, to my children and to my new generations to come; even if we are still living apart as different citizens. That's the reason why I would like to invite you today to look back together into our past in order to see our origins.

In my paper, I argue that our original name was "Chin", by applying ethno-symbolic theory, and defining the Chin people as a "nationality" or "ethnic nationality", and Chinland or Chinram as a "nation", but not as a nation-state, based on all the well-recognized theory that I have just mentioned and also based on the traditional Chin concepts of *Miphun, Ram,* and *Phunglam.* The meaning and concept of *Miphun* is an "ethnicity" or a "people" who believe that they come from a common descent or ancestor. *Ram* is a homeland, a country, or a nation with well-defined territory and claimed by a certain people who have belonged to it historically; and the broad concept of *Phunglam* is "ways of life", which includes almost all cultural and social aspects of life, religious practices, belief and value systems, customary law and political structure, and all kinds of aesthetic aspects of life such as dance, song, and even the customs of feasts and festivals, etc, all the elements in life that bind successive generations of members together as a people and a nationality, and at the same time separate them from others.

Under the subtitle of "The Chin Concept of *Miphun"* in my paper, I try to examine our "Collective Name of Chin", by arguing that the common proper name of the "Chin" is inseparably intertwined with "the myth of common descent" and the "myth of the Origins" of the Chin. According to the myth of the Origins, the Chin people emerged into this world from the bowels of the earth or a cave or a rock called 'Chinlung', which, as we will see below, is spelled slightly differently by different scholars based on various Chin dialects and local traditions, such as 'Chhinlung', 'Chinn-lung', 'Chie'nlung', 'Chinglung', 'Ciinlung', 'Jinlung', 'Sinlung', 'Shinlung', 'Tsinlung', and so on.

The tradition of 'Chinlung' as the Origins of the Chin has been kept by all tribes of the Chin in various ways, such as folksongs, folklore, and legends known in Chin as *Tuanbia.* For a people who had no writing system of their own, a rich oral tradition consisting of folksong and folklore was the most reliable means of transmitting past events and collective memories through time. The songs were sung repeatedly during all kinds of feasts and festivals, and the tales that made up Chin folklore were told and retold over the generations. In this way, such collective memories as the Origins myth and the myth of common ancestors were handed down from one generation to the next. Different tribes and groups of Chin kept the tradition of 'Chinlung' in several versions; and I have cited two songs from the Hmar group of the Mizo tribe, who now live in the Mizoram State of India, which I refer to in this study as West Chinram.

In addition to Folksongs and Folklore, I have also quoted a number of modern scholars, who generally agree with the traditional account of the Origins of the name "Chin" and that the word "Chin" comes from 'Chinlung'. Hrang Nawl, one of the most prominent scholars and politicians among the Chin, confirms that the term "Chin ... come(s) from Ciinlung, Chhinlung or Tsinlung, the cave or the rock where, according to legend, the *Chin* people emerged into this world as humans". Even Vumson could not dispute the tradition that the Chin "were originally from a cave called Chinnlung, which is given different locations by different clans."

The literal meaning of *Chin-lung* is "the cave or the hole of the Chin", and this has the same meaning as the Burmese word for *Chindwin* as in the "Chindwin River", that also is—"the hole of the Chin" or "the river of the Chin". However, the word *Chin-lung* can also be translated as "the cave or the hole where our people originally lived" or "the place from which our ancestors originated". Thus, the word *Chin* without the suffix *lung* is translated simply as "people" or "a community of people". A Chin scholar, Lian Uk, therefore defines the term *Chin* as follows: "The Chin and several of its synonymous names generally means 'People' and the name Chinland is generally translated as 'Our Land' reflecting the strong fundamental relationship they maintain with their land."

Similarly, Carey and Tuck, who were the first to bring the Chin people under the system of British administration, defined the word *Chin* as 'man or people'. They recorded that the term *Chin* is "the Burmese corruption of the Chinese 'Jin' or 'Jen' (pronounce Chin/Cin or Ciang/Chiang) meaning 'man or people'."

Evidently, the word 'Chin' had been used from the very beginning, not only by the Chin themselves but also by their neighbouring peoples, such as Kachin, Shan and Burman, to denote the people who occupied the valley of Chindwin River. While the Kachin and the Shan still called the Chin as "Khyan" or "Khang" or "Khiang" or "Chiang", the Burmese usage seems to have changed dramatically from "Khyan" or "Chiang" (ချင်း) to "Chin" (ချင်း). In a couple of stone inscriptions, erected by King Kyanzittha (1084-1113), the name Chin is spelled as "Khyan" or "Chiang" (ချင်း). As far as historical and linguistic records are concerned, these stone inscriptions are the strongest evidence indicating that the name Chin was in use before the eleventh century AD.

Prior to the British annexation in 1896, there have been at least seventeen written records in English regarding research on what was then called the "Chin-Kuki linguistic people" in the "Chin-Lushai Country". These early writings variously referred to what is now called and spelled, "Chin", as "Khyeng", "Khang", "Khlang", "Khyang", "Khyan", "Kiayn", "Chiang", "Chi'en", "Chien", and so on.

Here I quoted a number of scholars, including Father Sangermono, who lived in Burma as a Catholic missionary from 1783 to 1796 A.D. In his now classical book: *The Burmese Empire*, he spelled the name Chin as "Chien" and the Chin Hills as the "Chien Mountains".

I also quoted Reid (*Chin-Lushai Land*, 1893), C.A. Soppit (*Kuki-Lushai Tribe*, 1893), Shakespeare (*The Lushai-Kuki Clan*, 1912), Snodgrass (*The Burmese War*, 1824-1826, 1826), Sir Author Phayer (*History of Burma*, 1883), and finally, after convincing myself quite well, I concluded by saying that: It was in 1891 that the term "Chin", to be written as "CHIN", was first used by Major W.G. Hughes in his military report, and then by A.G.E. Newland in his book: *The Images of War* in 1894, and the conventional spelling for the name CHIN became legalized as the official term by *The Chin Hills Regulation* in 1896.

In this way, the canonical process of the term CHIN was completed in 1896.

Note: This is a verbal presentation of my paper: "Origins of the Chin" at the "Seminar on Exploring History, Culture and Identity of the Chin", organized by the Department of History and Ethnography, Mizoram University, Aizawl, and sponsored by the Euro-Burma Office in Brussels.

FIFTEEN

The Origin of the Chin

This paper is adapted from the first chapter of 'In Search of Chin Identity' *and presented at the seminar* 'Exploring History, Culture and Identity of the Chin' *organized by Mizoram University and the Euro-Burma Office, October 2008. The paper was published as chapter two* 'Chin: History, Culture and Identity' *edited by K Robin, Mizoram University, 2009*

Introduction

As the title indicates, this paper is a brief attempt to investigate the origin of the Chin by applying ethno-symbolic theory of ethnicity. In so doing, attention will be given to such simple questions as "Who are the Chins?" and "Why can they be described as an ethnic group? At the same time, this paper will try to answer the questions of "What makes a Chin a Chin?", "What are the chief features which distinguish the Chin people as an ethnic nationality from other human collectives or ethnic groups?" and "Which criteria makes it possible for them to be recognized as a distinctive people and nationality?" Ethno-symbolic theorists, such as A. D. Smith, suggest that there are six main features, which serve to define "ethnic nationality". These are: (i) a common proper name, (ii) a myth of common descent, (iii) a link with a homeland, (iv) collective historical memories, (v) one or more elements of common culture, and (vi) a sense of solidarity.[1]

In my previous study,[2] I have defined the Chin people as a "nationality" or "ethnic nationality", and Chinland or Chinram[3] as a "nation", but not as a nation-state, based on all the well-recognized theory that I have just mentioned, and also based on the traditional Chin concepts of *Miphun, Ram,* and *Phunglam.* The meaning and concept of *Miphun* is an "ethnicity" or a "people" who believe that they come from a common descent or ancestor. *Ram* is a homeland, a country, or a nation with well-defined territory and claimed by a certain people who have belonged to it historically; and the broad concept of *Phunglam* is "ways of life", which includes almost all cultural and social aspects of life, religious practices, belief and value systems, customary law and political structure, and all kinds of aesthetic aspects of life such as dance, song, and even the customs of feasts and festivals, etc, all the elements in life that "bind successive generations of members together" as a people and a nationality, and at the same time separate them from others.

I shall, however, in this paper limit myself within the first four features of ethnicity, which correspond to what is contained in the traditional Chin concepts of *Miphun* and *Ram. Miphun* involves the common name and the myth of common descent, and *Ram* covers what is involved in the concept of a common homeland and collective historical memories.

The Chin Concept of *Miphun*

A Collective Name

The common proper name of the "Chin" is inseparably intertwined with "the myth of common descent" and the "myth of the origin" of the Chin. According to the myth of the origin, the Chin people emerged into this world from the bowels of the earth or a cave or a rock called 'Chinlung',[4] which, as we will see below, is spelled slightly differently by different scholars based on various Chin dialects and local traditions, such as 'Chhinlung', 'Chinn-lung', 'Chie'nlung', 'Chinglung', 'Ciinlung', 'Jinlung', 'Sinlung', 'Shinlung', 'Tsinlung', and so on.

The tradition of 'Chinlung' as the origin of the Chin has been kept by all tribes of the Chin in various ways, such as folksongs, folklore, and legends known in Chin as *Tuanbia.* For the people who had no writing system of their own, a rich oral tradition consisting of folksong and folklore was the most reliable means of transmitting past events and collective memories through time. The songs were sung repeatedly during all kinds of feasts and festivals, and the tales that made up Chin folklore were told and retold over the generations. In this way, such collective memories as the origin myth and the myth of common ancestors were handed down from one generation to the next. Different tribes and groups of Chin kept the tradition of 'Chinlung' in several versions; the Hmar group of the Mizo tribe, who now live in the Mizoram State of India, which I refer in this study as West Chinram, have a traditional folk song, the lyrics of which follow:

> *Kan Seingna Sinlung* [Chinlung] *ram hmingthang*
> *Ka nu ram ka pa ram ngai*
> *Chawngzil ang Kokir thei changsien*
> *Ka nu ram ka pa ngai.*

In English it translates as: "Famous Sinlung [Chinlung]is my motherland and the home of my ancestors. It could be called back like chawngzil, the home of my ancestors."[5]

This folksong also describes that the Chins were driven out of their original homeland, called 'Chinglung'. Another folksong, which was traditionally sung at the *Khuahrum* sacrificial ceremony and other important occasions, reads as follows:

> My Chinland of old,
> My grandfather's land Himalei,
> My grandfather's way excels,
> *Chinlung's* way excels.[6]

Modern scholars generally agree with the traditional account of the origin of the name "Chin" and that the word comes from 'Chinlung'. Hrang Nawl, one of the most prominent scholars and politicians among the Chin, confirms that the term "Chin ... come(s) from Ciinlung, Chhinlung or Tsinlung, the cave or the rock where, according to legend, the *Chin* people emerged into this world as humans."[7] Even Vumson could not dispute the tradition that the Chin "were originally from a cave called Chinnlung, which is given different locations by different clans."[8]

In addition to individual scholars and researchers, many of the political and other organizations of the Chin accepted the Chinlung tradition not as a myth but as an historical fact. The Paite National Council, which was formed by the Chin people of the Manipur and Mizoram States, claimed Chinlung as the origin of the Chin people in the memorandum they submitted to the Prime Minister of India. The memorandum stated, "The traditional memory claimed that their remote original place was a cave in China where, for fear of enemies, they hid themselves, which is interpreted in different dialects as 'Sinlung' [Chinlung] in Hmar and Khul in Paite and others."[9] In this memorandum, they suggested that the Government of India "will take initiative as to group all Chin people inhabiting the Indo-Burma border areas within one country as specified and justified herein for the safe-guarding of their economic, social, political rights, etc."[10]

Other significant organizations that accepted the Chinlung tradition of the origin of the Chin as an historical fact include the Christian Evangelical Groups in Mizoram State of India. This produced a popular Gospel song that has, for all intents and purposes, become almost like a *Chin national anthem* on both sides of the Indo-Burmese border. The song recognized 'Chinlung' as the original homeland of the Chin, the verses are:

1. Unau te u in dam tlang lo maw?
    Rinumna chibai in dawng thin em?
    CHINLUNG chung zoram chevela mi te,
    Insuih khawm leh zai i rel ang uh.

Cho:

   Aw, thang leh fa te'n engnge kan ti tak ang le!
   Kan chanvo kan ngil neihna kong chu,
   Thawk chuak tur in engnge kan ti tak ang le!
   Insuih khawm leh zai i rel ang u.

2. Unau te u, han dawn ngun ve te u,
    Khuavel unau hmandang hriat tir zel in,
    Kan nih na chung Pathian lo rel ruat sa ang khan,
    Insuih khawm leh zai i rel ang u!

The plain translation is:

1. Brothers and sisters! Are you all in good health?
    Shall we speak to each other in trust?
    Yes, we all are the descendents of CHINLUNG,
    We are the children of our fatherland,
    Let us prepare for our re-unification.

Cho:

> Youth! What are your plans?
> Shall we call upon our responsibilities?
> Let us prepare for our re-unification!

2. Brothers and sisters! Let us think carefully,
    For the people surrounded us to understand,
    Like God has already planned,
    Let us prepare for our re-unification.

The literal meaning of *Chin-lung* is "the cave or the hole of the Chin", and this has the same meaning as the Burmese word for *Chindwin* as in the "Chindwin River", that also is—"the hole of the Chin" or "the river of the Chin."[11] However, the word *Chin-lung* can also be translated as "the cave or the hole where our people originally lived" or "the place from which our ancestors originated."[12] Thus, the word *Chin* without the suffix *lung* is translated simply as "people" or "a community of people."[13] A Chin scholar, Lian Uk, therefore defines the term *Chin* as follows:

> The Chin and several of its synonymous names generally means 'People' and the name Chinland is generally translated as 'Our Land' reflecting the strong fundamental relationship they maintain with their land.[14]

Similarly, Carey and Tuck, who were the first to bring the Chin people under the system of British administration, defined the word *Chin* as 'man or people'. They recorded that the term *Chin* is "the Burmese corruption of the Chinese 'Jin' or 'Jen' meaning 'man or people'."[15]

Evidently, the word 'Chin' had been used from the very beginning not only by the Chin themselves but also by their neighboring peoples, such as Kachin, Shan and Burman, to denote the people who occupied the valley of Chindwin River. While the Kachin and the Shan still called the Chin as "Khyan" or "Khiang" or "Chiang", the Burmese usage seems to have changed dramatically from "Khyan" or "Chiang" (ချင်း) to "Chin" (ချင်း).[16] In a couple of stone inscriptions, erected by King Kyanzittha (1084-1113), the name Chin is spelled as "Khyan" or "Chiang" (ချင်း).[17] As far as historical and linguistic records are concerned, these stone inscriptions are the strongest evidence indicating that the name *Chin* was in use before the eleventh century AD.

Prior to the British annexation in 1896, there have been at least seventeen written records in English regarding research on what was then called the "Chin-Kuki linguistic people". These early writings variously referred to what is now called and spelled, "Chin", as "Khyeng", "Khang", "Khlang", "Khyang", "Khyan", "Kiayn", "Chiang", "Chi'en", "Chien", and so on. One of the earliest Western writers to note the existence of the hill tribes of Chin in the western mountains of Burma was Father Sangermono, who lived in Burma as a Catholic missionary from 1783 to 1796 A.D. In his now classical book: *The Burmese Empire*, published one hundred years after his death, in 1833, he spelled the name Chin as "Chien" and the Chin Hills as the "Chein Mountains". He thus recorded:

> To the east of Chein Mountain between 20"30' and 21"30' latitude is a petty nation called 'Jo' (Yaw). They are supposed to have been Chien, who in the progress of time, have become Burmanized, speaking their language, although corruptly, and adopting their customs.[18]

In Assam and Bengal, the Chin tribes—particularly the Zomi tribe who are living close to that area—were known as "Kuki". The Bengali word for *Kuki* means "hill-people or highlanders", which was, as Reid described in 1893:

> ...Originally applied to the tribe or tribes occupying the tracks immediately to the south of Cachar. It is now employed in a comprehensive sense, to indicate those living to the west of the Kaladyne River, while to the

west they are designated as Shendus. On the other hand, to anyone approaching them from Burma side, the Shendus would be known as Chiang, synonymous with Khyen, and pronounced as 'Chin'.[19]

The designation of Kuki was seldom used by the Chin people themselves, not even by the Zomi tribe in what is now the Manipur State of India, for whom the word is intended. Soppit, who was Assistant Commissioner of Burma and later Sub-Divisional Officer in the North Cacher Hills, Assam, remarked in 1893 in his study of *Lushai-Kuki*:

> The designation of Kuki is never used by the tribes themselves, though many of them answer to it when addressed, knowing it to be the Bengali term for their people.[20]

Lt. Col. J Shakespeare, who was one of the authorities on the Chin, said in 1912 that:

> The term Kuki has come to have a fairly definite meaning, and we now understand by it certain ... clans, with well marked characteristics, belonging to the Tibeto-Burman stock. On the Chittagong border, the term is loosely applied to most of the inhabitants of the interior hills beyond the Chittagong Hills Tracks; in the Cachar it generally means some families of the Thado and Khuathlang clans, locally distinguished as new Kuki and old Kuki. Now-a-days, the term is hardly employed, having been superseded by Lushai in the Chin Hills, and generally on the Burma border all these clans are called Chin. These Kuki are more closely allied to the Chakmas, and the Lushai are more closely to their eastern neighbours who are known as Chin.

And he concluded, by writing:

> Nevertheless, there is no doubt that the Kukis, Lushais and Chins are all of the same race.[21]

In 1826, almost one hundred years before Shakespear published his book, Major Snodgrass, who contacted the Chin people from the Burma side, had already confirmed that Kukis and Lushai are of the Chin nation, but he spelled Chin as Kiayn. He also mentioned Chinram as "Independent Kiayn Country,"[22] in his *The Burmese War,* in which he described a detailed account of the First Anglo-Burmese War in 1824-26. Sir Author Phayer still spelt Chindwin as "Khyendweng" in his *History of Burma,* first published in 1883.[23] It was in 1891 that the term "Chin", to be written as "CHIN", was first used by Major W.G. Hughes in his military report, and then by A.G.E. Newland in his book: *The Images of War,*[24] and the conventional spelling for the name became legalized as the official term by *The Chin Hills Regulation* in 1896.

The Myth of Common Descent

Traditional accounts of the origin of the Chin people, of course, have been obscured by myths and mythologies. In fact, myths and mythologies—together with symbols, values and other collective memories—are important elements of what Clifford Geertz called "primordial identities" which so often define and differentiate the Chin as a distinctive people and nationality throughout history.[25] As noted already, one such myth was the traditional account that had been handed down through generations describing how the Chin "came out of the bowels of the earth or a cave called Chin-lung or Cin-lung."[26] According to some it was located somewhere in China,[27] others claimed it to be in Tibet,[28] and some suggested that it must be somewhere in the Chindwin Valley since the literal meaning of Chindwin is "the cave or the hole of the Chin."[29] I shall come back to the debate on the location of 'Chinlung', but here I shall concentrate only on the traditional account of the origin of the Chin.

Almost all of the Chin tribes and clans have promulgated similar but slightly different versions of the myth, which brings the ancestors of the Chin out from the hole or the bowels of earth. The Ralte clan/group of the Mizo tribe, also known as the Lushai, who are now living in the Mizoram State in India, have had a tradition of what is now generally known as 'Chinlung tradition', that brings their progenitors from the bowels of the earth. The story was translated into English and recorded by Shakespeare in 1912 as follows:

> [Once upon a time when the great darkness called *Thimzing* fell upon the world,] many awful things happened. Everything except the skulls of animals killed in the chase became alive, dry wood revived, even stones become alive and produced leaves, so men had nothing to burn. The successful hunters who had accumulated large stocks of trophies of their skill were able to live using them as fuel.
>
> After this terrible catastrophe, *Thimzing*, the world was again re-peopled by men and women issuing from the hole of the earth called 'Chhinlung'.[30]

Shakespeare described another similar story:

> The place whence all people sprang is called 'Chinglung'. All the clans came out of that place. The two Ralte came out together, and began at once chattering, and this made Pathian (*The Supreme God*) think there were too many men, and so he shut down the stone.[31]

Another very similar story of the origin of the Chin, which is also connected with the Chinlung tradition, as handed down among the Mara group of the Laimi tribe—also known as the Lakher—was recorded by N. E. Parry in 1932:

> Long ago, before the great darkness called *Khazanghra* fell upon the world, men all came out of the hole below the earth. As the founder of each Mara group came out of the earth he called his name. Tlongsai called out, "I am Tlongsai"; Zeuhnang called out, "I am Zeuhnang"; Hawthai called out, "I am Hawthai"; Sabeu called out, "I am Sabeu"; Heima called out, "I am Heima." Accordingly God thought that a very large number of Mara had come out and stopped the way. When the Lushai came out of the hole, however, only the first one to come out called out, "I am Lushai", and all the rest came out silently. God, only hearing one man announce his arrival, thought that

only one Lushai had come out, and gave them a much longer time, during which Lushais were pouring out of the hole silently in great numbers. It is for this reason that Lushais to this day are more numerous than Maras. After all men had come out of the hole in the earth God made their languages different, and they remain so to this day.[32]

All sources of Chin traditions maintain that their ancestors originated from 'Chinlung' or 'Cin-lung'. Sometimes the name for 'Chinlung' or 'Cin-lung' can be different, depending on the specific Chin dialect—such as Khul, Khur, and Lung-kua, etc.— but it always means 'cave' or 'hole' no matter what the dialect. The reason Chin-lung was abandoned, however, varies from one source to another. Depending very much on the dialect and local traditions, some said that Chin-lung was abandoned as a result of an adventure, or because of the great darkness called *Khazanghra, Thimzing* or *Chunmui*. In contrast to the stories above, some traditions maintain that their original settlement was destroyed by the flood. The Laimi tribe from the Haka and Thlantlang areas had a very well-known myth called *Ngun Nu Tuanbia*, which related the destruction of human life on Earth by the flood. The Zophei also had their own version of the story about the flood called *Tuirang-aa-pia* (literal meaning: "white water/river is pouring out or gushing"), which destroyed their original settlement. The story goes as follows:

Once upon a time, all the humankind in this world lived together in one village. In the middle of the village there was a huge stone, and underneath the stone was a cave that in turn was connected with the endless sea of water called *Tipi-thuam-thum*. In this cave dwelt a very large snake called *Pari-bui* or *Limpi,* which seized one of the village children every night and ate them. The villagers were in despair at the depredations committed by the snake, so they made a strong hook, tied it on the rope, impaled a dog on the hook and threw it to the snake, which swallowed the dog and with it the fish hook. The villagers then tried to pull out the snake, but with all their efforts they could not do so, and only succeeded in pulling out enough of the snake to go five times round the rock at the mouth of the hole, and then, as they could not pull out any more of the snake, they cut off the part that they pulled out, and the snake's tail and the rest of the body fell back into the deep cave with a fearful noise. From that night water came pouring out of the snake's hole and covered the whole village and destroyed the original settlement of mankind. Since then people were scattered to every corner of the world and began to speak different languages. And, it was this flood, which drove the ancestors of the Chin proper to take refuge in the Chin Hills.[33]

It is interesting to note that many of the Chin tribes called the Chindwin River, the "White River", that is in Chin—*Tui-rang, Tuikhang, Tirang, or Tuipui-ia*, etc; all have the same meaning but differ only in term of dialect. Thus, modern historians, not least Hutton, Sing Kho Khai and Gangte, believe that what the traditional account had remembered about the flood story, which destroyed the Chin's original settlement might be the flood of the Chindwin River, and they therefore claim that the Chin's original settlement was in the Chindwin Valley and nowhere else.

The Chin Concept of *Ram*

In traditional Chin thought, *Miphun* cannot exist without *Ram*. They therefore define themselves as a *Miphun* with the strong reference to *Ram*, that is—the original homeland, a particular locus and territory, which they all collectively claim to be their own. At the same time, they identify members of a community as "being from the same original homeland."[34] The inner link between the concepts of *Miphun* and *Ram* was strengthened in Chin society through the worship of *Khuahrum* at *Tual* ground. As Anthony Smith convincingly argues, "Each homeland posses a center or centers that are deemed to be 'sacred' in a religio-ethnic sense."[35] In Chin society, the *Tual* ground where the guardian god *Khuahrum* worshipped, were the sacred centers which stood as protectors of both men and land.

For the Chin people, the concept of *ram,* or what Anthony Smith calls the "ethnic homeland", refers not only to the territory in which they are residing, i.e. present Chinram, but also the 'original homeland' where their ancestors once lived as a people and a community. What matters most in terms of their association with the original homeland is that "it has a symbolic geographical center, a sacred habitat, a 'homeland', to which the people may symbolically return, even when its members are scattered...and have lost their [physical] homeland centuries ago."[36] Ethnicity does not cease to be ethnicity simply because of the fact that the Chin were expelled from their original homeland, or because they are artificially divided into different countries, "for ethnicity is a matter of myths, memories, values and symbols, and not material possessions or political powers, both of which require a habitat for their realization."[37] Thus, the Chin concept of *ram* as the meaning of the 'territory' and 'original homeland' are relevant to *miphun.* The relevance of the 'original homeland' is:

> Not only because of it is actually possessed, but also because of an alleged and felt symbiosis between a certain piece of earth and 'its' community. Again, poetic and symbolic qualities possess greater potency than everyday attributes; a land of dream is far more significant than any actual terrain.[38]

I shall therefore trace the history of the Chin's settlements, i.e. not only in present Chinram but also in their original 'homeland' in the Chindwin Valley, in the following sections.

Migration Patterns

As highlighted already in previous sections, all sources of the Chin tradition maintain that the ancestors of the Chin people originated from the cave called 'Chinlung'. However, in the absence of written documents, it is difficult to locate the exact place where Chinlung existed. Scholars and researchers therefore give various opinions as to the location of Chinlung.

K. Zawla, a Mizo historian from the India side of Chinram, or West Chinram, suggests that the location of Chinlung might be somewhere in modern China, and the "Ralte group [of the Mizo tribe] were probably one the first groups to depart from Chinlung."[39] Here, Zawla quoted Shakespeare and accepted the Chin legend as historical fact. He also claimed that the Chin came out of Chinlung in about 225 B.C., during the reign of Shih Hungti, whose cruelty was then at its height at the time he constructed the Great Wall of China. Zawla relates the story of the Ch'ing ruling dynasty in Chinese history in a fascinating manner. He uses local legends known as *Tuanbia* (literally: "stories or events from the old-days") and many stories which are recorded by early travelers and British administrators in Chinram, as well as modern historical research on ancient China. Naturally, this kind of compound story-telling has little or no value in a historical sense, but is nevertheless important in terms of socially reconstructing collective memories as identity-creating-resources.

A number of other theories have been advanced in this connection, more noticeably by Sing Kho Khai and Chawn Kio.[40] Both of them believe that the Chin ancestors are either the Ch'ing or Ch'iang in Chinese history, which are "old generic designations for the non-Chinese tribes of the Kansu-Tibetan frontier, and indicate the Ch'iang as a shepherd people, the Ch'ing as a jungle people."[41] Thus, according to Chinese history, both the Ch'iang and Ch'ing were regarded as "barbarian tribes."[42] Gin Za Tuang—in a slightly different manner than Zawla, Sing Kho Khai, and Chawn Kio—claims that the location of 'Chinlung' was believed to be in Tibet.[43] Gin Za Tuang, nevertheless, maintains that the Chin ancestors were Ch'iang, but he mentions nothing about the Ch'ing.

In fact, Gin Za Thang simply follows Than Tun's and G H Luce's theory of the origin of Tibeto-Burmans and other groups of humans, who were believed to be the ancestors of the Southeast Asian peoples. According to Professors Than Tun and Gordon Luce,[44] the Ch'iang were not just the ancestors of the Chin but of the entire Tibeto-Burman group, and they "enjoyed a civilization as advanced as the Chinese, who disturbed them so much that they moved south."[45] Regarding this, Professor Gordon Luce says:

With the expansion of China, the Ch'iang had either the choice to be absorbed or to become nomads in the wilds. It was a hard choice, between liberty and civilization. Your ancestors chose liberty; and they must have gallantly maintained it. But the cost was heavy. It cost them 2000 years of progress. If the Ch'iang of 3000 BC were equals of the Chinese civilization, the Burmans [and the Chin] of 700 AD were not nearly as advanced as the Chinese in 1300 BC.[46]

Before they moved to the wilderness, along the edges of western China and eastern Tibet, the ancient homelands of Ch'iang and all other Tibeto-Burman groups, according to Enriquez, lied somewhere in the Northwest, possibly in Kansu, between Gobi and northwestern Tibet.[47] Thus, it is now generally believed that the Tibeto-Burman group and other Mongoloid stock, who now occupy Southeast Asia and Northeast India, migrated in three waves in the following chronological order:

1. The Mon-Khmer (Talaing, Palaung, En Raing, Pa-o, Khasi, Annimite.)
2. The Tibeto-Burman (Pyu, Kanzan, Thet, Burman, Chin, Kachin, Naga, Lolo.)
3. The Tai-Chinese (Shan, Saimese, and Karen.)

The Tibeto-Burman group initially moved toward the West and thereafter subdivided themselves into several groups. They follow different routes, one group reaching northern Tibet, where some of them stayed behind, while others moved on until they reached Burma in three waves. These people were:

1. The Chin-Kachin-Naga group
2. The Burman and Old-Burman (Pyu, Kanzan, Thet) group
3. The Lolo group.[48]

This migration pattern theory is, as mentioned above, has mainly been adopted by historians like Than Tun and Gordon Luce. However, anthropologists like Edmund Leach believe that "the hypothesis that the Southeast Asian peoples as known today immigrated from the region of China is a pure myth."[49]

The main difference between the historical approach and the anthropological approach is that while historians begin their historical reconstruction with the origins and immigration of the ancestors, anthropologists start with "the development within the general region of Burma of symbiotic socio-cultural systems: civilizations and hill societies."[50]

However, both historians and anthropologists agree—as historical linguistics, archaeology, and racial relationship definitely indicate—that the ancestors of these various peoples did indeed come from the North. But, anthropologists maintain their argument by saying that, "they did not come as the social and cultural units we know today and cannot be identified with any particular groups of today."[51] Their main thesis is that the hill peoples and plain peoples are now defined by their mutual relationships in present sites, because, for anthropologists, ethnicity was constructed within the realm of social interaction between neighboring reference groups.

The anthropological approach could be very helpful, especially when we investigate the pre-historical context of the Chin people where no written documents recorded by the people themselves exist. Thus, based on ethnic and linguistic differentiation, not on a written document, Lehman was able to demonstrate that "the ancestors of the Chin and the Burman must have been distinct from each other even before they first appeared in Burma."[52] And he continues:

> Undoubtedly, these various ancestral groups were descended in part from groups immigrating into present Burma, starting about the beginning of Christian era. But it is also probable that some of these groups were in Burma in the remote past, long before a date indicated by any present historical evidence. We are not justified, however, in attaching more than linguistic significance to the terms 'Chin' and 'Burman' at such dates.

And he concludes, by saying:

> Chin history begins after A.D. 750, with the development of Burman civilization and Chin interaction with it.[53]

Chin anthropologists like T. S. Gangte seem eager to agree
with Leach and Lehman. Like Leach and Lehman, Gangte rejects
hypothetical theories proposed by Zawla and Gin Za Tuang, who
locate 'Chinlung' somewhere in China and Tibet, respectively,
as myths. "In the absence of any written corroboration or the
existence of historical evidence to support them," he said,
"such hypothetical theories are considered highly subjective
and conjectural. They are, therefore, taken with a pinch of salt.
They remain only as legends."[54] He nevertheless accepted the
'Chinlung' tradition as the origin of the Chin and even claims
that the Chindwin Valley is where Chin history begins. Similar
to Gangte, the "Khuangsai source of Chin tradition mentions
that the location of *Chin-lung* was somewhere in the Chindwin
area."[55]

The Chin's Homeland of Chindwin

Professor Than Tun claims that Tibeto-Burman groups of the
Burman came down into present Burma via the Salween and
Nmai'kha Valleys, and reached the northern Shan State before
AD 713. But before they were able to settle themselves in the
delta area of Irrawady Valley, "the rise of Nanchao checked their
movements soon after 713."[56] The Nanchao made continuous
war with neighboring powers such as the Pyu who had founded
the Halin Kingdom in central Burma. In 835 the Nanchao
plundered the delta areas of Burma, and in 863 they went
further east to Hanoi. However, by the end of the ninth century
the Nanchao power collapsed, because according to Than Tun
"they had exhausted themselves."[57] Only after the collapse of
the Nanchao, were the Burman able to move further South into
the plains of Burma.

The Chin, according to Professor Luce, descended from
western China and eastern Tibet into the South via the Hukong
Valley,[58] which is a completely different route than the Burman
had taken. Thus, Lehman's theory is quite convincing that the
ancestors of the Chin and the Burman were distinct from each
other even when they first appeared in Burma. There is ample
evidence that the Chin were the first who settled in the Chindwin

Valley. The Pagan inscriptions dating from the eleventh century onward refer to the Chin of the Chindwin Valley. There is also persistent reference in the legends of almost all the Chin tribes to a former home in the Chindwin Valley. Chin original myths uniformly refer to the ruling lineage when speaking of the original homeland in the valley.[59] Archeological evidence supports this interpretation.[60] Sing Kho Khai therefore claims that:

> The literal meaning of the name 'Chindwin' definitely suggests that the Chindwin area was primarily inhabited by a tribe called the Chin.[61]

Vumson goes even further by saying:

> When the Burman descended to the plains of central Burma, during the ninth century, the [*Chin*] people were already in the Chindwin Valley.[62]

As far as historical evidence of the Chin settlement in the Chindwin Valley is concerned, some of the most reliable sources come from the Burman inscriptions erected by King Kyanzzittha and other kings during the peak of the Pagan dynasty. According to Professor Luce, who was a expert on Pagan inscription, "Chins and Chindwin ['Hole or Cave of the Chins'] are mentioned in Pagan inscriptions from the thirteenth century."[63] The earliest Pagan inscriptions put the Burman in upper Burma in roughly the middle of the ninth century A.D. Professor Luce therefore suggested that the Chin settlement in the Chindwin Valley began in the middle of the eighth century, while allowing for the possibility of a date as far back as the fourth century AD. Lalthanglian, a Mizo historian, also gives the eighth century A.D. as the possible date for the Chin settlement in the Chindwin Valley.[64]

Before the Chin made their settlement in the Chindwin Valley, there had been kingdoms of the Mon and the Pyu in the major river valley of Burma, the Sak or Thet and Kandu in Upper Burma, and also the Shan in the eastern country, but no one occupied the Chindwin Valley until the Chin made their home there. The Burman fought against the other occupants of the area, such as Thet, Mon and Pyu, but they did not fight the Chin. G. H. Luce writes;

> The Pagan Burman had wars with the Thets (Sak), the Kandu (Kantú), the Mons, the Shans and the Wa-Palaungs, but he called the Chins 'friends'. Moreover, while he pushed far up the Yaw, the Mu and the Irawaddy, he apparently did not go up the Chindwin. I cannot identify any old place of the Chindwin much further north than Monywa. From all this I infer that in the Pagan period the home of the Chin was mainly in the Chindwin Valley above Monyaw.[65]

In his major writing: "Old Kyakse and the Coming of the Burmans", Professor Luce also mentioned the Chin settlement in Chindwin and their relation with the Burman as follows:

> If the Chins had joined the Thet peoples in opposing the Burmans, the latters' conquest of the central plains might have been precarious. But the Thets probably hated the Chins, whose descent from the Hukong Valley had cut off their western tribes in Manipur, and overwhelmed their tenure of Chindwin. Burman strategy here was to conciliate the Chins. They advanced up the Lower Chindwin only as far as Monywa and Alone, called the Chins *Khyan*, "friends", and seem to have agreed to leave them free to occupy the whole Upper Chindwin Valley. There is no mention of any fighting between the Chins and the Burmans; and whereas the Pagan Burmans soon occupied the *M'u* Valley at least as far as *Mliytú* (Myedu) and the *Khaksan*, *Yaw* and *Krow* Valleys as far as the *Púnton* (Póndaung) Range and perhaps *Thilin*, I know of no place up the Chindwin much beyond *Munrwa* (Monywa) and the *Pankli 10 tuik* (ten 'taik' of Bagyi), mentioned in Old Burmese. [66]

Based on the Burman inscriptions of the Pagan Kingdom, which refer to the Chin as comrades and allies in the Chindwin Valley, Prof. G. Luce even suggested that the word "Chin" might come from the Burmese word *Thu-nge-chin* "friend". But this is very unlikely, because the word Chin had already been very well-recognized not only by the Burman but also by other peoples such as Kachin and Shan, even before the Chin made their settlement in the Chindwin Valley. The Kachin, for instance, who never came down to the Chindwin Valley but remained in the upper Hukong Valley and present Kachin Hills, called the Chin *Khiang or Chiang*. So did the Shan. Thus, it is very obvious that the term "Chin" had been used to denote the Chin people long before the Chindwin Valley became the homeland of the Chin. And the term Chindwin comes from the 'Chin' as in "the hole of the Chin" or "the river of the Chin", but not the other way around.

Collective Memories of Chindwin

Over the course of time, the Chin people moved up from the eastern bank of the Chindwin River to the Upper Chindwin of the Kale Valley. Although we do not know exactly when and why, the date can be set approximately to the final years of the thirteenth century or the beginning of the fourteenth century. Until the fall of the Pagan dynasty in 1295, the Pagan inscriptions continuously mentioned that the Chins were in between the eastern bank of the Upper Chindwin and west of the Irrawaddy River. Thus, it can be assumed that the Chin settlement in the Kale Valley began just before the end of thirteenth century A.D. The reason is equally unknown. Perhaps the flood destroyed their settlement as oral traditions remembered it; or as Luce has suggested, "the Chin were left to themselves in Upper Chindwin."[67] As far as linguistic evidence is concerned, traditional accounts of the flood story seem more reasonable than Professor Luce's suggestion. The traditional Chin account from the Zophei group of the Laimi tribe has recounted the fact that the flood from the low valley had driven their ancestors to the mountains on other side of the river, that is, in Chin, *Khatlei, Khalei or Khale*. Thus, it is believed that the root word of Kale is *Khalei*, and the meaning, of course, is the "other side of the river."[68]

After their original settlement in the Chindwin Valley was destroyed by the flood, according to the traditional account, the

Chin moved over to Upper Chindwin, and some groups such as the Asho went as far as the Pandaung Hills and other hills near the western part of the Chindwin River. Since then the Chin people have been broken into different tribes and speak different dialects. Many different myths and legends exist that explain why they broke into distinct tribes and speak different dialects. One such story is recorded by B. S. Carey and N. N. Tuck:

> They [the Chin] became very powerful and finding no more enemies on earth, they proposed to pass their time capturing the Sun. They therefore set about a sort of Jacob's ladder with poles, and gradually mounted them higher and higher from the earth and nearer to their goal, the Sun. However, the work became tedious; they quarreled among themselves, and one day, when half of the people were climbing high up on the pole, all eager to seize the Sun, the other half below cut it down. It fell down northwards, dashing the people beyond the Run River on the Kale border and the present site of Torrzam. These people were not damaged by the fall, but suddenly struck with confusion of tongues, they were unable to communicate with each other and did not know the way home again. Thus, they broke into distinct tribes and spoke different languages.[69]

Another story from the Zophei area, also known as the leather book, relates not only the story of the Chins being broken up into distinct tribes but also how the written language of the Chin came into being:

> In the beginning, when the stones were soft, all mankind spoke the same language, and there was no war on earth. But just before the darkness called *Chun-mui* came to the earth, God gave different languages to different peoples and instructed them to write on something else. While the Chin ancestors carefully inscribed their language on leather, the Burman ancestors, who were very lazy, wrote their language on stone, which was soft. However, soon after they had made the inscription of their languages,

the 'darkness' came and the Sun disappeared from the earth. During the 'darkness' the stone became hard but the leather got wet. Before the Sun came back to the earth, and while the wet leather was still very smelly, a hungry dog ate up the leather, and in this way, the Chin ancestors lost their written language.

When the Sun came back to the earth, the Chin ancestors realized that while they had lost their written language, the Burman language which was written on the stone had turned into 'the magic of letters'. Moreover, while the sons of Burman spoke the same language, the sons of Chin spoke different dialects because their common language was eaten up together with the leather by the hungry dog. Thus, the ancestor of the Chin prepared to make war against the Burman in order to capture 'the magic of letters'. Although the Burmans were weaker and lazier, the Chin did not win the war because 'the magic of letters' united all the sons of the Burman. Since the sons of Chin spoke different dialects, their fathers could not even give them the war order to fight the Burman. It was for this reason that the Chin broke into distinct tribes and speak different dialects.[70]

Another story connected with the 'magic of letters' comes from the tradition of the Mizo tribe, which was recorded by Shakespeare in 1912. According to Mizo tradition, God gave mankind not only different languages but different talents as well: "to the ancestor of the Poi or *Laimi* tribe he gave a fighting sword, while the ancestor of the Lushai tribe only received a cloth, which is the reason that the Poi tribes are braver than the Lushais."[71] In contrast to the Zophei tradition, the Mizo story tells that 'the magic of letters' was given to the white man, not to the Burman. Shakespeare therefore concludes, by saying that "I was told he (the white man) had received the knowledge of reading and writing—a curious instance of the pen being considered mightier than the sword."[72]

From Chindwin Valley to Present Chinram

As far as historical evidence is concerned, the Chin lived peacefully in Upper Chindwin of the Kale-Kabaw Valley for at least a hundred years, from the fall of Pagan in 1295 to the founding of the Shan's Fortress City of Kale-myo in 1395. There is no historical evidence that, between those periods, the Chin's life in the Kale Valley was disturbed either by natural disaster or by political events. During that period, the Chin founded their capital at Khampat in the Kabaw Valley. Lalthanglian, a Mizo historian, and M. Kipgen, a Zomi historian, both claim that the Khampat era was "the most glorious period" in Chin history. "Most of the major clans, who now inhabit the Chin State of Burma, Mizoram, Manipur, Cachar and Tripura, are believed to have lived together there under a great chief having the same culture and speaking the same language."[73]

But in the year 1395 when "the Shan built the great city of Kalemyo with double walls," at the foot of what is now called the Chin Hills, 20 miles west of the Chindwin River, a century of peaceful life in the Kale Valley had broken up.[74] As a matter of fact, the Shan had become the rising power in the region of what is now called "Upper Chindwin" and "Central Burma" by the middle of thirteenth century. Before they conquered the Chin country of the Kale Valley, the Shan had already dominated the regions by conquering the then most powerful kingdom of Pagan in 1295. They continued to fight among themselves and with the Burman kingdom of Ava, which was founded after the fall of Pagan by King Thadominphya in 1364. The Shan finally conquered Ava in 1529. Although Ava was recaptured by the Burman King Bayinnaung in 1555, the Kale Valley remained under the rule of Shan until the British period. During the next century after they had conquered the Chin country of the Kale Valley, the Shan also annexed Assam and established the Ahong dynasty, which lasted for more than two centuries.

According to Sing Kho Khai and Lalthanglian, the Chin did not leave the Kale Valley soon after the Shan had conquered the region. The Chin traditions of the Zomi and Mizo tribes, which were accepted as historical facts by Sing Kho Khai (1984) and

Lalthanglian (1978) respectively, mentioned that the Chins lived in the Kale Valley side by side with the Shan for a certain period. Zomi tradition, as noted by Sing Kho Khai, goes on to relate that "while they were living in the Kale Valley, a prince came up from below and governed the town of Kale-myo. During the reign of that prince the people were forced to work very hard in the construction of the fortress and double walls of the town."[75]

The hardship of the forced labor was said to be so great, according to Naylor, that "the fingers of workers, which were accidentally cut-off, filled a big basket."[76] The tradition continues to relate that the Chins, who were unable to bear the hardship of manual labor, moved up to the hill region to establish new settlements such as "Chin New", which was located in the present township of Tiddim of the Chin State in Burma.[77] Professor D. G. E. Hall, a well-known historian, confirms that the Shans were the one who "drove the Chin out of the Chindwin Valley into the western hills" of present Chinram.[78]

According to the legend, which Lalthanglian accepted as historical fact, the Chin planted a Banyan sapling at the site of an altar where they used to worship their *Khuahrum*,[79] just before they were forced to abandon Khampat. They took a pledge at the sacrificial ceremony to their *Khuahrum* that "they would return to Khampat, their permanent home, when the sapling had grown into a tree and when its spreading branches touched the earth."[80]

We do not know exactly when the Chin left Khampat and the Kale-Kabaw Valley, to settle in the hilly region of Chinram. But we *can* trace, at least approximately, these periods from the Shan and the Burma chronicles from the East and the Manipur chronicles from the West. The Manipur chronicles first mentioned the Chin people, known to them as Kuki, in the year 1554.[81] Thus, it is certain that the Chin settlement in present Chinram began only after the founding of Kale-myo in 1395, and reached the far-most northern region of their settlement in the present Manipur State of India in about 1554.

According to Sing Kho Khai, the first settlement they made in present Chinram was called "Chin New" or "Cinnuai" as he spelt it. Carey and Tuck, however, spelt "Cinnuai" as "Chin New."[82] The Chins lived together in "Chin New" for a certain period. But they split into tribal groups because of "their struggle against each other for political supremacy."[83] Economics may have been the compelling reason, because Chin Nwe, a rather small, hilly region could not provide enough land for the self-sufficient agriculturally-oriented economic system of peasant society. Thus, one group had made their new settlement in "Lailung", which was located in the present township of Falam, and they eventually became the "Laimi tribe."[84]

Another group who first settled in "Locom" eventually became the Mizo tribe, who now populate part of the Mizoram State in India. From Chin Nwe some groups moved up to the North, and they are now known as "Zomi", meaning northern people, or highlanders. Prior to these settlements, there is no historical evidence that differentiates the Chin into the Liami, Mizo and Zomi tribes, etc. Only the national name of "Chin" is represented in the records. Until that time, there were no such tribal names as Asho, Chó, Khuami, Laimi, Mizo and Zomi. Thus, B. S. Carey, who knew very well about the Biblical story of the fall of mankind,[85] described Chin Nwe as the "the Chin Garden of Eden", which indicated "before the fall came upon the Chin people", to use the symbolic term.[86]

Some of the Chin tribes, however, did not move over to the hills but remained in the Chindwin Valley, especially in remote areas like the Gankaw Valley and the Kale-Kabaw Valley of Upper Chindwin. Even today they are still called by their original names but with suffixes like Chin-pun, Chin-me, etc., because of their old-fashioned tattooed faces. Asho groups, as mentioned earlier, split away from the main groups before they moved to Upper Chindwin. They first lived in the Pandaung Hills, and then scattered around the Irrawady Delta, Pegu Yoma, Arakan Yoma, and some of the Asho even reached the Chittagaung Hill Tracts in what is now Bangladesh.[87] In Arakan and Chittagaung they are still known by their old name as "Khyeng".

The Chin Split into Tribal Groups and *Tual* Communities

As far as historical evidence is concerned, the Chin were known by no other name than CHIN, until they made their settlement in Chin Nwe. However, after they were expelled from their original homeland, the Kale Valley in Upper Chindwin, by the flood as oral traditions recount it—or conquered by the Shan as modern scholars have suggested—the Chin split into different tribal groups speaking different dialects, with different tribal names.

Undoubtedly, a vast majority of the Chin people moved over to the hill regions of the present Chin State in Burma, the Mizoram and Manipur States in India, and the Chittagaung Hills Tracks in Bangladesh. But some groups, as mentioned, remained in their original homeland of the Chindwin Valley, and later scattered into such areas as the Sagaing, Maqwi, Pakukko and Irrawady divisions of present Burma.

Linguistically, according to the *Linguistic Survey of India* in 1904, the Chin dialects are divided into four major groups as the Northern, the Central, the Old Kuki, and the Southern.

1. The Northern Group: Thado, Kamhau, Sokte (Sukte), Siyin (Sizang), Ralte, Paite.
2. The Central Group: Tashon (Tlaisun), Lai, Lakher (Mara), Lushai (Mizo), Bangjogi (Bawmzo), and Pankhu.
3. The Old-Kuki Group: Rangkhol, Kolren, Kom, Purum, Hmar, Cha (Chakma).
4. The Southern Group: Chin-me, Chin-bok, Chin-pun, Khyang (Asho), M'ro (Khuami), Shendus (Yindu), and Welaung.[88]

Scholars generally agree that there are six major tribal groups of the Chin, namely the 1) Asho, 2) Chó or Sho, 3) Khuami or M'ro, 4) Laimi, 5) Mizo (Lushai) and 6) Zomi.[89]

The term "tribal group" in a Chin concept is "a social group comprising numerous families, clans, or generations together with slaves, dependents, or adopted strangers."[90] In other words, they are a group of the same people whose ancestors made their settlement in a certain place together, after their common original homeland in the Kale Valley was destroyed. The Laimi tribe, for instance, is made up of the descendents of the group who made their settlement at Lai-lung, after they were forced to leave the Kale Valley. Thus, the term "tribe" as a Chin concept does not refer to common ancestors or common family ties but to a social group of the same ethnic nationality, who settled in a certain place. As the names imply, the tribal groups among the Chin rather denote geographical areas and the ownership of the land; for example, Asho means the plain dwellers, Cho means southerners, Khuami may be translated as "the native people", Laimi means descendent of the Lai-lung or the "central people" as Stevenson defines it,[91] Zomi or Mizo means the northern people, and so on. The tribal group therefore is not a divisive term, it only denotes how the Chin are split into various groups because of having lost their original homeland of Chindwin.

Generally, tribal groups can be divided into smaller sub-tribes or groups as follows:

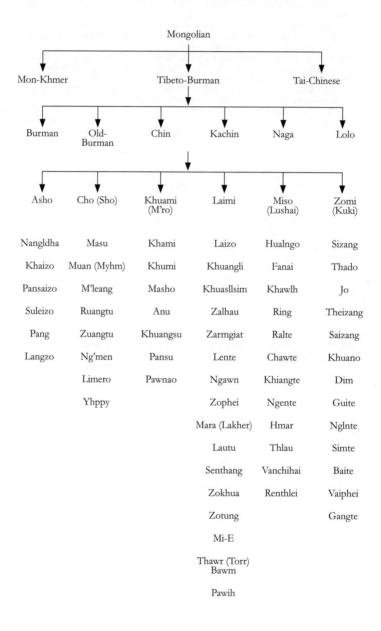

	Mongolian	
Mon-Khmer	Tibeto-Burman	Tai-Chinese

Burman	Old-Burman	Chin	Kachin	Naga	Lolo

Asho	Cho (Sho)	Khuami (M'ro)	Laimi	Miso (Lushai)	Zomi (Kuki)
Nangldha	Masu	Khami	Laizo	Hualngo	Sizang
Khaizo	Muan (Myhm)	Khumi	Khuangli	Fanai	Thado
Pansaizo	M'leang	Masho	Khuasllsim	Khawlh	Jo
Suleizo	Ruangtu	Anu	Zalhau	Ring	Theizang
Pang	Zuangtu	Khuangsu	Zarmgiat	Ralte	Saizang
Langzo	Ng'men	Pansu	Lente	Chawte	Khuano
	Limero	Pawnao	Ngawn	Khiangte	Dim
	Yhppy		Zophei	Ngente	Guite
			Mara (Lakher)	Hmar	Nglnte
			Lautu	Thlau	Simte
			Senthang	Vanchihai	Baite
			Zokhua	Renthlei	Vaiphei
			Zotung		Gangte
			Mi-E		
			Thawr (Torr) Bawm		
			Pawih		

241

Notes

[1] Anthony Smith, *Ethnic Origins of Nations* (Oxford: Blackwell, 1986), pp. 21-46; John Hutchinson and Anthony Smith, *Ethnicity* (Oxford and New York: Oxford University Press, 1996), pp. 6-7.

[2] See Lian H. Sakhong, *Religion and Politics among the Chin People in Burma, 1896-1949*, (Ph.D. dissertation: Uppsala University, 2000), especially Chapter One and Two. This paper actually is drawn from my dissertation.

[3] Here I use Chinland and Chinram interchangeably. At the "Chin Seminar", held in Ottawa, Canada, on 29th April to 2nd May 1998, Dr. Za Hlei Thang, one of the most outstanding politicians and scholars among the Chin, proposed the word ram in Chin should be used in stead of the English word land, as Chinram in stead of Chinland. It was widely accepted by those who attended the seminar.

[4] See... Lt. Col. J. Shakespeare, *The Lushai Kuki Clan*, (London: Macmillan & Co., 1912), p. 93-94; B. S. Carey and H. N. Tuck, *Chin Hills: A History of the People, British Dealing with them, their Customs and Manners, and a Gazetteer of their Country*, (Rangoon: Government Printing, 1896; reprinted in New Delhi: Cultural Publishing House, 1983), p. 142; N. E. Parry, *The Lakher*, (Calcutta:1932; reprinted in Aizawl: Tribal Research Institute, 1976), p.4

[5] *The Mizoram Encyclopaedia*, (1993), p. 328

[6] Cited by Mangkhosat Kipgen, *Christianity and Mizo Culture*, (Aizawl: Mizo Theological Conference, 1996), p.36

[7] Cited by Vumson, *Zo History* (Aizawl: Published by the Author, 1986), p. 3

[8] Vumson, *Zo History* (1986), p. 26; Vumson cannot accept the traditional account of the legend "as fact, because," for him, "it is contradictory to known facts of how man originated" (p. 26). He therefore proposed the word 'Zo' (meaning; 'hill people or highlander') to be used for the national name of the Chin.

[9] *Re-Unification of the Chin People: Memorandum Submitted by the Paite National Council to Prime Minister of India for Re-unification of Chin People of India and Burma under One Country*, (Imphal, Manipur: Azad Printing, 1960). The memorandum was signed by T. Goukhenpa, President, and S. Vungkhom, Chief Secretary, Paite National Council.

[10] Ibid. p. 2

[11] F. K. Lehman, *The Structure of the Chin*, (Champaign: Illinois University Press, 1963), p. 20

[12] Zapeng Sakhong, *Lai History* (M.A. thesis: Mandalay University, 1983), p. 7

[13] F. K. Lehman, "On the name of Chin, Lai and Zo" in *Chin National Journal* (No. 7, March 1999), pp. 92-97

[14] Lian Uk, *The Chin Customary Law of Inheritance and Succession as Practiced Among the Chins of Haka Area*, (Ll.B. thesis: Law Department of Rangoon University, 1968), p. 2

[15] B. S. Carey and H. N. Tuck, *Chin Hills: A History of the People, British Dealing with them, their Customs and Manners, and a Gazetteer of their Country*, (Rangoon: Government Printing, 1896; reprinted in New Delhi: Cultural Publishing House, 1983), p. 3

[16] It has to be noted that in Burmese a combination of alphabets 'KH' is pronounced as 'CH'.

[17] G. H. Luce, "Old Kyaukse and the Coming of the Burmans" in *Journal of The Burma Research Society*, Vol. XLII, June 1959, pp. 75-109.

[18] Father Vincenzo Sangermano, *The Burmese Empire* (Westminster: Archibald and Co., 1833; reprinted, Bangkok: White Orchid Press, 1995), p. 43.[Explanation within bracket is given by John Jardine, who wrote an introduction and notes when the book was first published in 1833, some one hundred years after Father Sangermano passed away. As John Jardine had explained quite clearly, what Sangermano described as "Jo" is not the "Jo" group of Zomi tribe of Chin, but the "Yaw" people who occupied the Gankaw Valley of Upper Chindwin. This particular point had been misinterpreted by many scholars, especially Zomi scholars including Vum Kho Hau and Sing Kho Khai, sometimes quite knowingly. Vum Kho Hau, for instance, writes in his book: Profile of Burma Frontier Man, "From time immemorial we call ourselves Zo (Jo, Yaw). This fact had been admirably recorded by Father V. Sangermano since the year 1783 when he made his headquarter at Ava." (1963:238)]

[19] Lieut. Col. S. Reid, *Chin-Lushai Land* (Calcutta: Government Printing 1893; reprinted Aizawl: Tribal Society, 1983), p. 5

[20] C. A. Soppit, *Kuki-Lushai Tribe*, (Calcutta: 1893, reprinted in Aizawl: Tribal Society, 1978), p. 2

[21] Lt. Col. J. Shakespeare, *The Lushai Kuki Clan*, (London: Macmillan & Co., 1912), p.8; cited also in G.S. Gangte, *Kuki of Manipur*, (Delhi: Gyan Publishing House, 1993), p. 21

[22] Major Snodgrass, *The Burmese War, 1824-1826*, (London: John Murray & Co., 1827), see map on p. 320

[23] Sir Arthur Phayer, *History of Burma*, (London: Trubner, 1883, reprinted New York: Augustus M. Kelly, 1967), p. 7

[24] Arthur George Edward Newland, *The Image of War: Service on the Chin Hills*, (Calcutta: Thacker & Sprink, 1894).

[25] Clifford Geertz, *The Interpretation of Cultures*, (London: Fontana Press, 1973), see especially "The Integrative Revolution: Primordial Sentiments and Civil Politics in the New States" in Chapter 10.

[26] T.S. Gangte, *Kuki of Manipur* (1993), op.cit., p. 14

[27] K. Zawla, *Mizo Pi Pu te leh an Thlaleh Cancin* (Aizawl: Published by the Author, 1976), p. 2

[28] Ginzathang, *Zomi Innkuan Laibu* (Rangoon: Published by the Author, 1973), p. 7

[29] K.S. Gangte, *Kuki of Manipur* (1993), op.cit., p. 14

[30] J Shakespeare, *The Kuki Lushai Clan*, (1912), op.cit., pp.93-94

[31] Ibid., p.94 [the italics within bracket is my explanation!]

[32] N. E. Parry, *The Lakher*, (Calcutta:1932; reprinted in Aizawl: Tribal Research Institute, 1976), p.4

[33] Ceu Mang, "Zophei Thawh-keh-nak" in *Lai Holh Reltu Magazine*, (Vol. 3, No.4, November, 1981), pp. 12-19. The Mara tradition of similar story was recorded by Parry in his book: The Lakher (1932), op.cit., p. 561 (part of the English text here is taken from Parry's translation!).

[34] Anthony Smith (1986), op.cit., p. 29

[35] Ibid., p. 28

[36] Ibid.

[37] Ibid.

[38] Ibid.

[39] K. Zawla (1976) op.cit.,p. 2. [Italic within bracket is my explanation1]

[40] Sing Kho Khai, *The Theological Concept of Zo in the Chin Tradition and Culture*, (BRE thesis: Burma Institute of Theology, 1984), and Chawn Kio, "The Origin of the Chin" in Ceu Mang, ed., *Krifa Bukbau* (Haka: CCLR Press, 1993), pp. 12-21. [in Chin!]

[41] Sing Kho Khai (1984), p. 53

[42] Ibid., p. 21

[43] Gin Za Thang (1973), op.cit., p. 5, cited also by Sing Kho Khai (1984), op.cit., p. 10; and T. S. Gangte (1993), op.cit., p. 14

[44] Both Professors Than Tun and Gordon Luce are regarded as the most well known scholars in the study of ancient Burmese history, including the Chin.

[45] Than Tun, *Essays on the History and Buddhism of Burma*, (Whiting Bay, Scotland: Kiscadale Publications, 1988), p. 3

[46] Cited by Than Tun (1988), p. 4

[47] C. M. Enriquez, *The Races of Burma*, (Rangoon: Government Printing, 1932), pp. 7-8

[48] Ibid.

[49] Cited by F. K. Lehman, *The Structure of Chin Society*, (Urabana: Illinois University Press, 1963), p. 11

[50] Ibid., p. 22

[51] Ibid.

[52] Ibid.

[53] Ibid., p. 22

[54] T. S. Gangte (1993), op.cit., p. 17

[55] Sing Kho Khai (1984), op.cit., p. 10

[56] Than Tun (1988), op.cit., p. 3

[57] Ibid.

[58] Gordon Luce, "Old Kyaukse and the Coming of Burma" in *Journal of Burma Research Society*, Vol. XLII, June 1959, pp. 75-109

[59] Lal Thang Lian, *History of Mizo in Burma* (MA thesis: Mandalay University, 1976), p.9

[60] Vumson in his *Zo History* (1986) mentioned that the "remains of Chin settlements are still found today in the Chindwin Valley. Two miles from Sibani village, not far from Monywa, is a Chin ritual ground. The memorial stone was, in earlier days, about

thirteen feet (4.3 m) high, but now decayed from exposure. The Burmese called it Chin paya or Chin god." (p. 34)

[61] Sing Kho Khai (1984), op.cit., p. 36

[62] Vumson (1986), op.cit., p. 35

[63] G. H. Luce, "Chin Hills—Linguistic Tour (Dec. 1954)—University Project" in *Journal of Burma Research Society* (Vol.XLII, June 1959), pp. 19-31

[64] B. Lalthanglian, *A History of Mizo in Burma*, (Aizawl: Zawlbuk Agencies, 1997), p. 71

[65] Ibid.

[66] G.H. Luce, "Old Kyaukse and the Coming of the Burman" (1959), op.cit., p. 89

[67] Ibid.

[68] The term Kale is Myanmarnized/Burmanized version of Khalei. Literal meaning of Kale or Khale in Burmese is "Children" which make no sense for geographical name. Thus, linguistic study confirmed not only the Chin traditional account of flood story, but also the root word of the name 'Kale Valley'.

[69] B. S. Carey and H. N. Tuck, *The Chin Hills* (1896), p. 146

[70] Pu Sakhong, *Kan Pupa Thawh-keh-nak Kong* (Aibur: Manuscript, 1969), (quotation here is my translation)

[71] Lt. Col. J. Shakespeare, *The Lushai Kuki Clan* (1912), op.cit., p. 95

[72] Ibid.

[73] Mangkhosat Kipgen (1996), op.cit., p. 39

[74] G.H. Luce, "The Chin Hills Linguistic Tour" (1959), op.cit., pp. 26-27

[75] Sing Kho Khai (1984), op.cit., p. 43

[76] L. P. Naylor, *A Practical Handbook of Chin Language*, (Rangoon: Government Printing, 1937), p. 3

[77] Carey and Tuck, *The Chin Hills* (1896), op.cit., p. 127

[78] D. G. E. Hall, *A History of South East Asia* (London: St. Martin's Press, 1968), p. 158

[79] According to M. Kipgen, the Banyan tree was "at the palace site" (1996:40).

[80] M. Kipgen (1996), pp. 40-41; This is said to have actually happened in 1916, in which year Saingunvaua (Sai Ngun Vau) and his party left for Mizoram for Khampat in Kabaw Valley where they made a new settlement in order to fulfil the old prophecy. Now, Khampat once again become the center of the Chin community in Kale-Kabaw Valley, and more than one-half of the inhabitant's population in Kale-Kabaw Valley are Chins. See Lalthangliana (1976: 87-89).

[81] See Lt. Col. J. Shakespear, "The Kuki Lushai Clan" in *JRAI*, (Vol. 11, No. 1, 1955), pp. 94-111, cited also by F. K. Lehman (1963), op.cit., p. 25

[82] See Carey and Tuck, *The Chin Hills* (1896), op.cit., p. 127

[83] Sing Kho Khai (1984), op.cit., p. 41

[84] Zapeng Sakhong, *Lai History*, (M.A.thesis: Mandalay University, 1983), p. 5

[85] B. S. Carey was the grandson of Dr. William Carey, a prominent English Baptist missionary to Serampore in India in 1794.

[86] B. S. Carey and H. N. Tuck, *The Chin Hills*, (1986), p. 127

[87] Lian Uk (1968), op.cit., p. 7

[88] G. A. Grierson, *Linguistic Survey of India, Vol.111: Tibeto-Burman Family, Part 111*, (Calcutta: Government Printing, 1904, reprinted Delhi: Motilal Banarsdass, 1967), p. 67

[89] Vumson (1986), op.cit., p. 40

[90] Merriam Webster's Collegiate Dictionary

[91] See Stevenson, *The Economics of Central Chin Tribe* (1943), which is exclusively about the Laimi tribe of Chin.

SIXTEEN

Christianity and Chin Identity

This paper is adapted from the last chapter of my doctoral dissertation 'Religion and Politics among the Chin Peoples' *and presented at the Sixth International Conference on Burma Studies at Gothenburg University, Sweden, 2003. It was first published as chapter ten in* 'Exploring Ethnicity in Burma', *edited by Mikael Gravers, Nordic Institute of Asian Studies, 2007*

Introduction

In 1999 when the Chin people in Burma celebrated the centennial anniversary of the arrival of Christianity, more than eighty percent of the Chin population proclaimed their faith in Jesus Christ as their Lord and Savior. In West Chinram of Mizoram State in India, church growth has been even faster and Christian life was even more vigorous than in the Chin State of Burma. This means that within the time span of a mere century, almost the entire Chin population has accepted the Christian faith, and the church has become deeply rooted in the socio-cultural tradition of the people.[1]

Such unusually fast growth of Christianity on both sides of Chinram during the twentieth century and the vitality of its practice, or what Chin theologian Mangkhosat Kipgen called, "a uniquely *Chin* form of Christianity", and a link between indigenization of Christianity and the rapid growth of church in Chinram are the factors I intend to explain theoretically in this paper. In doing this, I am going to argue that a link between indigenization and the growth of Christianity was one of the reasons why Christianity could provide the Chin people a means of preserving their identity and promoting their interests in the face of powerful forces of change.

Christianity in East Chinram is a fruit of the work of the American Baptist Mission. There have also been significant indigenous Chin missions, more notably the Chins for Christ in One Century (CCOC). I will argue in this paper that the growth of Christianity in East Chinram during the first five decades of the twentieth century was based on the contribution of at least three factors, namely: 1) the socio-political change represented by the British colonial power 2) the missionary factor (both foreign and indigenous) and 3) the theological similarity between Christianity and traditional Chin religion, which meant that conversion was not a radical change but a religious transformation from *Khua-hrum* oriented ritual practices to a *Khua-zing* oriented worship service within the same conceptual pattern of belief system.[2]

This paper is divided into three parts. The first part is dealing the socio-cultural change, and second part explains a link between socio-cultural change, or what I called Gospel and a new society, and the formation of a new ethnic identity, and in part three, I am going to explore the theological continuity between the traditional Chin religion and Christianity, which served as a means of preserving the Chin ethnic identity in the midst of multi-ethnic, multi-religious, and multi-cultural context of modern nation-state of the Union of Burma.

Socio-Cultural Change

Prior to British annexation in 1896, the Chins were an independent people ruled by their own traditional tribal and local chiefs called Ram-uk and Khua-bawi, respectively. Surrounding kingdoms like Burman or Myanmar, Bengal and Assam (India) never conquered the Chin people and their land, Chinram. As a result, Buddhism, Muslim and Hinduism never reached the Chin. The Chin traditional religion was the only social manifestation of people's faith, which bound the community together. Although all the tribes and villages followed the same pattern of belief systems, the ritual practices in traditional Chin religion—called *Khua-hrum worship*—were very much mutually exclusive, and could not serve to unite the entire Chin people under a single religious institution. Thus, until the British occupation, the Chin society remained in a tribal society and the people's identification with each other was tribally exclusive, and their common national identity remained to be searched.

By the turn of twentieth century, however, Chin society was abruptly transformed by powerful outside forces of change. The British conquered Chinram, and the Christian missionaries followed the colonial powers and converted the people. Within this process of change, the Chin people found themselves in the midst of multi-ethnic and multi-religious environments, which they did not welcome. They also realized that their country was not the central of the universe but a very small part of a very large British Empire. After the colonial period, they found themselves again being separated into three different countries—India, Burma, and Bangladesh—without their consent. While West Chinram of present Mizoram State became part of India, East Chinram of present Chin State joined the Union of Burma according to the Panglong Agreement signed in 1947. The smaller part of Chinram became part of what they then called East Pakistan, that is, present Bangladesh.

The primary agent of change, in my hypothesis, was the modern political systems represented by British colonial power and its successors—namely, independent India and Burma. The political development, of course, was the only agent with necessary power to force change. In tribal society, "distinction cannot easily be made between religious, social, cultural and political elements."[3] Anything that effects one aspect of life can strongly affect every aspect of life. In fact, "tribal society can only be maintained through traditional instruments of integration, if they remain in fundamental isolation from other societies."[4] When centuries-old isolationism in Chinram was broken up by the British colonial power, the traditional way of maintaining the tribal group's identity was no longer effective, and the process of de-tribalization had begun.

The process of de-tribalization could be a dangerous moment because that process could either become what Frederick Downs called the process of "dehumanization,"[5] or a process of what Swedish scholar Eric Ringmar called a "formative moment."[6] If the process became a process of dehumanization, that is, "to rob them of their essential life" of the "people's soul", as Down puts it, then the existence of tribal peoples could really be endangered. There are many examples, according to Dawns, in the Americas, Africa, other parts of Asia and India where many tribal peoples have ceased to exist.[7] On the other hand, the process of de-tribalization could become a "formative moment" if the people could find any other alternative, instead of seeking "to revitalize the old culture."[8]

In my hypothesis, the process of detribalization in Chin society has transitioned into such a "formative moment", that is—at a time in which new meaning became available and people suddenly were able to identify themselves with something meaningful. It was Christianity, which provided the Chin people the new meanings and symbols within as described in the "formative moment" theory, but without "a complete break with the past."[9] It is, therefore, interesting explore how Christianity helped the Chin people—no longer as a divided tribal groups, but as the entire nationality of Chin ethnicity—to maintain their identity, and how did Christianity itself became a new creating-force of national identity for the Chin people within this "formative" process of powerful changes.

Gospel And A New Society

Conversion to Christianity was not a single event but a long and gradual process of adjustment to the demands of the new faith as opposed to the old ritual habits, and also to the necessities of life. These adjustments to the new life always began with the abandonment of all the ritual systems connected with their traditional religion of *Khua-hrum worship*. The abandonment of old ritual systems included not only the sacrificial ceremonies but also many kinds of feasts and festivals which were regarded as practices of the "old life", what the Chin called *Lai phung*.

Moreover, all the converts were expected to stop the practice of polygamy and the consumption of intoxicants, *Zu le Zuhui*.

The missionaries also encouraged the early Chin Christians to separate the "new ways of life", that is, Christian ways of life, *Krifa Phung*, from the "old ways of life", that is, the traditional Chin ways of life, *Lai Phung*, and they portrayed the "old life" as sinful in nature and full of unhappiness and permanent unrest, while the "new life" was brightly colored and full of happiness and peace. Thus, when people converted to Christianity they located themselves in the "new life" and conceived their identity in terms opposing the old *Lai Phung* to the new *Krifa Phung*. It was due to the fact that nineteenth century evangelicalism represented by nearly all the Protestant missionaries, including the American Baptist Chin mission, "placed emphasis upon Christianity as a way of life, a lifestyle". For them, 'doctrine was important but meaningless if not associated with a transformed life'. Thus, as Frederick Downs observes, "the idea of becoming a Christian meant adopting a new mode of life."[10] In this way, conversion to Christianity and the adoption of new ways of life were inseparably linked to each other.

Within this long process of adjustment, at least three new forms of imagining the social world appeared—Sunday worship services, singing from the same hymnbooks, and reading the Holy Bible.[11] In fact, these three characteristics of the social world were related to their new ritual systems in Christianity and the expectation of salvation in Christ's life after death in *Mithi-khua*. The observation of the Sabbath, Sunday, was the very first step the Chin Christians took to "imagine" themselves as "living lives simultaneous with other lives in an homogenous time", measured not only by Biblical teaching about the Holy Sabbath (Genesis 2: 2, and Exodus 20: 8), but also by modern clocks and calendars. It was novel, yet effective and meaningful for the Chin Christians to create an "imaginary community" beyond their clan and tribal boundaries. As they observed Sunday, they also practiced the same rituals of singing from the same hymn-books and reading the same Holy Bible everywhere in Chinram. Whether they sung hymns or read the Holy Bible, congregations

249

at the Sunday service knew that they were singing and reading what many other believers were singing and reading at the same time with the same hope and faith they had in one God. Thus, the observation of Sunday services, singing from the same hymnbooks, and reading the same Holy Bible gradually became the most powerful sources for the creation of an "imaginary community," and thereby the creation of a common national identity for all the Chin Christians.[12]

New Rituals and Phenomena in Chin Society

The moment of conversion was not the end of the story but the beginning of a long process of adjustment to the demands of a new faith in relation to the ritual habits of traditional religion it supplanted. In this long process of adjustment, the adoption of a new faith and new identity was marked by some sort of ritual. The most observable phenomenon for the converts among the Chin was what we call in Chin *inn-thianh*, that is, "cleansing the house". The *inn-thianh* ritual was the first observable phenomenon of conversion and was usually followed by baptism.

The procedure of the *inn-thianh* ritual is almost the same everywhere in Chinram. Since the procedure of this ritual is always the same, I shall quote from the eyewitness account of Dr. East, reported in 1910. He described "cleansing house" in the Tiddim area as follows:

> Mr. Cope and I were now in Tang Nu Kwa [Thangnuai village] by invitation. We were called there by people, as seven families have accepted "the new way" and have asked us to help them break down the altars and all emblems of evil spirit worship, to remove all heads of animals sacrificed and all bamboo resting places for evil spirits. This is quite a job as there are many altars and many skulls, sometimes numbering fifty to a hundred, and as we have to take the initiative in order to embolden the people to touch things formerly held sacred and to help us in this most destructive breaking down of spiritualism and building up of Christianity. It took us from about 2 P.M. until the lengthening of the shadows.

The last house we sanctified to God belonged to an old couple, and when all emblems had been taken out and readied to be burned, the old man asked, "Will I dare to sleep in this house tonight since the spirits are not here to protect us and they have no resting place?" We then knelt and I placed my hands upon their heads and prayed that Jehovah God should now and thereafter dwell with them to protect them against sickness and all harms. Now they were ready to go back into the house and were not afraid, as God was greater than the evil spirits.

Dr. East concluded his letter to his wife:

My dear, it is not an easy thing to break loose from an age-old custom and imprinted beliefs. Man's heart is hungry for atonement. Man's heart is seeking a resting place. Man's heart is only satisfied when it knows that it is protected by one stronger than himself. And so a tremendous struggle takes place in the hearts and minds of these people when they awaken from age-long ignorance and face God.[13]

When the Chins converted to Christianity, they wanted to abandon their traditional ways of life. This was also encouraged by missionaries. Their traditional religion, after all, was inseparably linked with every aspect of life. In Chin traditional concept, a house was not just a home for people, it was also an abode for the household god called *chung-um*. Thus, when they wanted to become Christians, the first thing the Chins needed to do was to let their guardian god leave the house. In order to do this, they needed to clean their house and destroy the traditional sacrificial artifacts called *Kho le Kheng*. That was the reason people used to say, "*Kho le Kheng kan thlak cang*", or destroy the '*Kho le Kheng*' when they became Christians.

For many able-bodied people, destroying *kho le kheng* was not enough. They even rebuilt their houses completely and usually changed the architectural style as well. Thus, most of the Christians' houses are not in the traditional long-house style, but resemble the house Dr. East built in Haka. They also usually shifted away from their old house sites when they became Christians for they knew that the sites themselves were associated too much with their guardian god. When a whole village became Christian, they even moved off their old village site, which was inseparably linked with the village guardian god, *Tual Khua-hrum*. In the new village, the Church was at the heart of the community instead of the *Tual* or *Tlenlai Lung* that had been the communal sacrificial stone or altar.

From the traditionalist point of view, this new phenomenon of the *inn-thianh* ritual was a painful memory of the destruction of centuries-old institutions of Chin society. Today the Chin people view this painful memory from a different perspective. They now remember those stories as a symbolic departure from the "old ways" (in *Chin Laiphung* or *chan hlun*) and portray the epoch as an abrupt juncture, a fold in the course of social history marked by sharp changes in the ethos of everyday life. In a nutshell, these new phenomena or rituals such as *inn-thianh* and baptism, which are part of the conversion process, are the key social and ritual activities through which the transformation of identities and communities are accomplished.

Finding Common Ground and Common Knowledge

The views of the first missionary couple, Arthur and Laura Carson, on traditional Chin religion, culture, and custom were completely negative. Thus, Arthur Carson would write bluntly, "the Chin had no word for God, grace, mercy, forgiveness", or even "love". Mrs. Carson also wrote that "sacrificing to evil spirits" was "their only religion and system of medicine."[14] They passed, as Johnson points out, "this attitude along to young Dr. East" and other missionaries. The reason, according to Johnson, is that "when Laura and Arthur Carson first came to the Chin Hills, they were so struck by the backwardness of the people that they overreacted."[15]

Dr. East seemed to have changed his view after staying nine years in Chinram and traveling widely among many tribes of the Chin. In 1909, he met "a man over one hundred years old" at Roshi in the Falam area. He mentioned this old man in his letter, and that he would not be surprised "if he was even older" than one hundred years. This old man told him about the origin of the Chin and also the story of *Pa Lo Tuanbia*, which Dr. East translated as "The Story of Fatherless", and other myths and legends. Here I would like to relate the story of *Pa Lo Tuanbia*, which was recorded by Pu Sakhong of Aibur.

Once upon a time, a young lady who was still a virgin was collecting firewood far away from her village. On her way home, she found a fruit called *Khuhlu* on the village sacrificial stone called *Tlenlailung*. Without thinking much about the consequences, she just picked up the fruit and ate it because she was so thirsty from working the whole day under the hot sun. However, the fruit was not just ordinary fruit, since it had been left there by *Khua-zing*, the Supreme God. Moreover, *Khua-zing* had mixed His own fluid with the juice of the fruit, for *Khuhlu* was a very juicy fruit. So the young lady conceived without knowing man and gave birth to a baby boy. Since she was unmarried, the baby was simply named Pa Lo, meaning "Fatherless". Pa Lo was extraordinarily strong and handsome. When he grew old enough, he asked his mother who his father was, where he lived, and so on. His mother told him that his father lived in heaven without mentioning His name. Their conversation was overheard by God from heaven. God had another son in heaven. So he sent his son in heaven to visit his younger brother on earth. Pa Lo's brother from heaven did not stay long on earth, but during his short stay he made all kinds of domestic animals out of clay, and then he turned them all to living animals. In this way, Pa Lo became the richest man in the world and performed all kinds of feasts and festivals such as *Bawite-bawi* and *Khuang-cawi*.[16]

Dr. East was also told the story of Theizam, which is similar to the Biblical story of the Tower of Babel and the story of Ngun Nu, which is similar to the Biblical story of the Flood. Thus, he wrote on February 4, 1909:

To me it seems that the easiest way of getting into their hearts is to meet them where we have common ground and common knowledge. I was led to believe that these people had no knowledge of God, no word for love, and no word for heaven. However, I could not accept that idea as I very thoroughly believe in racial unity and that 'God made all men out of one blood', and it is therefore unreasonable to believe that any part of that race should be absolutely destitute of all knowledge of the Creator. It is a certainty that the wild Chins believe in the God of Heaven as Creator. This knowledge is universal among them.[17]

From the Chin's point of view, however, the most attractive common ground and common knowledge between their own traditional religion and Christianity consisted not only of stories such as the one about the Tower of Babel, the Flood, the Virgin Mary, and Pa Lo, as Dr. East pointed out, but also the theological similarity between the traditional Chin religious teaching of life after death in *Mithi-khua* and the Biblical teaching of heaven or paradise. Among missionaries, however, only Dr. Strait applied this similar theological concept of eschatology in his ministry after Dr. East left the field. As a matter of fact, Dr. Strait did the first scholarly work on traditional Chin religion for his doctoral dissertation, *A History and Interpretation of Chin Sacrifice*, in 1933. His knowledge of traditional Chin religion helped not only in his ministry of preaching the Gospel but also when he translated the Holy Bible and Hymns. He could apply the idioms and concepts of the Supreme God and life after death in Mithi-khua to help the Chin find common ground.

In Chin traditional religious concept, there was not a problem at all in reaching heaven after death, for their religion taught them that one must surely reach heaven if one died an ordinary death. The problems concerning heaven, which bothered the Chin most, were, "Are we going to be rich or poor? What kinds of house are we are going to live in?" According to traditional Chin religious teaching, the house they built here on earth was the image of the house in their future life in *Mithi-khua*. If one could build a very big and good house here on earth, then one would surely have a very big and good house in the future life.

But now the Chins were told by Christian missionaries that if they became Christians they would have a very big and good house glittering with silver and gold, a house prepared for them by God Himself. They did not need to build homes on earth for life in heaven, they were told, but they must abandon their own traditional way of life to become Christian! And they were told that if they did become Christians, their homes in heaven would be like the missionary house in Haka built by Dr. East in 1907. Such concrete examples and promises were most attractive to the first generation of Chin Christians. Thus, for the first and second generation Chin Christians, one of the most popular hymns translated by Dr. Strait was:

> *Ni nak in a ceu khua a um ko,*
> *Zumnak in a hnu ah kan hmuh lai,*
> *Khi khin kanmah kanpa hngak len ko,*
> *Kannih umnak a ser lio dah ngai.*
> (There is a place brighter than the Sun,
> And we will reach it by faith,
> Our Father is preparing a house for us,
> That is glittering as silver and gold).[18]

Secondly, the most attractive Christian teaching for the Chin was the substitute death of Christ on the cross for sinners. According to traditional Chin religious teaching, if one died an accidental or violent death, his soul must go to *Sarthi-khua*. No soul can be redeemed from Sarthi-khua except with a substitute violent death, that is, revenge for his or her death. To illustrate my point here, I would like to relate a story of an accident that took place in the early 1950s, in Leitak in the Zophei area.

Leitak was the principal village of the Zophei area and used to be ruled by a very powerful chief, Mang Hnin of the Hlawn Ceu clan. When Mang Hnin died, he had only one son by his principal wife, *Nutak*. This son was to inherit his power and wealth although he had many more sons from his minor wives, called *Nuchun*. Unfortunately, a son of a former slave of Mang Hnin accidentally killed the heir of Mang Hnin's house, Lian Hei. According to the traditional Chin religious belief of *Laiphung*, Lian Hei would become the slave of his slayer, no

255

matter who he was. For his mother, Pi Khuang Cin, it was completely unacceptable that her beloved son, the heir of Mang Hnin, to become the slave of her own former household slave. Thus, Pi Khuang Cin, Regent of Mang Hnin's house, gathered together all her relatives from far and near and ordered them to take revenge on her son's death. At that time the government strongly prohibited such action, but Pi Khuang Cin was determined to take revenge no matter what. She was ready to make war if the government of newly Independent Burma intervened in any way.

On that occasion, Pu Sakhong, who was married to Lian Hei's elder sister, convinced Pi Khuang Cin that revenge had already been taken for Lian Hei, for he was a Christian. Lian Hei converted when he was in mission high school at Insein near Rangoon where his uncle, Lt. Tial Khuai, served in the Chin Hills Battalion of the British-Burma army. Pi Khuang Cin asked who had taken that revenge for his son, and she was then told about the substitute death of Jesus Christ on the cross. Pi Khuang Cin was convinced because Jesus was crucified on the cross. She would not have been convinced if Jesus had died an ordinary death, for she knew according to her religious teaching that only a violent death by pouring blood could substitute for her son's death. Thus, she was converted and baptized by Rev. Heng Cin, who was once expelled from Leitak by her late husband, Chief Mang Hnin.[19] In this way, the theological similarity between traditional Chin religion and Christianity, especially the substitute death of Jesus Christ on the cross for sinners, opened the doors for the conversion of the Chin people, even for people who were the heads of the Chins' religious and political institutions like Pi Khuang Cin.

Gradual Adjustment to the New Ways of Life

In this section, I am going to discuss how Christianity helped the Chin people not only to adjust to the change thrust upon them, but to create a new society based on the Gospel, and how Christianity provided a means of promoting the self-awareness of the Chin through its ideology and ecclesiastical structures.

(i) The Formation of a New Ecclesiastical Structure

Although all the Chin people professed the same religious doctrine and belief system before they became Christians, their ritual practices, which centered upon the sacrificial worship of Khua-hrum divided them into many groups of clans and tribes. When they gradually became Christians, however, the Chin people were not only provided with the same religious doctrine and belief system but also with a single ecclesiastical structure where all the tribes and clans of the Chin could join as members of a single community of believers. Thus, one of the most significant things that their new religion of Christianity provided for the Chin people during the pioneer missionary era was the formation of the "Chin Hills Baptist Association" (CHBA) at Haka in March 1907. Officially, the CHBA was formed by the election of its executive committee during a meeting of the representatives of the young churches and individual Christians, most of them new converts who attended the meeting in order to receive baptism. 'From a worldly standpoint', as Johnson observes, 'it was not a very important matter—just thirty-four people gathered to effect a little organization to bind scattered believers' in Chinram. But "this was the tiny seed that later grew into today's Chin Baptist Convention, one of the largest church groups in Burma."[20]

In "Baptist polity", as Johnson explains, "an association brings together Baptist churches, not individuals, into an organization for fellowship. It is not an authority over churches, but provides a forum for the discussion of issues, for encouragement in the faith and acts as a body to for providing advice to churches on ordination."[21] At that time in Chinram, however, there were very few organized churches and only a group of believers scattered in six or seven villages. Thus, the significance of the formation of the CHBA was that it was a "binding medium" to these new and often weak Christians. Since the CHBA functioned as a binding medium throughout East Chinram, it could hold and unite all the Chin Christians who came from many different tribes and clans within a single community of faith. It meant that, unlike their old religious institution of *Khua-*

hrum, the CHBA could accept people from different tribes and clans as believers of the same faith within a single ecclesiastical structure. In joining the CHBA, the Chin people were therefore encouraged to seek their self-awareness and national identity of *Chin-ness* through membership in a new Christian community. To put it another way, when they became Christians and joined the CHBA, the meanings and values of tribal and clan affiliation based on their traditional religion of *Khua-hrum* worship, which had been so effective in the Chin's resistance against the British, lost its strength. Thus, the national identity of *Chin-ness* gradually surpassed the meaning and effectiveness of clan and tribal identity.

From the very moment of its formation, the CHBA even challenged the notion of tribal identity, and "racism begins to break down", as Johnson put it. As mentioned, no Chin would allow the presence of a stranger from another tribe at any kind of traditional religious ceremony. But the Christians in Haka now welcomed strangers from other tribes—especially the Zomi tribe from the Sizang and Kamhau groups in the Tiddim area—to their new religious ceremonies as their own brothers and sisters in Christ. This event was very significant in Chin history; Johnson observes:

> The Hakas were used to calling the Sizang and Kamhau by the appellation 'Thaute', a derogatory term, and could not understand how Christians could accept these Thautes as brothers. The superstition that the Tiddim area people possessed the power of the 'evil eye' was still strong, and so the Hakas tended to shun them.[22]

Recognizing the effect of this event, the missionaries and Chin Christians not only held an Association Meeting as a recurring annual religious ceremony and festival, they also routinely shifted it from one place to another. In this way, the Association Meeting, also known in Chin as *Civui*, eventually became one of the most important religious activities for the Chin Christians and the most well-known religious festival in Chinram. At the *Civui* festival, different tribes and clans of Chins who formerly had never shared any kind of religious ceremony could now freely share their inner feelings and experiences in one faith, and also the same ritual practices through the church. And the Civui itself therefore constituted one of the identity-shaping sources which not only provided for the individuals' epistemological characteristics, i.e. his beliefs and basic values, but also catered to interpersonal relationships and brought about a sense of total solidarity between the individual and his fellow Christians who, in turn, shared his own ethnic nationality. Thus, the formation of the CHBA gradually provided the Chin people not only with a single ecclesiastical structure but also its related religious festival called *Civui*, and both of them constituted sources for the creation of their national identity in a new society, Christian Chinram. Moreover, these new religious institutions also transformed Chin society gradually from "tribal and clan-oriented" society to the "community of faith" in Jesus Christ.

(ii) The Feast as Worship

According to traditional Chin belief systems and ritual practices, there was no worship without feasts. Moreover, the feast was not just the sharing and partaking of food, but sharing the source of life (*zing-dangh*), and therefore a communion between god and man as well as between men. Since the Chin viewed the feast as sharing the source of life, there was no feast without animal sacrifice, known in Chin as *Sathi luan lo cun Do a si lo* (literally, "there is no feast without pouring blood"). The concept of pouring blood is very important because blood, according to traditional Chin religion, was the source of life, which must be shared as communion not only between the family, clan, and tribe, but also between them and their guardian god *khua-hrum*. In other words, pouring sacrificial animal blood was a symbol of communion between the guardian god *Khua-hrum* and man, and the sharing and partaking of the flesh and blood of sacrificial animals at the feast was a communion between men which united not only members of the community with each other but also with their god, *Khua-hrum*. The idea of animal sacrifice in the worship of *Khua-hrum* could be compared with the idea of animal sacrifice in the Hebrew Bible. According to

259

W. Robertson Smith:

> The leading idea of animal sacrifices of the Semite was not that of a gift made over to the god, but an act of communion in which the god and his worshipers united by partaking together of the flesh and blood of a sacred victim.[23]

When they became Christians, the Chin concept of communion as sharing the "source of life" (*zing-dangh*) was gradually transformed into the concept of communion with the "giver of life" (*Khua-zing*), that is, the Supreme God. Together with such a transition in belief, missionaries introduced a new ritual practice of "Holy" Communion between the Supreme God and man, which was simply a symbol without any animal sacrifice or real feast. Since there was no sharing and partaking of a real meal at Christian Holy Communion, it was only a communion between man and the giver of life, that is, the Supreme God *Khua-zing*, and not a communion between men. In traditional Chin religious concept, there was no communion between men without sharing and partaking of "the flesh and blood of a sacred victim" because the Chin considered it a source of life that must be shared between men so that the members of a family, clan, and tribe who shared the same source of life could be united as one. By contrast, the Christian "Holy Communion", which was usually held on the first Sunday of the month, did not bond people together as the same family or clan or tribe but rather as a community of believers. Moreover, the missionaries discouraged almost all traditional Chin feasts and festivals, which, of course, were in one way or another related to traditional ritual practices and belief systems. Thus, to become Christian during the missionary era was to abandon the traditional Chin ways of life, *Lai-phung*.

However, how could life be possible without feasts and festivals for the people who viewed the feast as worship to god? The spiritual life of the Chin people could not survive without feasts and festivals even in Christian churches. Traditional Chin religion received "its own rhythm through the regular changes of the agrarian year", and people had to renew their spiritual life through the rhythm of seasonal changes which were usually marked by many feasts and festivals. Feasts and festivals are the ancient rhythm through which people can renew their spiritual life without ceasing. Thus, the Chin church, as in Africa, "... has adapted itself to this ancient rhythm but has also created new festivals and given the year a new meaning."[24] In this way, Christmas (*Krismas*), New Year (*Kumthar*), and Easter (*Tho*) became the most important social feasts and festivals for the new Chin Christian community. As mentioned, they also created a new festival called *Civui*. Although Christmas, New Year, and Easter are seasonal festivals, the Chin celebrate them rather like feasts, and a single family usually hosts the festival for the entire community.

(iii) Krismas, Kumthar, and Tho

Although there was a transition from the Chin traditional ways of life to the new community of faith, the conversion to Christianity did not break down the ties of family, clan, and tribe in Chin society overnight. Instead, a good relationship between members of the family, clan, and tribe were somehow strengthened by the teaching of Love in the Christian Gospel. The only thing that was needed for the new converts among the Chin was to create a new ethos of how to express such Love and good feelings among themselves.

In their old culture, Love and good feelings were expressed in feasts and festivals, which tied family, clan, and tribe strongly together. Since Christian teaching encouraged good relationships and strong ties among members of the family, clan, and tribe, feasts and festivals were also needed for newly converted Chin Christians so that they could express their Love and ties not only between members of the family, clan, and tribe but also among members of the Church who shared the same faith in Christ the Savior. The only difference between the two— the old and the new—was that in the old culture, feasts and festivals were centered upon family, clan, and tribe, emphasizing the difference between one family and another, one clan and another, one tribe and another, and so on. Hence, it reinforced

261

clan and tribal identities, which in the long run resulted in deep separation between different tribes of the same people. In the new Christian society, however, feasts and festivals were centered upon a love that transcended the boundary of family, clan, and tribe; they emphasized the Love of God and humanity, which everybody could share and enjoy freely. Thus, the celebrations of Christmas, New Year, and Easter Sunday in the new Chin society were not just the celebration of seasonal feasts and festivals but the transformation of Chin society from "clan and tribal groups" to "the religious community of the Church" with no boundaries. In this way, the Chin society was gradually transformed from "clan and tribal oriented society" to "the community of faith in Christ".

In present Chin society, *Krismas*, *Kumthar* and *Tho* are celebrated like many other feasts and festivals in the old culture. Normally, a family who has a harvest as good as expected declares that they will host *Krismas* or *Kumthar* or *Tho*, whichever is most appropriate for them. Most families prefer to host *Krismas* and *Kumthar* because *Tho* usually occurs during the farmers' busiest time, when they need to prepare their fields for sowing before the monsoon rains comes in the middle of May. Even when the harvest is not as good as expected, a Christian family still offers a portion of money or food to the church and the church arranges to make the feast as best as they can. Thus, *Krismas*, *Kumthar* and *Tho* are really community events for the new Chin society, and also a time for community fellowship and reunion. Even today, when things are changing rapidly, the Chin people still prefer to celebrate those feasts, especially *Krismas*, in their birthplace.

During the feast, the host family has to prepare meals for the entire community, but cooking and preparing food are the responsibility of the community as a whole, especially the youth, as it was in their old culture. As long as the feast lasts, there are many activities in which almost all of the community or church members have to participate, such as song contests for both solo and choir, dramas, speeches and sermons, etc. Villagers and the community commonly employ these events not only to recall the past but also to share their faith and the rituals that define the new Chin society. In this way, those feasts and festivals gradually continue to help to create a new identity for a new society.

(iv) Civui and the Religious Festival

If *Krismas*, *Kumthar* and *Tho* are feasts and fellowship events for a single village or a single town, *Civui* is a festival for a larger community in which at least three villages participate. This is not just a religious festival but an expression of how the ecclesiastical structure of the Baptist church in Chinram created "new festivals and has given the season a new meaning". Moreover, this is about how Christianity helped the Chin people overcome "clan and tribal barriers"—which confined them separately in their history—and created a new tie and a new national identity for the whole Chin people. In other words, it is how Christianity has helped Chin society make the transition from a "clan and tribal oriented society" to a church-oriented community, which transcends the old tribal identity.

As mentioned already, *Civui* means "meeting", but it implies "any Church administrative meeting which is larger than the local Church meeting."[25] Thus, based on the ecclesiastical structure of the Baptist Church in Chinram, there are three levels of *Civui*: 1) Area *Civui*, 2) Association *Civui*, and 3) Convention *Civui*. Area *Civui* is held annually but Association and Convention *Civuies* are held tri-annually. (In some areas, especially in the Mizoram State in India, *Civui* is known as *Khwam-pui*, meaning "big gathering".)

Indeed, *Civui* is a good combination of Church administrative meeting and religious festival for the new society in Chinram. For Area *Civui*, the Church business meeting usually starts on Thursday, but at the Association and Convention levels, where much more business is to be done, the meeting usually starts on Monday. In both cases, however, ordinary pilgrims (*Civui a zawh mi*) must arrive on Friday when the Church administrative business is over. In fact, Friday is the real beginning of *Civui*. Usually, there are at least seven worship services during the *Civui*: one on Friday night, three on Saturday and three on Sunday. The intervals between worship services are used for fellowship and games. During the services, there are many speeches, sermons, choirs, and at night services, even dramas. The churches send their choir groups to highlight this special event, and the host village is responsible for providing room and board throughout the *Civui*. Nowadays, Area *Civui* is mainly held in rural areas, and Association and Convention *Civuis* are usually held in more urban areas—in towns such as Haka, Falam, Tiddim, etc. For the new Chin society, *Civui* has become a religious festival from which people can receive both spiritual and social benefits.

Civui is also a time when villagers and communities commonly recall their past, discuss their present, and share visions for their future together in one hope and one faith. This is a time when people do not identify each other as members of family, clan, or tribe but only as members of the community of faith. This is a time when people share not only their experiences both past and present, but even their emotions and faith. When people can freely share their experiences, emotions and faith, these are remembered not only as personal memories but also as common memories or socially reconstructed narrative events. And when personal memory becomes common memory, this is called social history, a factor that holds "history and identity together". In this way, the Chin people do "identity work" together, especially during such events as the *Civui*.

Concluding Remark

In this paper, I have argued that conversion to Christianity in Chin society was the product of a long-term process of change resulting from the pressures of external forces. Scholars from various disciplines have already affirmed the fact that there is a connection between religious change and social pressure in society. Social anthropologist Raymond Firth, for instance, writes, 'Religious change has often been a result of social pressures upon guardians of the doctrine and ritual.' He continues:

> Religion, like other social institutions, is continually in a process of change, due partly to external pressures of

an economic or political kind, or to internal pressures of doctrinal debate or personal ambition.[26]

Secondly, I have tried to analyze the paradoxical continuity between traditional Chin religion and Christianity. Doing this, I am mindful of the fact that if 'change is a lawful fact of social life', as scholars like Geertz have argued, how do we account for continuity? Scholars from various disciplines have tried to grapple with the problems of continuity within the process of change.

In my hypothesis, continuity between traditional Chin religion and Christianity was possible because of the two religions' similar theological concepts and belief systems, especially the traditional Chin concept of a Supreme Being, *Khua-zing*, and the Christian understanding of a Supreme God, the creator of all things in this universe. Traditionally, the Chin had a clear concept of the Supreme God, *Khua-zing*, but they did not worship Him because He was good and did not require any sacrificial appeasement like *Khua-hrum* and *Khua-chia* did. Thus, traditional Chin religion was centered upon the worship of *Khua-hrum* (guardian gods) and *Khua-chia* (evil spirits), not upon *Khua-zing*, the Supreme God.

When the Chin converted to Christianity, they inevitably passed through a long-term process of adjustment between the demands of a new faith and the ritual habits of their traditional religion. In this long-term process of change and adjustment, the Chin people completely abandoned almost all their traditional ritual practices of sacrificial ceremonies and their related value systems. This process of change also made deep inroads into the original patterns and structures of traditional religion, and thereby society itself. The belief system, however, was transformed from *Khua-hrum*-centric to *Khua-zing*-centric within the same conceptual pattern of belief system. In other words, the worship of *Khua-hrum* was transformed into the worship of *Khua-zing*, or the worship of the lesser god to the Supreme God.

In order to highlight the Chin response to the new religious challenge and how they did become Christians, I have approached my study from the Chin local perspective. Thus, instead of investigating purely institutional development of the

Chin churches, I investigated the gradual shift from traditional Chin religion to Christianity as an integrating factor in the development of Chin self-awareness. In this way, I analyzed the local stories that people tell about their society and about the past, especially events personified in ancestors and other historic figures. Through such stories, small and large, personal and collective, the Chin people do much of their "identity work" together. In other words, such "stories hold history and identity together."[27]

The most prominent and frequently repeated local stories are, of course, about the moment of the first confrontation with colonial power and the Christian mission, and subsequent conversion to Christianity. The stories of conversion are repeatedly told and retold, often in narrative accounts as writings, songs, sermons and speeches passed on during such occasions as religious feasts, celebrations, and worship services. These are times when people engage in exchange practices that define social and political relations. Although the wars against British annexation (1872-1896), the Anglo-Chin War (1917-1919), the Second World War and Japanese invasion (1939-1945), and the Independence of Burma (1948) are also significant junctures in temporal consciousness, the events of Christian conversion are uniquely important in the organization of a socio-historical memory.

In present Chin society, telling dramatic versions of the conversion stories has become almost a ritual practice during Sunday worship services and the annual Local and Association Meetings called *Civui,* where villages and communities commonly gather to recall the past. Narratives of shared experience and history do not simply represent identity and emotion, they even constitute them. In other words, histories told and remembered by those who inherit them are discourses of identity, just as identity is inevitably a discourse of history. Thus, "history teaching", as Appleby claims, "is identity formation."[28] Especially for the people who live in communities transformed by powerful outside forces, the common perception of a threat to their existence as well as the narrative accounts of socio-religio-cultural contact with the outside world had created identity through the idiom of shared history. However, just as history is never finished, neither is identity. It is continually refashioned as people make cultural meaning out of shifting social and political circumstances. I have analyzed how the old tribal and clan identities were gradually replaced, and how Christianity provided a means of preserving and promoting the self-awareness of Chin identity through its theological concepts and ideology and its ecclesiastical structure; and how the Chin people gradually adjusted to Christianity through an accelerated religious change in their society.

In addition to the theoretical framework which I have applied; another dimension which needs to be taken into account is the political developments after independence that strongly impacted on the Christian movement in Chinram was especially the promulgation of Buddhism as a state religion of the Union of Burma in 1961 by the U Nu government. This state religion issue provoked the Chin's religiously motivated liberation movement led by the "Chin Independence Army" in the 1960s. Viewing that Christian missionaries were the one who kept "imperialism alive" and agitated separatist movements among the Chin and other ethnic nationalities in Burma, General Ne Win, who came to power in 1962 through a military coup, not only expelled foreign missionaries but also intensified its military campaign against the Chin and other ethnic nationalist movements.

Ironically, when the military aspects of the Chin nationalist movement was suppressed from both sides of India and Burma, the indigenous form of Christianity, that is, the church without foreign missionaries, became a more valid expression of ethnic identity of the Chin in Burma. Moreover, the Christian movements under the dictatorship, especially "Chins for Christ in One Century", which was launched during at the peak of Ne Win's era in 1980s, became a symbolic expression of Chin national identity.

The present military junta in Burma, aware that Christianity and Chin identity are inseparably intertwined with each other, is relying on religious persecution as a means to eliminate the Chin's distinctive identity. The Burma Army destroy churches, removes Christian symbols of the cross—which is also a Chin national symbol—from mountain tops and holy places. They convert Chin Christians to Buddhism by force, and use forced labor to construct pagodas. The military junta has arrested and also killed a number pastors and Church leaders who boldly protested for their freedom of belief.[29]

The Chin Christians view the religious persecution that they are suffering as "part of the plan of providence of God, and an integral consequence of following Jesus Christ", and they proclaim that "the blood of the martyrs are the seeds of the Church and the Chin nation."[30] Through this irony the Chin Baptist Churches have shown spiritual vitality against the revolutionary changes under General Ne Win's regime and religious persecution under the current military junta. In fact, Chin Christians have manifested their own true character through an indigenous Chin church in the midst of a multi-ethnic and multi-religious cultural environment in the Union of Burma.

Notes

[1] During the first three decades of the twentieth century, "the great majority of" the Chin people in Mizoram State of present India had become Christian already. See Mangkhosat Kipgen, *Christianity and Mizo Culture*, (Jorhat, Assam and Aizawl: Mizo Theological Conference, 1996). For the church growth in East Chinram of Chin State in Burma, see Lian H Sakhong, *Religion and Politics among the Chin People in Burma, 1896-1949* (Uppsala University: Studia Missionalia Upsaliensia, 2000), Lian H. Sakhong, *In Search of Chin Identity: A Study in Religion, Politics and Ethnic Identity in Burma* (Copenhagen: Nordic Institute of Asian Studies, 2003), and Pum Suan Pau, *Growth of Baptist Churches in Chin State: The Chins for Christ in One Century Experience* (Manila: Union Theological Seminar, 1998).

[2] See my doctoral dissertation, *Religion and Politics among the Chin People in Burma, 1899-1949* (Uppsala University, 2000).

[3] Frederick S. Downs, *Essays on Christianity in North-East India*. (New Delhi: Indus Publishing Co., 1994), p. 4.

[4] Frederick Downs, *Essays on Christianity in North-East India* (1994), p.4

[5] Frederick Downs, *Essays on Christianity in North-East India* (1994), p.4

[6] Eric Ringmar, *Identity, Interest and Action: A Cultural Explanation of Sweden's Intervention in the Thirty Years War*, (Cambridge: Cambridge University Press, 1996), p. 145

[7] Frederick Downs, *Essays on Christianity in North-East India* (1994), op.cit., p. 24

[8] Frederick Downs, *Essays on Christianity in North-East India* (1994), p. 24

[9] Frederick Downs, *Essays on Christianity in North-East India* (1994), p. 29

[10] Frederick Downs, *History of Christianity in India: North East India in the Nineteenth and twentieth Centuries, Vol. V, Part 5* (Bangalore: 1992), p.146

[11] I borrowed the theme of "imagining social world" from Benedict Anderson's *Imagined Communities: Reflection on the Origins and Spread of Nationalism*, rev. ed. (London, 1991), especially pp. 9-36

[12] Cf. Benedict Anderson, *Imagine Communities* (1991), especially chapter 3.

[13] East 1990: FM-186, and also Johnson, *History of American Baptist Chin Mission*, Vol. 1 (1988), pp. 259-60.

[14] Laura Carson, *Pioneer Trails, Trails and Triumph* (New York: Baptist Board Publication, 1927), p. 161

[15] Robert Johnson, *American Baptist Chin Mission* (1988), p. 263.

[16] Pu Sakhong, *Kan Pupa Thawhkehnak Kong* (Aibur: Manuscript, 1971), p. 11

[17] East, FM-186, 1908-1919

[18] This hymn is inscribed on the gravestone of Pu Hreng Kio of Aibur who became a Christian in early 1930s and passed away as a church leader of Aibur in 1961.

[19] Interviewed with Pi Men Tang, Lian Hei's sister, on December 27, 1990

[20] Robert Johnson, *American Baptist Chin Mission* (1988), p. 145

[21] Robert Johnson, *American Baptist Chin Mission* (1988), p. 145

[22] Robert Johnson, *American Baptist Chin Mission* (1988), p. 145

[23] William Robertson Smith, "Sacrifice: Preliminary Survey" in *Lectures on the Religion of the Semites: The Fundamental Institutions* (2d ed.; London: Black, 1894), reprinted in C. E. Carter and C. L. Meyers (ed.,), *Community, Identity, and Ideology: Social Science Approaches to the Hebrew Bible* (Winona Lake, Indiana: Eisenbrauns, 1996), pp. 43-64.

[24] Bengt Sundkler, *Bara Bukoba: Church and Community in Tanzania* (London: Hurst & Company, 1980), p. 181

[25] Cung Lian Hup, *Innocent Pioneers and Their Triumps in a Foreign Land* (Chicago: Lutheran School of Theology, 1993), p. 105

[26] Raymond Firth, *Religion: A Humanist Interpretation* (London: Routledge, 1996), p. 199

[27] Cf. Geoffrey M. White, *Identity Through History*, (Cambridge University Press, 1995)

[28] Joyce Appleby, "The Power of History" in *The American Historical Review*, Volume--, No. 1. February 1998, pp.1-14

[29] The Chin Human Rights Organisation (CHRO) has compiled hundred of cases of religious persecution in Chin State, committed by current military junta in Burma. See *Religious Persecution: A Campaign of Ethnocide against Chin Christians in Burma* (Ottawa: CHRO, 2004).

[30] See *Religious Persecution*, report by CHRO.

SEVENTEEN

The Future of Indo-Burma Relations: A View from Divided Peoples

This paper was presented at the 9th International Conference on Burma Studies, University de Provence, Marseilles, France, 6-10 July 2010. This is its first publication.

Introduction

Burma and India share a 1,643 km-long land border, which divides the homelands of three major ethnic groups in the region, namely, the Chin, Kachin and Naga. Modern international boundaries divide the Chin into Chin State, Sagaing Division and Magwe Division in Burma, Mizoram and Manipur States in India, and Bawm Area of Chittagong Hills Track in Bangladesh. The Kachin are divided into Kachin State, Shan State and Sagaing Division in Burma, Arunachal Pradesh State in India, and Yunnan Province in China. The Naga are divided into Nagaland and Manipur States in India, and Sagaing Division in Burma. Before the colonial period, these ethnic groups and their homelands were never annexed or conquered by either India or Burma/Myanmar.

During the colonial period, the British authorities promulgated two separate constitutions for these ethnic groups: the Kachin Hill Tribes Regulation of 1895, which was applied mainly to the Kachin; and the Chin Hills Regulation of 1896, which was applied not only to the Chin in what they then called the Chin Hills District, Chittagong Hills District, and Lushai Hills District, but also for the Naga in the then Naga Hills District and other areas. After the promulgation of the 1935 Burma Act and India Act in 1937, which officially separated British India and British Burma, the Chin Hills Regulation for the Lushai Hills District and Naga Hills District was renamed as the Assam Frontier Tract Regulation for the Lushai Hills and Naga Hills. For the Chin Hills District, the name Chin Hills Regulation remained until the Chin joined in Burma's independence in 1948. Unfortunately for those peoples, the British administrative boundaries that divided their homelands became the international boundaries when India and Burma gained their respective independence from British colonial power.

In this paper, I shall examine the future of Indo-Burma relations from the perspective of these three ethnic groups: the Chin, Kachin, and Naga. I will argue in this paper that the future of Indo-Burma relations, especially the Indian "Look East Policy", depends very much on how the Burmese military junta and the Indian government approach these ethnic problems, including on-going territorial-based ethnic conflicts in North East India and a six decades long civil war in Burma. They all have armed groups and while the Chin and Kachin are fighting against the military junta in order to gain greater autonomy within a federal arrangement of the Union of Burma, the Naga, from both India and Burma, have been fighting for their freedom since the end of the colonial period.

Without solving these ethnic problems in North East India and Burma, India cannot effectively apply its "Look East Policy". The Look East Policy, as Pudaite argues, is part of "India's response to the process of globalization...initiatives India and its eastern partners take for expanding mutual cooperation spanning over and through the NE region" (Pudaite, 2010: 179). India cannot look east without "looking at the NE region" including the Chin, Kachin and Naga regions in Burma. Without ending sixty years of civil war and solving the root cause of the political crisis in Burma, which is mostly rooted in ethnic issues; the military junta in *Naypyidaw* cannot hope for the stability of the region and the long term developments that they dream of, even by establishing good relationships with its neighbours, especially with India.

For the past sixty or so years, those ethnic nationalities have been able to protect and promote their heritage and way of life through armed resistance. Consequently, they were able to prevent the degradation of their culture, religion and language from successive governments of the Union of Burma and India. However, due to the changing geopolitics after the end of the cold war, it has become very difficult to sustain armed-struggle as an ethnic nationalist movement.

Moreover, it is not easy to resist the forces of globalization, represented not only by the governments of India and Burma but by multi-national companies, trans-national corporations, and international-financial institutions, etc. This paper will, therefore, argue that for those ethnic nationalities, even if they are not willing to abandon armed-struggle, it is time to look at other alternative means and ways to sustain their heritage, way of life, freedom, and the development of their homelands.

The future of Indo-Burma relations, in a nutshell, depends very much on how India and Burma approach ethnic issues in the region, and how those ethnic groups will respond to the forces of globalization, and whether they are able to find alternative solution to armed-struggle.

Historical Background: The Crown Colonial Scheme

In 1937, when the Burma Act of 1935 was officially implemented and Burma was separated from the Province of India, Sir Robert Reid, the Governor of Assam, strongly protested against the policy of the British India government, which had adopted the administrative boundaries of the homelands of Chin, Kachin and Naga as the boundary between Burma and India, and later between India and Bangladesh as well. He thus wrote to the London government that '. . . the separation of Burma from India on lines of the present frontiers will permanently divorce portions of tribes [Chin, Kachin and Naga], which naturally should comprise a single unit' (R. Reid 1942: 6).

From the very beginning, Sir Robert Reid, like B. S. Carey who drafted the Chin Hills Regulation, was in favour of forming what later came to be known as a "Province of Commonwealth" for those peoples and were strongly opposed to the idea of dividing them into three administrative units and thereby three countries. Foreseeing the dangerous consequences of dividing those peoples, in 1935 he updated the provision of the "Inner Line Regulation" of 1873 in order to protect the Chin, Kachin, Naga and other ethnic groups in what is now called "Northeast India" from the exploitation of outsiders. As a matter of fact, the inner line regulation was adopted by the British colonial power not only to prohibit permanent residence in the area by persons not native to it, but designed as a recognition of the pre-colonial independent status of the Chin, Kachin, Naga and other peoples in the region.

In 1941, Sir Robert Reid made his strongest proposal, which became known as the "Crown Colonial Scheme of 1941". He declared that '. . . they [the Chin, Kachin and Naga] are not Indian in any sense of the word, neither in origin nor in outlook, and it is a historical accident that they have been taken into an Indian province' (R. Ried 1942: 6; cited also by Symleah 1981: 172–78). He thus proposed to form a separate colonial province, what he called the "Chin-Lushai Province", for the peoples and regions covered by the Chin Hills Regulation, which would have had its own governorship and the same political and administrative status as the governments of Assam, Bengal and Burma. His proposal was accepted by the Conservative Party in London led by Sir Winston Churchill. Unfortunately, World War II prevented the implementation of Sir Robert Reid's proposal of the Crown Colonial scheme in 1941.

Soon after the Second World War, the British returned to Burma with new colonial schemes, including the "Crown Colonial Scheme of 1941" which intended to create a separate British colonial province, the "Chin-Lushai Country". The British officers who had had a friendly relationship with the Chin, Kachin and other ethnic groups during the war, particularly Sir Dorman-Smith, Governor of British Burma, and H.N.C. Stevenson, Director of the Frontier Areas Administration, reminded the London government of its commitment to implement Sir Robert Reid's Crown Colonial Scheme (cf. Sakhong, 2003: 186-187).

The "Crown Colonial Scheme", however, was updated in accordance with the changing political situation during the war, which favoured the formation of a separate colonial country called the "Province of the Commonwealth" between India and Burma. While Robert Reid's original "Crown Colonial Scheme" was aimed at the creation of the "Chin-Lushai Country" only for the Chin, the up-dated proposal included the Chin Hills District (the present Chin State in Burma), Lushai Hills District (the present Mizoram State in India), the Chittagong Hill Tracts (in present Bangladesh), Arakan Hill Tracts (Paletwa Township of present Chin State), Naga Hills District (present Nagaland State), Manipur, North Cachar and Mikir areas, parts of the Chindwin District (present Naga Hills in Burma), the west bank of the Chindwin (present Kale, Kabaw, Kankaw, and Tamu Valleys in Sagaing Division of Burma), Kachin Hills (present Kachin State in Burma, but excluded Myitkyina, Bamaw and Kata Townships), the hill areas of Sadiya and the hills of Tripura.

Thus, in 1945, Mr R. Coupland, a Professor in the History Department at Oxford University and an expert on constitutional law, was sent again to study the possible implementation of the resolution to make a separate country for those peoples into what he called a "Province of the Commonwealth". He gave his affirmative report to the British government under the Crown Colonial Scheme (Cf. Coupland 1946: 201–205).

However, before this project was implemented, the Conservative Party was defeated in the first post-war general election by Clement Attlee's Labour Party. The Labour Party, which had long had the independence of India and Burma as part of its program, wanted to give away the entire subcontinent and the creation of a "Province of the Commonwealth" between India and Burma was out of the question for the new government. Eventually, Attlee annulled the Conservative Party's "Crown Colonial Scheme" when he came into power in 1945 (cf. Sakhong, 2003: 186-187, and pp. 206-208).

The Status of Chin, Kachin and Naga in Newly Independent Burma and India

After the end of World War II, the Chin, Kachin, Naga and other ethnic groups in Burma, such as the Karen and Shan expected better treatment from the British government in the way of social, cultural, economic and, most importantly, political development projects for their homelands. They had, after all, served with great loyalty on the British side during the war. They were not prepared for the rapidly changing political situation after the Second World War, nor for independence of their respective homelands. While Indian and Burman nationalists had been fighting hard to gain freedom and become sovereign nation-states, the Chin, the Kachin and the Karen were still willing to remain under British rule.

In the early stage of the post-war period, the colonial powers strongly highlighted the rights and interests of the Chin, Kachin, Karen and other non-Burman nationalities from the so-called Frontier Areas. But in 1945, soon after he came to power, Attlee decided to replace former governor Dorman-Smith with Major-General Hubert Rance, who had administered Burma during the temporary military administration in 1945. Rance arrived in Rangoon on August 30, 1946, and immediately informed London that "the White Paper is now out of date". He also cabled directly to Attlee that "The AFPFL is the only horse to back" (M. Smith, 1991: 77). Thus, together with the replacement of Governor Dorman-Smith, who closely associated himself with the Conservative Party, the Labour Government in Britain "reversed its policy, and Burma's political agenda became largely a matter of bilateral negotiation between the British and Aung San's AFPFL" (Christie, 1998: 155).

In December 1946, the British only invited Aung San and his delegation from Burma Proper to London without a single representative from the Frontier Areas to discuss "the steps that would be necessary to constitute Burma as a sovereign independent nation" (Aung San Suu Kyi, 1991: 23). Since Attlee's Labour Government had already prepared to grant Burma's independence "either within or without the Commonwealth", the London talks were largely a formality, at most putting into more concrete form the principles to which they already had agreed. The only stumbling blocks were the issues relating to what they then called the Frontier Areas (Cf. U Maung Maung, 1988: 253).

When the Chin, Kachin, Shan and other ethnic groups became a major issue in post-war Burma, Stevenson, Director of the Frontier Areas Administration, organized what came to be known as the First Panglong Conference in March 1946. Later, at the Second Panglong Conference, held in February 1947, the Chin, Kachin, Shan and the Interim Burmese Government led by General Aung San signed the historic Panglong Agreement, the purpose of which it declares in its preamble:

> Believing that freedom will be more speedily achieved by the Shans, the Kachins, and the Chins by their immediate co-operation with the interim Burmese government.

For the Chin, Kachin and Shan, the essence of the Panglong Agreement was to speed up their own search for freedom together with the Burman and other nationalities in what became the Union of Burma, based on the principles of equality, mutual trust and recognition. As a condition for joining the Union of Burma, the Chin, Kachin and Shan demanded that the right of secession must be included in the 1947 Constitution of the Union of Burma, which was duly proclaimed in Chapter X, Article 201, and 202:

Chapter (X): The Right of Secession

201. Save as otherwise expressly provided in this Constitution or in any Act of Parliament made under section 199, *every state shall have the right to secede from the Union* in accordance with the condition hereinafter prescribed.

202. The *right of secession* shall not be exercised within ten years from the date on which this Constitution comes into operation.

Although Chapter 10 of the 1947 Constitution guaranteed the rights of secession for all member states of the Union, the clauses in the same constitution for the Chin Affairs (Chapter IX, Part V), and the Kachin Affairs (Chapter IX, Part. III) omitted the right of secession. Only the clauses for the Karenni and Shan States Affairs reaffirmed the right of secession.

Unfortunately, the Naga in Burma were more or less side-lined when the negotiations for the future status of the non-Burman/Myanmar ethnic nationalities were conducted. The same was true for the Chin in India inwhat they then called the Lushai Hills District when Indian nationalists negotiated with the British for independence. However, the Naga in India were capable of negotiating their own future status both with the British and Indian nationalists.

In 1947, the Naga National Council (NNC), under the leadership of Angami Zapu Phizo, went to New Delhi and negotiated the Naga claim for independence with both the British and Indian nationalists, including Mahatma Gandhi. Phizo and his NNC submitted a Memorandum to the [British] Government of India, in which they asserted their "right of self-determination and amending the setting up of an Interim Government of the Naga people for a period of Ten Years" (NNC 1993: 17-18).

After submitting the Memorandum, Phizo was able to secure what came to be known as "The Naga-Akbar Hydari Accord", which was signed by Sir Akbar, the Governor of Assam, and the Naga leaders in Kohima on 28 June 1947. The "Naga-Akbar Hydari Accord", also known as the "Governor's Nine-point Agreement", recognized "the right of the Naga to develop themselves according to their freely expressed wishes" (Hazarika, 1994: 97). The accord also mentioned that after ten years of the agreement's implementation, "the Naga National Council will be asked whether they require the above agreement to be extended for a further period, or [if] a new agreement regarding the future of the Naga people [should be] arrived at" (Ibid.)

Knowing the attitude of the Indian nationalists who intended to oppose the "Naga-Akbar Hydari Accord", Phizo and his NNC declared Naga independence on 14 August 1947, just one day a head of India's independence. On 9 July 1948, Phizo was arrested and jailed in Calcutta. He was released after one year on humanitarian grounds, but "Phizo was undeterred" (Hazarika, 1994: 98). As soon as opportunity presented itself, Phizo and his NNC conducted "a referendum where the Naga were asked whether they wanted to live in India or resume their separateness. The vote was ninety-nine percent in favour of independence" (ibid). Thus, Phizo once again declared Naga independence in 1956, and a fully fledged war broke out between the Naga and the Indian government.

Indo-Burma Relation as Joint Operations against Ethnic Insurgencies

The war in Nagaland continues today. In this on-going war, as Hazarika observes,

> Churches were burned, villages were razed, and aircrafts were used to bomb and harass the Nagas. Women were raped and continue to be molested even these days by troops, nearly forty years after the first shots of Naga uprising were fired (Hazarika, 1994: 101).

In late 1950s, while the civil war in Nagaland was in a full swing, another ethnic insurgency arose in North East India, this time in Mizoram State, or what they then called the "Lushai Hills District" led by the Mizo National Front (MNF).

The MNF began its movement as the Mizo National Famine Front (MNFF) in 1959, when the famine called "*Mautam*" struck Mizoram. The *Mautam,* is a periodical event, related with the bamboo plants that flower every fifty years and form a sort of seed resembling paddy seeds. Although the flowers heighten the rugged beauty of the landscape, they are also the harbingers of starvation and death. Not only the bamboo seeds, but also the flowers themselves, attract rats like "honey draws bees". Millions of rats swarm into the jungle and rice and vegetable fields of the *jhum* or *Lo,* devouring everything in their wake. This was the most important cause of the great famine that periodically visits Mizoram (Cf. Hazarika, 1994: 111).

In October 1958, the Mizo District Council predicted the imminence of famine following the flowering of the bamboo and passed a resolution to take precautionary measures. It asked the governor of Assam to sanction the sending of Rs 150,000 in relief funds for the Mizo district, including the Pawi-Lakher region. However, the Assam government rejected the request, "possibly assuming that the prediction of famine was a primitive people's tradition" (ibid.). But tradition proved right. The bamboo flowered in 1959, and the next year rats multiplied in millions and ate up grain, fruit and everything else that was edible. The catastrophe occurred suddenly and so comprehensively that the governor of Assam was taken by surprise.

Exasperated by the Assam government's failure to bring in assistance in time, the Mizo Cultural Society and various denominations of Christian churches formed famine-fighting squads. The most prominent of these groups was the Mizo National Famine Front (MNFF), launched by a young bank clerk called Laldenga. In fact, most of the relief and aid came from foreign missionaries who had been working among the Mizo for many years, such as the American Baptist Mission and the Scottish Presbyterian Mission. During that period of suffering, the MNFF helped the villagers by making sure they received their share of missionary and government aid. In doing so, they became so popular that the villagers recognized them as their real leaders, especially Laldenga, who was seen as a national hero. Sanjoy Hazarika writes:

> In order to help his people Laldenga developed a network of workers and supporters who distributed food and travelled to the remotest villages with relief and a message. The message was simple: the state and Central Government did not care for the Mizos and this was shown in its shoddy response to the famine; that the Mizo District Council, the main political forum, had

failed to rally support at a time of crisis and was now unrepresentative of Mizo aspirations; that the area was integrated into Assam as late as 1898 under a political officer who acted as a representative of the Viceroy; and that the Mizos, like the Nagas, were a nation and deserved a place of their own, away from India. The response was electrifying (Hazarika, 1994: 111).

On October 28, 1961, after the famine was over, the MNFF eventually converted itself into a political party called the Mizo National Front (MNF), with independence—and hence the reunification of all the Chin people living in Burma, India and East Pakistan (now Bangladesh)—as its goal. Thus, from the very beginning the MNF had advocated for independence, or what some historians call the philosophy of "Greater Chinram", which indeed became very popular among the Chin people in both India and Burma. The policy of the MNF was clearly described in the "Mizo Memorandum", submitted to the Prime Minister of India on October 30, 1965.

The Mizos, from time immemorial, lived in complete independence without foreign interference . . . Their administration was like that of the Greek City State of the past . . . Their territory or any part thereof had never been conquered or subjugated by their neighbouring states . . . The Mizo are a distinct nation, created and moulded and nurtured by God and nature. The Mizo had never been under the government of India. Therefore, the Mizos demanded the nation of Mizoram, a free sovereign state to govern itself, to work her own destiny and formulate her own foreign policy (cited by Vumson, 1986: 279).

On February 28, 1966, the MNF began the Biblically code-named "Operation Jericho". All the towns in Mizoram were encircled by the Mizo National Army, to strike at zero hour, one o'clock on March 1, 1966. Before the next day dawned, the MNF Army had occupied the entire region of Mizoram. The Government Treasury, radio station and police station at Aizawl, the capital of Mizoram, fell into their hands. The MNF therefore solemnly declared the independence of Mizoram on March 1, 1966, and West Chinram, of Mizoram State in India, became a free nation, at least for a short period of time (cf. Vumson, 1986: 286).

As the ultimate goal of the MNF movement was independence for the entire Chin people they planned to capture and set free the whole of Chinram. That is, not only Mizoram in India but also Chin State in Burma and the Chittagong Hills Track in Bangladesh, where the Chin people are artificially divided. They, thus, widened their operations into Burma to capture all the important towns in East Chinram. In this operation, from April to June 1966, the MNF captured Tiddim, Tamu and Falam. Since Falam was the capital of what was then called the Chin Special Division, its liberation symbolized the freedom of the whole of East Chinram in Burma. Thus, by capturing Aizawl and Falam, at least for a short period, the MNF was symbolically able to liberate both East and West Chinram (Chin State and Mizoram State) in 1966.

Even before the Naga and Mizo (Chin) from the North East India started their armed-struggle against the New Delhi government, ethnic nationalities in Burma had already started their armed resistance against the central government in Rangoon. Although the right of secession was included to safeguard ethnic rights in the 1947 Constitution of the Union of Burma, none of the ethnic nationalities in the country were satisfied with the real constitutional arrangement. When they signed the Panglong Agreement, they had envisaged a federal system where they could enjoy a combination of "self-rule" for their respective ethnic states and "shared-rule" for the whole Union. But what happened with the 1947 Constitution was a mixture of both federal and unitary systems with strong centralization. With this, they felt, that they had lost their autonomous status in an independent Burma. Therefore, beginning with the Karen in 1949, one ethnic group after another revolted against the central government.

In addition to the constitutional crisis that they have faced since independence, Chin, Kachin and Karen Christians were also confronted by another problem when U Nu's government promulgated Buddhism as a state religion in 1961.The most serious armed rebellion as a direct result of the adoption of Buddhism as a state religion was that of the Kachin Independence Army (KIO), which emerged soon after the state religion of Buddhism act was promulgated in 1961. The "Christian Kachin", as Graver observes, "saw the proposal for Buddhism to be the state religion as further evidence of the Burmanization of the country" which they had to prevent by any means, including armed rebellion (Graver, 1993: 56). The Chin rebellion, led by Hrang Nawl, was also related to the promulgation of Buddhism as the state religion, but the uprising was delayed until 1964 owing to tactical problems.

After several months of training in East Pakistan, the Chin National Liberation Army, under the leadership of Hrang Nawl, was ready for action. But before they took any action against the Burmese government, they discussed all the matters with their blood brothers from the Mizo National Front (MNF) led by Laldenga. The main purpose of the meeting was to discuss whether they would need to combine their forces into a single political organization and fight both India and Burma under the same command. The meeting was held at Tuisang on March 23, 1965. The MNF's delegation was led by Maj. Gen. Lalliana the commanding officer of the MNA (Mizo National Army) Special Forces, Senator Subloa, a member of the Central Committee of the MNF, and Brigadier Biakchhunga, a veteran of the Burma Army's Chin Rifles. At the meeting they agreed that, because of the geopolitical nature of India and Burma, they would not combine their forces but would fight separately for the same purpose, and they also agreed not only to cooperate with each other in military operations but also to exchange and share any information they would need for such operations.

While the MNF launched "Operation Jericho" and occupied the entire West Chinram of Mizoram and the Capital of East Chinram, Falam;, Hrang Nawl and his Chin Liberation Army attacked Haka, the present Capital of Chin State, Tiddim, Rih, Thlantlang, Matupi and other towns and areas. The 700 strong force of the Chin Liberation Army, under the command of General Tual Zen and Col. Son Kho Pau, a former Burma Army officer, were divided into two groups, Northern Command and Southern Command, and they virtually controlled most of East Chinram in March 1965.

Alarmed by the Chin rebellion on both sides of Chinram, Mizoram and Chin States, and also by the Naga liberation movement; the Indian Prime Minister Lal Bahadur Shastri visited Burma and discussed the situation with General Ne Win and with "rebel movements along the India-Burma borders. . . they agreed to cooperate with each other to prevent any sinister attempt at secession or disintegration" (Vumson, 1986: 235). As geopolitics played a major role in the region, Burma too was alarmed by the Chin nationalist movement on both sides of its border with India. General Ne Win, thus, visited India in March 1968. There "he agreed with Mrs. Indira Gandhi, then Indian Prime Minister, to joint security measures against resistance groups on both sides of the boundary. They agreed to exchange information and to coordinate their patrols in the Naga-Mizo-Chin border areas"(ibid. P.237).

In 1969, the Burma and Indian Armies launched a joint operation against the Chin nationalist movement. In Shillong, Hrang Nawl, Son Kho Pau and TunKho Pau were all arrested by the Indian authorities and deported to Burma in accordance with the Indo-Burma Agreement. Hrang Nawl, Son Kho Pau and other Chin nationalist leaders were immediately handed over to the Burmese government but Tun Kho Pau, who was an Indian citizen, was not deported but brutally killed by the Assam Rifles of the India Army. Son Kho Pau passed away a few months after he was released from a Burmese jail after serving more than ten years imprisonment without trial. Hrang Nawl also served over ten years without trial and was released two years after General Ne Win promulgated a new constitution in 1974.

As the physical movement of the Chin National Liberation was virtually ended by the Indo-Burma joint operation in 1969, the Indian Army launched another military operation against the MNF. In 1971 when the Indian Army invaded East Pakistan and declared the independence of Bangladesh, the MNF headquarters in East Pakistan was forced to move into the Arakan Hills Tract in Burma. Laldenga was evacuated to Karachi in West Pakistan, where he was helped and protected by Z. A. Bhutto's government. Later, with the help of his missionary friend Michael Scott, Laldenga moved to London and lived there in exile.

In October 1984, Indira Gandhi invited Laldenga for talks. Mrs Gandhi died and her son Rajiv Gandhi signed the Mizo Peace Accord in 1985. As a result of this accord, Laldenga entered Aizawl as a victorious leader of the Mizo tribe of the Chin in India. He became the Chief Minister of the Interim Mizoram Government in 1986. Soon his MNF party was victorious and on Chin National Day (February 20) in 1987, Laldenga became the elected Chief Minister of Mizoram. On that very same day, Mizoram was declared a full autonomous State within the federal system of India (Cf. Chatterjee, 1990: 541–542).

The Changing Dynamic in Indo-Burma Relations

Since both countries emerged as sovereign nation-states, India and Burma adhered to the five principles of peaceful co-existence, formulated at Bandung Conference in 1954 as the core of their foreign policies. These were: (1) Mutual respect for each other's territorial integrity and sovereignty; (2) Mutual non-aggression; (3) Mutual non-interference in each other's internal affairs; (4) Equality and mutual benefit; and (5) Peaceful co-existence. Both countries were also active in the non-alliance movements as founding members in 1950s.

The foreign policy for every sovereign country is fundamentally intended to safeguard their national interests abroad, and, as such, it is more or less the extension of domestic policies, which can broadly be described as: (i) consolidation and preservation of national independence, (ii) safeguarding of national security, and (iii) national development (cf. Pudaite, 2010: 215). As part of their respective "national security" interests, bilateral relation between India and Burma has mainly focused on "cooperation in combating insurgencies" along the Indo-Burma border, especially the Chin, Kachin and Naga insurgent groups (cf. K. Yhome, 2008: 85).

The Chin, Kachin and Naga nationalist movements have always been a major concern for both countries. Although the physical movement of the Chin National Liberation was curtailed in 1969, and the Mizo National Front was converted into a normal political party when Mizoram became a full autonomous state in 1987; the Kachin and Naga armed-struggles continue to exist. However, in 1980, the Naga National Council split into two factions; Thuengaling Muivah, who was picked up by Phizo for his chief aide in 1966, split away from Phizo's NNC. Together with Isak Swu, Muivah founded the National Socialist Council of Nagaland (NSCN) on the Burma side of Nagaland. The NSCN split into two factions again; one group is led by Muivah and Isak Swu, therefore known as NSCN (M-I), and another faction is led by Khaplang, therefore known as NSCN (K).

After the student-led democracy uprising in Burma in 1988, another insurgent group emerged from Chin State in Burma. The Chin National Front (CNF) was founded by Chin students from Rangoon and Mandalay universities, who were involved in the 1988 democracy movement but escaped to the India border after the military coup in 1989. The CNF's military wing the Chin National Army (CNA) received military training from the Kachin Independent Organization (KIO) in early 1990s and established a strong network with other ethnic insurgent groups from Burma and joined the National Democratic Front (NDF), founded in 1976, the largest alliance of ethnic armed groups in Burma,. They also become a member of the "Ethnic Nationalities Council", the largest ethnic political alliance which includes both armed groups and political parties of all of Burma's ethnic nationalities. The CNF has made it clear that their policy has been to establish a genuine democratic federal union of Burma. And, as such, they do not interfere nor disturb Indian sovereignty in its policies.

Although CNF policy is aimed at the establishment of a democratic federal union of Burma, the Indo-Burma joint military operations did not spare them. In 1995, when the Indian and Burmese army launched a joint security operation code named "Operation Golden Bird" against the Naga armed groups, the CNF was accused of helping both the NSCN (MI) and NSCN (K) to transport arms through the border between the two countries. The Vice-Chairman of the CNF, Salai Sang Hlun, was captured by the Assam Rifles and killed on 23 April 1995. In the early to mid- 2000s, the CNF suffered two more joint military operations launched by Burmese and Indian forces. In 2005 they lost "Camp Victoria" one of their most important military camps in what was the most severe setback suffered by the CNF since its inception.

Indian and Burmese joint military operations against ethnic insurgent groups intensified after the formation of the "Indo-Burmese Revolutionary Front" which united various armed groups from both sides of the border; "the KIO, the NSCN-IM, the ULFA (United Liberation Front of Asom), the UNLF-M (United National Liberation Front – Meghen, of Manipur) and PLA (People's Liberation Army, also of Manipur) The Revolutionary Front was able to launch a number of joint attacks against Indian authorities (Egreteau, 2003: 62-63). While the Indian army was engaged in military campaigns against the CNF and other groups on the Indian side of the border, the Burmese army attacked the general headquarters of the NSCN (K) in Eastern Nagaland of Sagaing Division in early 2007. The "NSCN (K) acknowledged that ten of its cadre were killed during raids and some others sustained injuries" (Yhome, 2008: 79).

As joint military operations were conducted more often it has become clear that, "military-to-military ties between the two countries have been growing over the years. High-level visits of military officials have been part of the process of strengthening ties between the two militaries" (Yhome, 2008: 78-79). In April 2007, the Burmese (Myanmar's) Naval Chief, Vice Admiral SoeThein, visited India. That visit was followed by the visit of Lieutenant General Tin Aung MyintOo, the Quartermaster of SPDC Armed Forces, who replaced Gen SoeThein as Secretary-1 of the SPDC in October 2007, when he met "his Indian counterpart Lt. Gen Sudhir Sharma and the then Vice Chief of Army Staff Lieutenant General Deepak Kapoor". At that meeting the SPDC General asked "India to sell infantry weapons and ammunition in return for Myanmar's help in flushing out insurgent groups based along the border region" (ibid.).

India has reportedly sold two British made Islander aircraft, light artillery, T-55 tanks and small arms, including assault rifles, light machine guns, and handguns to the regime. Indian military officers have also "promised aid and training for Myanmar's troops". Security imperatives of both countries in their border areas, as Yhome observes, "strengthen the military supply relationship between the two countries" (ibid. p. 79). In addition to "military-to-military relations", the improvement of Indo-Burma relations could, in early 1990s, be viewed within a broader perspective of the changing dynamic of Indian foreign policy, from "idealism" to "realism", or from a moral-value-based approach to a more pragmatic one.

The Indian Look East Policy

India was the only Asian country that officially condemned "through its official channel" the SLORC's bloody crackdown on the student-led democracy demonstrators in 1988 and openly supported the pro-democracy movement in receiving "Burmese student refugees with open arms."(Yhome, 2008: 76). All this was done in accordance with the so called the "idealism" approach of the Indian foreign policy establishment, through which India, as the largest democratic country in the world, supported democracy movements not only in Burma but around the world. However, this approach was soon ended by the Narasimha Rao's government which adopted the more pragmatic approach of realism in its foreign policy towards Burma (cf. Egreteau, 2003: 132-133).

India had obviously changed its foreign policy towards Burma for several reasons, including: (1) the perceived need to contain the Chinese influence in South East Asia, especially in Burma, (2)an urgent need to obtain energy supplies, especially natural gas, from Burma, and (3) the long term need to secure cooperation with the Burmese military regime in combating insurgencies in North East India (cf. Yhome, 2008: 85).With this changing new policy, India "officially put to an end ... radical isolation of Myanmar", and decided to "follow the diplomatic model of 'Constructive Engagement Policy' conducted by ASEAN countries" (Egreteau, 2003: 133). To open a new diplomatic door, Mr. J. N. Dixit, Deputy Foreign Minister, visited Rangoon in March 1993.The Rao's government reaffirmed the Indian fundamental principle of "non-interference in the internal affairs of any country" to the military junta in Burma, when Foreign Minister Mr. Pranab Mukherjee visited Rangoon in March 1996. Mukherjee also confirmed to the generals in Rangoon that "India considered the Burmese democracy movement Myanmar's internal affairs" (ibid.). In this way, India demonstrated that "it has become aware of [the] importance of establishing a dialogue" with Burma and ASEAN countries (ibid.).

In line with this new foreign policy, India adopted its "Look East Policy" which eventually transformed not only in to an "idealism-oriented" Indian foreign policy, but also changed its approach to the North East region. Since independence, the North East region is not only "poorly connected" with mainstream India but neglected by successive governments of India in New Delhi. Until the late 1970s, political issues of the region, including insurgent problems, were dealt with by the External Affairs Ministry of the Government of India, not by the Home Ministry (cf. Hazarika, 1994: 91). India seemed to have adopted, and continuously applied, British colonial policy in its dealing with the Chin (Mizo), Naga and other ethnic groups in the North East region and thereby recognized the pre-colonial independent status of those ethnic groups. However, "compared to the pre-Independence land and waterways connectivity available for the North East, the existing channels of trade and transport routes are far from adequate to have any opening impact on the overall insularity of the region" (Pudaite, 2010: 182).

The immediate reason for changing Indian foreign policy from "idealism" to "realism" seemed to be related also to the end of cold war and the collapsed of the Soviet Union. During the cold war, India depended heavily on the Soviet Union for trade, economic and financial assistance to military, technological and diplomatic matters. When the Soviet Union collapsed, India lost its last remaining Western-*Sahib*. It was a huge mental shift for Indian elites, who still wanted to worship the Western-*Sahib*. And now that the *Sahib*s were gone, Indian elites tried to readjust to the new reality and looked towards the East, instead of the West; there they discovered that Asia's Tiger economies were booming. When Delhi looked eastward, India found the reality of the North East and realized that without opening its door to the East, there was no way to develop the landlocked regions of North East India. And without any form of development that could facilitate finding a political solution, there was no way to end the on-going ethnic conflicts in the region. India was thus forced to include the "Look East Policy" as both foreign and domestic policies in the North East region.

When India started serious engagement with South East Asia, especially with Burma, Mr. Lal Thanzaua Pudaite, who belonged to a Hmar dialect group from the Mizo tribe of Chin, was appointed as the Indian Ambassador to Burma in 1995-1996, and Indian Trade Representative in Taiwan in 1997-2000. Pudaite described in his posthumously published book that India had taken several initiatives during his tenure as Ambassador in Rangoon, including:

> Joint venture for hydro-power project on Chindwin River; Reintroduction Indian Airlines flight from Kolkata to Rangoon; Joint exploration of Myanmar's gas deposits in Arakan; Multi-model project for development of Highway; Inland Waterway on Kalodyne River; Sittwe Port and Hydro-power generation from a dam on Kalodyne; Railways to link Myanmar via Jiribam-Imphal

valley through to Kalewa (Tahan) in Myanmar; Highway to be constructed by India from Champhai to Falam in Myanmar; Reconstruction of the Stillwell Road or old Burma Road from Assam via North Myanmar to Yunnan in China, etc. (Pudaite, 2010: 178).

India has also taken a proactive role in the following projects:

1. In 1992, UN's Economic and Social Commission for Asia and Pacific region (ESCAP) based in Bangkok endorsed the Asian Land Transport Infrastructure Development (ALTID). Thereafter, it revived the Asian Highway (AH) and the Trans-Asian railway (TAR) projects, which had been held in abeyance since 1959 and 1960 respectively. Inter-governmental agreements were concluded: for AH on 18 Nov 2003, and for TAR on 4 July 2004.

2. Agreement on Bangladesh-India-Myanmar-Singapore-Thailand Economic Cooperation (BIMSTEC) was established in 1997. Its principal aims are eventual free trade, investments, tourism and technical cooperation.

3. Kunming Initiative (1999): a meeting of non-official think tank group as well as businessmen was convened at Kunming, the capital of Yunnan Province, China, to explore ways for sub-regional economic and cultural cooperation. Representatives from Bangladesh, China, India and Myanmar (BCIM) participated and the group now called "BCIM Economic Cooperation Forum" has been meeting at various locations in one of the 4 countries every year. The main objective of this group is to generate ideas and device mechanisms for sub-regional cooperation extending over Southwest China, Myanmar, Bangladesh and Northeast India.

4. Free Trade Agreements with Thailand, Singapore, Indonesia and Brunei by 2011 and with Philippines, Cambodia, Laos, Myanmar and Vietnam by 2016.

5. Mekong-Ganga Cooperation, etc.

There are a number of cooperation agreements at bilateral level too. For instance, an Indo-Myanmar bilateral agreement for far-reaching significance to Northeast is the Multi-modal Inland Waterway-cum-Highway project on the Kalodyne River, estimated to cost $104 Million. Under this project, Sittwe Harbour in Rakhyne, Myanmar and navigation on Kalodyne as also Highway from south Mizoram will be developed so that Northeast is directly linked to seaport. All the attendant protocols to the agreement have been signed and the project is ready to take off (Pudaite, 2010: 178-179).

After his retirement, Pudaite co-founded the "Center for North-East Studies and Policy Research", and established his own NGO called "Tribal Welfare Agency". He proposed "Vision NER – 2020", in which he outlined, among others, the following points:

a. Upgrade, and integrate Mizoram's transport network into existing proposal for Trans-Asian Railways (TAR) and Asian Highway systems; e.g. additional AK linkage from Bangladesh via Agartala – Aizawl – Champhai – Tiddim/Falam – Mandalay (The original proposals for TAR and AH systems do not cover Tripura, Mizoram and Chin State of Myanmar).

b. Connect NH-54 from south Mizoram to Haka, [the capital of Chin State].

c. Enhance quality of maintenance of all existing roads to at least all weather level and upgrade load bearing capacity of bridges in all major roads to national standard.

d. Early execution of the Multi-Modal Highway-cum-IWT project on Kolodyne.

e. Railways (broad-gauge) expansion from Chaparmukh (Assam valley) to Hailakandi (Cachar), by passing 39 tunnels and 179 bridges in the Lumding to Badarpur sectors, then extend railways to Bairabi (Mizoram) up to Lawngtlai/Myanmar border in south Mizoram.

f. To bypass Sonupur area, where the highway frequently blocked by land/mudslides throughout rainy seasons, another highway link from Assam valley to Surma valley is essential.

g. Open up Inland Water-cum-Rail/Road transit routes from Mizoram to West Bengal via Bangladesh, and also to access Chittagong port.

h. Direct air links en route some Northeast cities to Southeast Asian cities like Kunming, Yangon, Mandalay, Bangkok, etc.

Pudaite suggested that in pursuit of India's Look East Policy; "Vision for NER – 2020" will transform the "Northeast India Region" into a major gateway between South Asia and Southeast Asia, and will eliminate the "isolation and remoteness" of the region. Since he saw the "Look East Policy" as an Indian response to globalization, Pudaite insisted that "we cannot avoid or escape from this inexorable process of globalization, for the NE is too insignificant a region to influence this massive international game. India has decided to be an active participant in this game and all we need to do, therefore, is to prepare for the challenges we must face" (ibid, p. 180).The challenges are already there, and how the peoples from the region will respond is a critical issue that requires careful analysis.

Paradigm Shift in Indo-Burma Relations: Searching for a Solution!

The challenges posted by the forces of globalization are huge and real. The indigenous peoples from the region, especially the Chin, Kachin and Naga, must respond to these challenges whether they like it or not. In such a situation, a paradigm shift in Indo-Burma relations is needed, but, how to find a political solution for the ethnic nationalities in the region is much more important.

Under current political circumstances and existing laws from both sides of India and Burma, the indigenous peoples from the region will not be able to reap the benefits of globalization.

Unless both countries can find political solutions to end the on-going civil war and ethnic conflict and repeal repressive laws that are imposed on the people due to these circumstances there is no way to empower the peoples in the region. Without empowering the peoples, railways and highways may pass through the region but the common people will just be by passed and they will not have the capacity to make use of the new opportunities brought about by globalization and its connectivity.

There are two legal issues that require serious political consideration, especially in North East India, which also concerns the peoples from Burma. The first one is: "Restricted Areas Permit" (RAP) and the second is: "Inner Line Regulation" (ILR). The "Restricted Areas Permit for Foreigners" is a regulation imposed by the New Delhi government to prevent foreigners, especially Christian missionaries from abroad, entering the region. The "Inner Line Regulation" was promulgated by the British authority in 1873, in order to prevent the influx of outsiders, especially Indians, to the region. Both laws are now in need of review within the context of current political demands from those indigenous ethnic groups in the region, especially the Chin, Kachin and Naga.

(1) Restricted Areas Permit for Foreigners

The reason for imposing the "Restricted Areas Permit for Foreigners" in North East India was directly or indirectly linked with the prohibition of "Foreign Christian Missionaries" activities in the region.

During the colonial period, the Chin (especially among the Mizo tribe), Kachin, and Naga were converted to Christianity en masse by foreign missionaries, mainly from the United Kingdom and United States of America. For many years, the Christian missionaries were in the region not only as spiritual leaders but also as educators and social workers. They knew the needs of local peoples, spoke the local languages, and identified themselves with the local peoples as brothers and sisters in Christ. When the nationalist movements emerged after World War II, those missionaries could not avoid providing to the needs of the people, and some of those missionaries became unofficial advisors to the leaders of ethnic nationality movements, especially among the Chin, Kachin and Naga.

Although this was not intentional on the part of the Christian missions, Christianity or at least Christians have played a prominent role in the ethnic struggle for political liberation among the Chin, Kachin, and Naga. For better or for worse, Christianity has become the "established" religion among those ethnic groups, in both India and Burma (cf. Dawns, 1992).A unique feature of political developments among the Chin therefore is "the prominent role played by Christians": such as, Phizo (Naga National Council), Laldenga (Mizo National Front), Hrang Nawl (Chin Liberation Army), and Zau Tu and Zau Dang, the two brothers who founded the Kachin Independence Organization. There were many Christian leaders who led the Karen National Union (KNU) in Burma as well.

Among the Foreign Missionaries, Michael Scott, Presbyterian Missionaries from Britain, was a prominent figure who was personally involved both as a peace maker and helper. When the Naga nationalist movement was at the peak, Michael Scott founded a "Peace Mission" together with Jayaprakash Narayan, a leading follower of Gandhi, and Prasad Chaliha, the Chief Minister of Assam, and tried hard to negotiate between the Phizo's Naga National Council and the Indian government. However, the "Peace Mission" failed because Michael Scott was accused of acting "too openly toward the Naga cause" (Hazarika, 1994: 102). As mentioned, Michael Scott also helped Laldenga in his exile to London. He also arranged meetings for Hrang Nawl with the British and US Consulates in Calcutta in 1965, and later provided shelter when Hrang Nawl was hiding in Shilong.

The involvement of Christians in the nationalist movements among the Mizo (Chin) and Naga, especially when these movements erupted into violent rebellions, "has reinforced the suspicion of the Indian public," as Downs observed, that "Christians, at least in that region, are anti-national in the larger sense of Indian nationalism" (Dawns, 1992: 29). The same is also true in Burma, since the Chin, Kachin and Karen, who are predominantly Christians, have fought against the central government of Burma in Rangoon.

Alarmed by the Chin (both MNF and CLA), Kachin and Naga nationalist movements, the governments of India and Burma agreed, during the visit of the Indian Prime Minister Lal Bahadur Shastri to Rangoon in 1965, to cooperate to deal with the rebel movements along their mutual border. They also discussed the role of Christianity in these separatist movements, especially among the Chin and the Naga. Making no effort to understand the roots of the Chin, Kachin and Naga nationalist movements and the real cause of the rebellions, the two governments simply made Christian missionaries the scapegoat for all these nationalist movements, saying: "in fact Christian missionaries are there not for advocating a faith but for keeping imperialism alive" (S. P. Sinha in K. S. Singh (ed.), 1972: 62; Downs, 1992: 30).

· Apparently out of fear of the Chin, Kachin and Naga movements along the Indo-Burmese border and other separatist political activities in both countries, Indian Prime Minister Lal Bahadur Shastri and the Burmese military government leader General Ne Win agreed "to remove all the foreign missionaries from the black region", or what were referred to in India as the "restricted areas" (Downs, 1992: 29). As a result, the Indian government expelled all foreign missionaries from West Chinram (Mizoram), Manipur, and Nagaland. While the Indian authorities classified these parts of the country as "restricted areas" and removed foreign missionaries from these areas alone, General Ne Win expelled all foreign missionaries, not only from Eastern Chinram (Chin State) but from the whole of Burma. Thus, on March 23, 1966, a deportation order was issued for all missionaries, bringing to an end the 150-year history of the American Baptist Mission in Burma.

Although foreign missionaries were expelled from North East India and Burma, the churches of the Chin, Kachin and Naga demonstrated their spiritual vitality in the face of revolutionary change and manifested their own true character of indigenous churches in the midst of the multi-ethnic, multi-religious and multi-cultural environments of Burma and India. In present day, almost one hundred percent of the peoples of the Chin (especially among the Mizo), Kachin and Naga have declared their faith in Jesus Christ as their Lord and Saviour (Cf. Sakhong, 2000).

The vibrancy of the Christian Churches in Mizoram State and Nagaland State, without foreign missionaries, demonstrate that the "Restricted Areas Permit for Foreigners", which was put in place for forbidding the activities of foreign missionaries in the region, no longer serves its original purpose. However, so long as the regulation remains in force, "no foreigner, even if he or she has a valid visa for entry to India, can visit much of the areas of the NER hills, without first obtaining an RAP from the Home Ministry of India or Home department of state concerned. No Indian missions abroad are authorized to issue this permit to visit the specified areas in NER without the clearance of the Home Ministry" (Pudaite, 2010: 186). Under such restriction of this regulation, "promotion of tourism for the region, for example, seems meaningless", and as Pudaite suggests, this "Restricted Areas Permit regulation for foreigners should be withdrawn" (ibid. P. 187).

(2) Inner Line Regulation

The "Inner Line Regulation" is politically more sensitive than the Restricted Areas Permit. The INR requires a "Inner Line Pass" (ILP) for outsiders of the region, including Indian citizens, as a kind of entry visa to Arunachal, Mizoram, and Nagaland States. As mentioned, the "Inner Line Regulation" was promulgated by the British colonial power as the recognition of the pre-colonial independent status of the Chin (Mizoram), Kachin (Arunachal), and Naga (Nagaland).

Since the "Inner Line Regulation" was passed on political grounds, it should not be viewed only in terms of the "the protection the native peoples in the regions from the exploitation of outsiders" and the "prohibition of the permanent residence in the areas for non-native persons". The political essence of the

"Inner Line Regulation" can be compared with the "Panglong Agreement", signed by the Chin, Kachin and Shan with the Interim Burmese Government led by Gen Aung San, on 12 Feb 1947. The essence of the "Panglong Agreement", like the "Inner Line Regulation", is the recognition of the pre-colonial independent status of the Chin, Kachin and Shan, who could thus regain their sovereignty and independence without any attachment to Burma Proper, but agreed that they would join in the independence of Burma for the sake of speeding up their own search for freedom (cf. Preamble of Panglong Agreement).

The recognition of pre-colonial independent status, from both political and legal points of views, was meant "to guarantee the rights of internal self-determination" for those indigenous ethnic nationalities: which includes the right of "self-rule" for their respective homelands; the right of full autonomous status endowed with legislative, judiciary, and administrative powers for their respective states; the right to promulgate the state constitutions for their own respective states within a legal-framework of the federal union; and the rights to protect, preserve, and promote their culture, language, religion, heritages, ways of life and national identity. The core of "internal self-determination" in a federal system is the right to promulgate the "state constitution" through which the indigenous ethnic nationalities from member states of the federal union can protect and promote all other rights.

In today's context, if the "Inner Line Regulation" is approached only from the perspective of "prohibition of the permanent residence in the areas for non-native persons"; the main concern will be "the problem of illegal immigration" and the "danger of being swamped by the outsiders" (Pudaite, 2010: 187). The problem of "illegal immigration" is sensitive but not unsolvable. The danger here is not merely "illegal immigration" but the power game: if the power game is shifted from the hands of indigenous ethnic nationalities in Arunachal, Mizoram and Nagaland to New Delhi, the Chin (Mizo), Kachin, and Naga peoples will forever lose their "rights of self-determination" which are protected by the "Inner Line Regulation" on the

Indian side of the border. As the government of the Union of Burma has no right to abolish the "Panglong Agreement", which was signed before independence; the government in New Delhi cannot repeal or abolish the "Inner Line Regulation" without the consent of the peoples, namely, the Chin (especially the Mizo and other Chin tribes who are in Mizoram State), the Kachin (and other ethnic groups in Arunachal Pradesh State), and the Naga.

In the light of India's "Look East Policy" and the unstoppable forces of globalization, the "Inner Line Regulation", which was promulgated more than a century ago, may be in need of review but it should be done without losing its original purpose. Under the current political circumstances, the best means to do this seems to be by granting the rights to promulgate separate state constitutions for the states which are now under the protection of the "Inner Line Regulation", *albeit* within the legal-framework of the Indian Constitution. In this way, the State Constitutions, which would be drafted and promulgated by the peoples themselves through their respective State Assemblies, will be able to protect and promote the rights that are meant to be protected by the "Inner Line Regulation". The "Inner Line Regulation" was meant to be the protection of the "rights of self-determination" for the indigenous ethnic nationalities in the region, but it was never fully implemented after independence. By replacing this regulation with the "State Constitution", the peoples from these three states will be able to enjoy full "rights of internal self-determination" within the federal arrangement of the Indian Constitution.

In order to grant the right to adopt separate constitutions for the three states that are protected by the "Inner Line Regulation", India must also upgrade its constitution, from a quasi-federal system to genuine federalism. The India Constitution, of course, has granted its member states the legislative, judiciary and administrative powers. The main flaw, however, is that the Indian states do not enjoy the right to promulgate their own separate constitutions. Instead, all the affairs of the states are incorporated into the Union Constitution, exactly like the 1947

Constitution of the Union of Burma. Such constitutional arrangements indicate that "whatever powers the government of states enjoy and exercise are given to them by the central government", which indeed is one of the main characteristics of a unitary, not a federal, system. In a unitary system, power lies in the hands of the central government; and state powers are derived from the center (cf. Sakhong, 2005: 17-18).

In addition to the absence of state constitutions, the India Constitution adopted a peculiar system of "unelected State Governor", appointed by the President. Constitutionally, the state executive power is vested in the Governor, and the Governor not only has the right to dissolve the State Legislative Assembly but appoint the Chief Minister of the State in a situation where no single party or leader commands majority support (cf. Kashyap, 2009: 197-200). Such powerful head of a provincial State, but unelected, is not only undemocratic but a political system usually practiced only in Imperialism and monarchy, not in a republic or a federal system.

Without a State Constitution, compounded by an all-powerful State Governor, no State in India can claim that they have the right of "self-determination", albeit "internal self-determination". Unless the right of internal self-determination is granted, which is guaranteed in a federal system by the State Constitution; there is no other means to substitute the "Inner Line Regulation". Thus, if the Delhi government wanted to find a political solution in Northeast India, and genuinely wanted to promote development through its "Look East Policy", India must take a huge step or paradigm shift in constitutional change.

The same is true for Burma but the problem is bigger. In addition to the constitutional crisis created by the 1947 Constitution and the 1974 Constitution, the peoples of Burma, especially ethnic nationalities, have faced sixty years of on-going civil war and military dictatorship. Recently in 2008, the military junta promulgated a new constitution, which creates another level of constitutional crisis. As the military regime is posing several levels of threat to the peoples of Burma, there have emerged strong opposition groups who want to solve the country's political crisis through peaceful means. Since the 1988 pro-democracy movement, all ethnic nationalities and democratic forces, led by Daw Aung San Suu Kyi, are struggling together for democracy and genuine federalism. Such unity in purpose has never occurred in Burmese history since independence, and ethnic nationalities are no longer alone in their struggle for democracy, equality, and internal self-determination through a federal arrangement. The best hope for Burma, therefore, is that there are reliable and united political forces from both ethnic nationalities and democratic groups, who want to solve the political crisis in Burma through the constitutional means of establishing a genuine Federal Union of Burma.

Conclusion

Because of historical accidents that occurred at the end of the colonial period, many ethnic nationalities and their homelands are divided into different countries. In this paper, I have analyzed the cases of the Chin, Kachin and Nagain the light of the future of Indo-Burma relations, and also from the possible long term effects of globalization, currently represented by India's "Look East Policy" and the Burmese military junta's response to it.

For the past six decades, ethnic nationalities in Burma and Northeast India have been fighting against the governments of Burma and India, respectively. Both Indian and Burmese governments, therefore, must consider how to solve these ethnic conflicts and on-going civil wars seriously. Sixty years of negative experiences indicate that these problems cannot be solved through military means alone, and a political solution is needed.

To find a political solution, what the Indian and Burmese governments should do first is to recognize the pre-colonial independent status of the Chin (Mizo in India), the Kachin and the Naga peoples and their homelands. No matter what kind of political systems they had practiced then, there were independent peoples and their homelands were never part of either Burma or India. Secondly, they should be granted "internal self-determination" for their homeland, so that they may be able to practice "self-rule" for their respective states while they will also be a part of "shared-rule" in larger federal unions, either in India or Burma depending on which side they live. Thirdly, in order to grant "internal self-determination" for those ethnic peoples through a federal arrangement, both India and Burma should practice a genuine federal system, so that all member states of the federal union of India and Burma would be able to enjoy political rights of legislative, administrative, and judiciary powers which they should apply through State Legislative Assembly, State Government, and State Supreme Court. Fourthly, in order to secure "internal self-determination", all member states of both countries shall be granted the right to promulgate their own separate State Constitutions within the constitutional framework of the Federal Union of either India or Burma.

For the past sixty years, ethnic armed-resistant movements in Burma and Northeast India have been seen as the means to regain the rights of self-determination for their homelands, to protect the dignity and identity of the peoples, and to preserve and promote the culture, language, religion and way of life of all these unrecognized peoples. What most of all these ethnic nationalities are fighting for is not necessarily an independent sovereign state for their respective homelands but for the dignity of the people; for their long held traditions, heritage, and way of life; and for their national identity. Even if some groups are fighting for a sovereign nation-state, it should be re-evaluated in the light of contemporary international political trends and the forces of globalization.

Contemporary international political trends indicate that a sovereign nation-state is not the only means to serve the people best, and the power of absolute sovereignty is diminishing slowly, at least in Europe where the modern form nation-state first emerged. The sovereign nation-sates in Europe are "coming together" as members of the "European Union" in order to serve their own peoples more effectively, and create peace and harmony in the region and in the larger world. By doing this, members of the European Union are consciously giving up a certain level of the absolute power of the sovereign nation-state. This is a lesson that can be learned both by governments and ethnic armed-groups in Northeast India and Burma.

In this paper, I have argued that the best means to solve political crisis in Burma and ethnic conflicts in Northeast India is to grant those ethnic nationalities, who were independent peoples before the colonial period, an "internal self-determination" through a federal arrangement. For those ethnic nationalities, especially, the Chin, Kachin and Naga, I suggest that armed-resistance is not the only means to serve the people best, and if "internal self-determination is granted", they therefore must find some alternative means and ways to preserve, protect and promote the long term interests of their peoples.

If both governments and ethnic insurgent groups could find a political solution, and create peace and harmony in the region then Northeast India, Chin State, Eastern Nagaland, Kachin State and all the western valley of Upper Chindwin could become not only the gateway between Northeast and Southeast Asia, but the region can also become the place where the value of unity in diversity is practiced and the beauty of pluralism can flourish.

References:

Aung San Suu Kyi (1991), *Freedom from Fear* (London: Penguin Books)

Chatter, Shuns (1990), *Mizoram Encyclopedia* (New Delhi & Bombay: Jaycee Publishing House).

Christie, Clive (1998), *Modern History of South East Asia* (London: Tauris Academic Studies)

Coupland, Robert (1945), *The Future of India* (Oxford: Oxford University Press)

Downs, Frederick, S (1992), *History of Christianity in India: North East India in the Nineteenth and Twentieth Centuries* (Vol. V, Part 5) (Bangalore: The Church History Association of India)

Egreteau, Renaud (2003), *Wooing the Generals: India's New Burma Policy* (New Delhi: Authors Press)

Hazarika, Sanjoy (1994), *Strangers of the Midst: Tales of War and Peace from India's Northeast* (New Delhi: Viking-Penguin India)

Kashyap, Subhash, C. (2009),   *Concise Encyclopaedia of Indian Constitution* (New Delhi: Vision Books)

Maung Maung, U (1989),   *Burmese Nationalist Movements, 1940–1948* (Honolulu: University of Hawaii Press)

Pudiate, L. T (2010),   *Mizoram and Look East Policy* (New Delhi: Akansha Publishing House)

Reid, Robert (1942),   *A Note on the Future of the Present and Partially Excluded Areas of Assam* (I.O.L: 1942, reprinted, Aizawl: Tribal Research Institute, 1976)

Sakhong, Lian H. (2000),   *Religion and Politics among the Chin People in Burma, 1896-1949*,(Uppsala:DoctoralDissertationatUppsala University)

Sakhong, Lian H. (2003),   *In Search of Chin Identity: A Study in Religion, Politics and Ethnic Identity in Burma*, (Copenhagen: Nordic Institute of Asian Studies)

Sakhong, Lian H. & David Williams, (2005)   *Designing Federalism in Burma* (Chiang Mai: UNLD Press) ed.,

Smith, Martin (1991),   *Burma: Insurgency and Politics of Ethnicity* (London and New York: Zed Books Ltd)

Symleah, D. R (1942),   *Crown Colonial Scheme,* reprinted as *"Proceeding of North East India"* (New Delhi: History Association, Second Edition)

Vumson,(1986),   *Zo History* (Aizawl: Published by the author)

Yhome, K (2008),   *Myanmar: Can the Generals Resist Change?* (New Delhi: Rupa & Co.)

PART FOUR

PERSONAL REFLECTIONS

EIGHTEEN

In Loving Memory of
Dr. Chao Tzang Yawnghwe:
Our Beloved Uncle Eugene

The following eulogy was given at the funeral of Dr. Chao Tzang Yawnghwe on Saturday, 31 July 2004, at Burquitlam Chapel, Vancouver, Canada and published in 'Independence' the magazine of the Shan Herald Agency for News.

Uncle Eugene was my mentor; intellectual advisor, political leader, and intimate personal and family friend. In fact, he was like my father. When Harn called me and broke the news of his demise just a few hours after he passed away (coincidentally I was holding his picture to hang on our sitting room wall), the sadness overwhelmed me all day long. In every single minute, his loving memory comes back to me – the sound of his voice, his smile, his laughter, his jokes, even the way he used to eat and the smell of his cigar. I remember him with love, pride, admiration and respect in my own special way.

I will always treasure so many sweet memories. I remember so many roads that we had travelled together during the past three years; in every kind of weather, in all kinds of circumstances, so many miles of journey to so many countries all over the world and speaking so many words for the peoples of Burma, which came from the deepest level of our heart. The words we uttered mostly were about peace, reconciliation and freedom; and he was a voice for and the voice of the voiceless people of Burma, especially ethnic minority groups. Although his voice was for peace and reconciliation, the way he expressed those words were not always smooth. There always were a number of disturbances, confrontations and conflict that we had to encounter, for we are dealing with the most brutal regime in the world. But no matter what kind of difficulties we faced, Uncle Eugene never lost his patience and optimism.

It was rather a long journey for him (and for those of us who endeavored the same journey with him) because peace was so far to reach; the atmosphere usually was unkind and tedious because there were so many harsh situations involving politics and power struggles that brought different opinions to be reconciled and build consensus even before we confronted the real enemy. Politically violent and stormy days were quite often, and too long, because the truth was so difficult to find. We knew from the very beginning that the path to freedom was not paved with flowers, but firmly believed that truth shall one day make us free.

I know that Uncle Eugene should not be idolized, or enlarged today beyond what he was in life. He should be remembered simply as a good and decent man; he was the one who saw injustice and fought for justice. He saw so many things that went wrong in our society and tried to make it right; he saw the suffering of our people and tried to heal them; he saw and experienced five decades of civil war in our country and tried to stop it, even by holding arms. He was born into a Shan Royal family and was the son of the first democratically elected President of Burma but chose to live a humble life in the academic world; his life was blessed with fame and wealth but he identified himself with the poor and the oppressed. He was the one who dared to abandon a promised life under bright lights with neon signs in order to fight for the freedom of his homeland. Instead of spending glorious nights sipping ruby red wine and mingling with friends, he opted for a jungle life to free his people. Instead of enjoying an academic life in the first world, he came back to the jungle for the second time to join the struggle for democracy, human rights and freedom in the very country where he and his family were persecuted and denied their basic rights of dignity and governing power.

I first met Uncle Eugene in 1998 at a conference in Ottawa, Canada. After a chat, we soon engaged in a serious intellectual and political debate on Burma; beginning with certain historical facts which quickly led us into the question of "why". The question of "why" in history did not satisfy him, but I maintained my position quite firmly. We quickly resumed our debate when we met again in Thailand after one year in 1999, all the way from Bangkok to Mae Sot. It was the time we formed the National Reconciliation Program (NRP) for Burma, and the NRP remained very close to his heart until his final days. I later realized that his main concern (during our debate) was not merely historical fact and the question of "why" in history, but he seemed to be trying to shift the entire paradigm of Burmese studies by challenging the old school of history and political science in the context of Burma. He challenged, as I also did from my own ways, the very notions of "nation-building" and "national integration" for the term "nation" is a subjective value which cannot be shared objectively between two different people or ethnic groups, which therefore is very problematic in multi-ethnic plural societies like Burma. As we went along the same journey for the same struggle, we boldly proposed "state-building" instead of "nation-building", suggested "unity in diversity" instead of "ethnic assimilation", and opted for "federalism and democratic decentralization" instead of a centralized unitary version of absolute sovereignty.

Although I have been deeply involved in Burma's democracy movement since 1988 as a student, and later as a political activist, and have attended several meetings and conferences in exile, I was quite reluctant to go back to the jungle and work fulltime for the movement after I finished my doctorate study at Uppsala University. Uncle Eugene did not force me to rejoin, but he once wrote a letter to me and related his life story, in which he mentioned how he escaped assassination attempts at least twice. He also mentioned the reason why he believed in democracy and was ready to sacrifice his life for the cause. In short, he wrote the reason why he never surrendered to evil power and willingly continued to live the struggling life of a freedom fighter. He completely committed his time and life for the poor and the oppressed people of Burma. I let my wife read his letter, and she burst into tears. For me and my family, we have our own commitment and readiness to sacrifice for the struggle of freedom in our country; but Uncle Eugene was the one who, one way or another brought me back to the jungle life of a freedom fighter, and to the democracy movement in Burma.

Since January 2001, I worked with him. We travelled together all over the world, camped together in the jungle, shared hotel rooms in many cities around the world, and rented a small apartment together in Chiang Mai. I saw his humbleness not only in the small room that we shared but also in big hotel lobbies and grand dinners with dignitaries. I saw his courage and leadership quality when we were faced with unbearable hardship and difficulties. I saw his intellectual genius and wisdom not only in jungle conferences but also in academic seminars around the world. I saw his loving kindness and caring attitude when we met with oppressed, marginalized and less fortunate fellow human beings. He was a loving father and husband who deeply cared for his family and loved his children. I realized how committed a family man he was, especially after he visited us in Uppsala in June 2003. He fondly loved children, including my kids, and used to send nice presents to them. The following letter is one of example, which he wrote to me on September 20, 2003:

Dear Lian

There are two packs of dried lamiae fruits in my room, I think. They are for you, Aapen, and the kids. Never got around to telling you. I was going to, but you were not around, and even when I see you, there were so many other things that I forgot. Sorry for not remembering. I recalled the fruits only after I got back (yesterday, 19th, at 3 pm). I hope you will be back in office, and will take them back home.

Best, UncleE/CTY

Although we worked very closely during the past three years, we rarely found enough time to talk about our personal matters.

Instead, we exchanged notes via e-mail or telephone. In his loving memory, I would like to mention his last letter to me, in which he mentioned his creed, which reflects his real portrait and who he was. I didn't know that this letter would be his last letter to me. The letter was dated on February 7, 2004.

Dear Lian

By the time you read this, you will presumably be at home with your loving family. My regards to Aapen and the kids.

First, I hope you got the book, *Good Morning Buddha* by Phra Phillip, the English monk. I put it on your bed. It is a very useful book, a must.

Second, I am happy we had the short phone conversation before you left, appreciate your honesty.

I am a person who does not believe that anyone owes me anything, not even loyalty, gratitude nor love. My behavior towards everyone is based on the concept that all are fellow human beings, nothing more, nothing less. Hence, no one is perfect. I come into this world alone, perhaps incidentally or accidentally. This is my creed.

But at the same time, I believe that some human beings are noble in spirit and at heart, but some are really despicable, while the majority decent and neither very good nor very bad.

It is my sacred obligation, I believe, to help all fellow human beings, but as a political person, it is my obligation to help, facilitate, mentor, guide the up-coming persons of promise and capabilities, to foster and bolster his/her potentials. And this is what I always do.

You are – in my judgment – one of the leaders and builders of the future Union – the kind of vision I devoted my life to. So, I hope you recognize the burden or cross you will have to bear if you want to give meaningful leadership.

Being a leader is being a politician, as importantly as being a good human being above all – not a good Christian, a pious Buddhist, or a devout Muslim. Religion serves to make a person a whole human being – not to show the path to paradise, heaven, or nirvana. Religion should be a very personal moral guide and framework.

To be a good human being, a whole Man, this is the holy grail of a political leader. It is not courage so much, nor intellect, nor is it heroic deeds and words. These are incidental.

Believe me, in my eventful life spanning many decades of turmoil and turbulence, I have met and dealt with thousands of people – the good, the bad, and the ugly. You wouldn't believe the evil I have confronted, the really bad, and truly ugly, the cold-blooded killers, the cold eyed back-stabbers, and such. I haven't survived merely through luck.

You can be assured that I will stand behind you and other up-and-coming hopes of our people – providing that you try to overcome your personal turmoil and emotional immaturity. It is the fate of politicians to have his heart broken, again, and again, countless times. You have not only to bear this cross, but also to recognize it, and embrace it.

I hope you are not offended by my frankness – as a true friend. I am sure that your wife will agree with me if you show her this letter.

Best, UncleE/CTY

Uncle Eugene was an irreplaceable mentor, leader and friend; his death is a great personal loss to me, and it is a great loss also for the continuing fight for equality, self-determination, federalism and democracy in Burma. I feel very heavy and saddened that he will no longer be with us in the rest of our struggle. This reminds me once again that we can not get hold of everything that we wanted in life. Sorrow and emptiness have taken away days and nights with no explanation.

As I recall the loving memories and gladness that he had brought to me, I am very proud and honoured that I have had the privilege to work with him during his last but finest hours in life. He was a great noble freedom fighter, a genius academic, a true believer in democracy, human rights and freedom. He is gone now, but his legacy will live on! His courage, wisdom, hard work and dedication to the cause of peace and freedom in Burma will be firmly rooted in the living history of our country. He will always be remembered as a leader, a hero, a revolutionary and intellectual activist who dedicated all his life for the freedom of the people of Burma. We respect the dignity and legacy of Uncle Eugene and the Yawnghwe family.

With great honour I salute Uncle Eugene!

NINETEEN

A Struggle to be an Authentic Human Being Again: The Martin Luther King Prize Acceptance Speech

The following speech was delivered in honor of receiving the Martin Luther King award at the Salem Baptist Church, Stockholm, Sweden, on the evening of the 15 January 2007. On that occasion, I had given two speeches, more or less the same text: one was delivered when the award was given and the second one was prepared for Evening Worship Service at the Salem Baptist Church. This is a shorter version that I delivered at award given ceremony.

Your Excellencies, Ladies and Gentlemen, and Dear Friends:

I am standing before you to accept a prize bearing the name of one of the persons I most admire, Dr. Martin Luther King, Jr. This indeed is a great honor for me, and at the same time I do realize that this award is given not only to me but to the peoples of Burma as the recognition of our struggle for democracy and human rights, peace and justice, freedom and equality, federalism and *internal* self-determination in ethnic homelands.

Even as I speak, thousands of my compatriots are sacrificing their freedom and well-being, and our leader Daw Aung San Suu Kyi, as you all know, is still under house arrest. My dear friend Khun Htun Oo, a Shan leader, is still serving his sentence of 96 years imprisonment in the most notorious jail in Burma. Many more had sacrificed their lives already in the on-going sixty years of civil war; or on the streets of our capital and other cities while they demonstrated for their free will; or in the notorious prisons in Burma. They sacrificed their lives, their freedom, and their well-being so that Burma may have a future with freedom. And here in Sweden, a very peaceful country, you have recognized our struggle because you know that "injustice anywhere is a threat to justice everywhere", as Martin Luther King said.

I felt extremely honored when I was told that I had been awarded the Martin Luther King Prize for 2007. Martin Luther King was one of my heroes since my university days in Rangoon. This brought back many fresh memories of student life when we were young and dared to think and challenge almost everything under the Sun, including military dictatorship in our country. We also remember how the regime sent troops into our cmpus and killed hundreds of our fellow students. Martin Luther King, Jr. and Dietrich Bonhoeffer were the two theologians who inspired me personally, daring in order to know "the cost of discipleship" while having "a dream" to make the world a better place to live, in the midst of bloody events like what happened at our campus in 1988.

Just before the fateful events of the student-led uprising in 1988, I was reading at Theological Seminary for my term paper about the non-violent strategy of Martin Luther King and the ethics of Dietrich Bonhoeffer. Both of them dared to challenge unjust laws, and both did not survive their struggle. Both of them are my inspiration; and both of them received their inspiration from the teachings of Jesus Christ, who proclaimed that

> The Spirit of the Lord is upon me,
> Because he has anointed me,
> To proclaim good news to the poor.
> He has sent me to proclaim liberty to the captives,
> And recovering of sight to the blind,
> To set at liberty those who are oppressed.

Since I joined the movement, I have written so many letters and statements calling for the release of Daw Aung San Suu Kyi, Hkun Tun Oo and all political prisoners in Burma but to no avail. After the popular uprising in 1988, the entire people of Burma "are the prisoners in our own house" as Aung San Suu Kyi said. Burma under this military regime is just like a blind man who lost his sight for power and greed, and covered by absolute darkness and overwhelmed by an extremely negative attitude. We must, therefore, recover the sight of our country, and restore the vision of our nation. Still, there are millions of oppressed to be released and their freedom restored. This is what our struggle is all about.

This is a struggle for freedom: freedom from oppression and injustice. Freedom for us is to live a certain areas of our life without any interference from the state or the authority or other persons. We believe that some portions of our human existence must remain independent; as such, we must preserve, protect, and promote a maximum area of our personal freedom if we don't want to degrade ourselves or deny our human nature. At the very least: freedom of expression, freedom of belief, freedom from fear, and freedom from want must be guaranteed in any human existence as the fundamental freedom.

But, in my country – Burma; we are deprived from all these fundamental freedoms. We want "freedom of expression" because freedom of expression is a huge crime under military regime. We have over one thousand political prisoners in Burma, who committed no crime but dared to express their free will. We want "freedom of belief" because religious minority groups in Burma, especially Christians and Muslim, are suffering religious persecution under this military regime. We want "freedom from fear" because we live our lives under this military regime in constant fear. We want "freedom from want" because the peoples of Burma are destitute living under extreme conditions of impoverishment, hunger and disease without remedy in a land that used to be known as the "rice bowl of Asia".

There is no political freedom in Burma, especially for ethnic nationalities. We are prevented from attaining our right to *internal* self-determination: the right to rule ourselves in our respective homelands, the right to manage our livelihood, the right to take responsibility for our destiny, and the right to preserve, protect and promote our culture, our language, our religion, our heritages and our ways of life. In order to defend our ways of life and our homelands, we, ethnic nationalities in Burma, have no choice but engaging in almost sixty years of civil war.

The root cause of political crisis in Burma is not just ideological confrontation between military dictatorship and democracy; it also involves constitutional problems rooted in the denial of *internal* self-determination for ethnic nationalities who joined the Union as equal partners at the Panglong Conference in 1947.

So, our struggle is a struggle for *internal* self-determination through federal arrangement so that we may be able to enjoy the rights to rule ourselves in our respective homelands, and, at the same time, the right to rule together and share responsibility for the union as a whole. And we believe that in a multi-ethnic country and a plural society like Burma, a genuine federalism is the only system that can guarantee the fundamental rights for all citizens of the Union, political equality for all ethnic nationalities, and the right of *internal* self-determination for all member states of the Union.

In this struggle, we also challenge the notion of "nation-building" in which the concept of "nation" is blended with the doctrine of "one ethnicity, one language, and one religion". As such, "nation-building" belongs to what social scientists call "subjective values", that is, culture, language, religion, ethnicity, homeland, shared memories and history, etc., which differentiate one group of people from another — values that cannot be shared objectively between different peoples. From its process, the very notion of "nation-building" excludes other ethnic groups, cultures, religions and everything related to the concepts of pluralism and "unity in diversity".

In the name of "nation-building", the successive governments of the Union of Burma have violated not only basic human rights and individual freedom but also all kinds of collective rights for ethnic nationalities. In the name of absolute national sovereignty, the rights of *internal* self-determination for ethnic nationalities are rejected; in the name of national integration the right to follow different religious teaching, to practice different cultures, and to speak different languages are deprived; and in the name of national assimilation, the rights to up-hold different identities and traditions are denied.

In this struggle, we are calling for "unity in diversity" instead of "national assimilation" because we believe that "unity in diversity" as political value would allow us to live as different ethnic groups, different religious groups, and different cultural and language groups peacefully together. In this struggle, we are calling for "decentralization" instead of "centralization" where power is concentrated only in the hands of dictators.

In this struggle, we are calling for a negotiated-settlement through political dialogue. Instead of fighting each other and killing each other, we want to solve our political problems through political means on a dialogue table, not on the battlefields. So, what we are saying is "stop fighting", "stop killing"; killing innocent lives will not solve the problem, denying human rights will not make the country free, and destroying human and natural resources will not make any benefit for the future of Burma. However, by finding a common ground through dialogue, negotiation, and compromise; we can solve all of our problems together.

And above all: what we want is to live just like a human being, to live with human dignity, and reflecting the image of God. We believe that we — the human being — are the creation of God according to His own image. The image of God in human life is reflecting through freedom that God has given to us together with responsibility. But the image of God in human existence has been distorted and damaged because of injustice and oppressions, because of deprivation of freedom, because of violation of fundamental human rights, and because of the denial to take responsibility.

So, our struggle is a struggle for freedom and justice: so that we may be able to take responsibility for our own destiny as an individual human being, and collectively as a people and a nation. Our struggle is a truggle for human dignity and equality because we believe that all human being are created equal, and as such we all are endowed with human dignity equally. This struggle is a struggle to be recognized as an authentic human being again.

In conclusion, I would like to take this opportunity to express my sincere thanks to the Martin Luther King Prize Committee for your recognition of our struggle, the people of Sweden for your support and solidarity that you have shown to the people of Burma time to time, and all of you: my dear friends in Sweden.

I would like to acknowledge also my colleagues at the Ethnic Nationalities Council, United Nationalities League for Democracy, Chin National League for Democracy, Chin National Council, Federal Constitution Drafting and Coordinating Committee, and National Reconciliation Program; and individually I would like to thank Harn Yawnghwe, Jack Sterken, Sao Seng Suk, and Sai Mawn: although they are not here today, I must say that without you guys I would not be able to survive in the jungle of the Thai-Burma border.

And I would like to express my love and gratitude to my wife, Aapen, and my children: David and Laura. Without your support, understanding and love; I would not be able to stand here, and would not be able to work for what I believe and for the oppressed people of Burma.

I thank you for your recognition of our struggle! With all your help, and with the unity and strength of the people of Burma, "We shall overcome some day"!

Thank you!